THE CAMPER VAN BIBLE

Bloomsbury Publishing

An imprint of Bloomsbury Publishing Plc

50 Bedford Square London WC1B 3DP UK
1385 Broadway, New York NY 10018 USA
29 Earlsfort Terrace, Dublin 2, Ireland

www.bloomsbury.com

First published 2016

British Library Cataloguing-in-
Publication Data

A catalogue record for this book is
available from the British Library.

Library of Congress Cataloguing-in-
Publication data has been applied for.

ISBN: PB: 978-1-4729-2-6548

    ePDF: 978-1-4729 -2-6555

    ePub: 978-1-4729-2-6562

15 14 13 12 11 10 9

Designed by Austin Taylor
Illustrations © David Broadbent
Typeset in Scala

Printed and bound by Bell & Bain Ltd.,
  Glasgow G46 7UQ

To find out more about our authors
and books visit www.bloomsbury.com

THE
CAMPER VAN
BIBLE

LIVE · EAT · SLEEP · (REPEAT)

MARTIN DOREY

BLOOMSBURY
LONDON · OXFORD · NEW YORK · NEW DELHI · SYDNEY

Contents

LIVE

16

EAT

146

SLEEP

276

354

(REPEAT)

For Dave.

The famous little red and white camper van.

    Who carried us so far, rarely moaned and was loved by all who sailed in him. He took us to the ends of the known world and beyond on a series of fantastic adventures that we will never forget. For a few short years of his long life we were lucky enough to be graced with Dave's presence outside our house, sitting patiently, waiting for us to come sprawling out with our mess and shoes and bikes and marshmallows and dreams. He carried them all.

    We shall miss him and wish him well with his new life in the North-East.

◤ **The little camper** that took us to the end of the known world. If you want to know whether or not it's possible to travel with 4 people in a Type 2 for 10 weeks, with surfboards, bikes, awnings, tents and snorkels, then I am happy to say it is. Very much so. Good old Dave. TV star, featured in books and magazines and loved by us.

Introduction

Thanks for finding this book.

If you own a camper, dream of owning a camper or are in the process of trying to own a camper, then this is the book for you. And if you love campers, camping, waking up to lovely views, watching the stars at night and sharing good times with friends, then it's definitely for you, too. And even if you enjoy a little more than the basic luxuries on your travels, dare I say it, this is even meant for you.

Why? Because everyone loves a camper.

The camper van – whether a micro camper, a rat look classic, a concourse ready show van, a stealth camper, a coach built or even an A Class – is more than just a bed on wheels. It's a universal symbol for the open road, free spiritedness, love, peace and harmony that

everyone and anyone can relate to – even if the road ahead seems impassable sometimes.

The camper van is about getting out, off the couch and living life. It's about taking you to the places you love the most, to the places that you haven't seen before or the places you yearn to see one more time before work, life and the mortgage drag you back again.

Yes, so it's just a vehicle with an engine and a steering wheel.

But, if you already own one, I'll bet it's got a name. Am I right? And if I am, what does it tell you about the way you feel about it and what it does for you?

It's more than just a vehicle.

I rest my case.

WHAT'S INSIDE
(other makes are available)

For once it's okay to judge the book by its cover. *The Camper Van Bible* is, as the title would suggest, a book all about camper vans. It's also a book about all camper vans.

While many might think of a camper van as a classic VW Split Screen, other makes are most definitely available. Besides, something shiny that looks great on the concourse might not be right for you, your pocket or the way you need to travel. If it makes you happy and gets you where you want to go, who says it's any better or worse than any other camper van? Not me. In my camper van-owning career I have owned

a classic and three not so classic campers. I've also made do with a few camper 'conversions' that shouldn't have been allowed. And no, you can't make a decent camper out of a Citroen 2 CV. Trust me, I tried.

Inside this book you'll find lots and lots of very useful and practical information and advice about living, eating and sleeping in all kinds of camper vans. We'll talk about buying a camper, a few layouts, facilities and even a few tips to help you get a great night's sleep – and to get up in the morning. If we've got it right, this will be broken up with images, illustrations and snippets of facts, figures and stuff you didn't know about living on four wheels. We've even put together a glossary so, if you feel the need, you can talk camper vans around the campfire to your heart's content.

I'd like to think that at least some of the pictures you'll find between the covers will make you reach for the phone or your tablet or even to the person sitting next to you to make arrangements for your next (or first) camping trip to somewhere absolutely amazing. I've got some ideas for that, too.

If you do feel inspired to hit the road, then don't forget to take this book with you. You might need it along the way. It might well save your life, your marriage, a little bit of face or time, or possibly even a small fortune. At the very least I promise it'll get you out of a foodie fix if you run out of ideas, with a bunch of no nonsense, back to basics recipes that anyone could make and enjoy.

Ready? Let's do it.

LIVE

Hot sand on toes, cold sand in sleeping bags,
I've come to know that memories
Were the best things you ever had
The summer sun beat down on bony backs
So far from home where the ocean stood
Down dust and pine cone tracks

INTRODUCTION

Welcome! In this first section you'll find all kinds of information about campers, from a potted history of the camper to what a camper is likely to cost you over its lifetime. It's all about life with a camper, from finding one, to planning a conversion, to deciding what to take on your adventures (and how to fit it all in). It's a celebration of all things camper, and, if you don't mind me saying, I have had a whale of a time doing it.

Why?

In writing this book I've met some brilliant people. I have met someone who sleeps in a Daihatsu Hijet at work during the week and then drives home at the weekend. It works for him. But then, at the weekends he still goes out for trips in the van, such is his love of camping and camper van living.

I met a couple with a beautiful Bedford CF motorhome. It's slow and shabby (chic) and leaks when it rains. But it's still a thing of beauty, made even more beautiful by the fact that it's loved, well used and appreciated by all who sail in her.

Live

18

↗ **Paul and Sarah Greening's camper, Margot,** a classic Bedford CF, drove up to Bristol from their home in Devon to allow me to photograph her. As Margot is a little slow they camped overnight and 'made a weekend of it' proving they can't get enough of the camper van lifestyle.

I spent evenings under the stars with people who also like to spend nights under the stars. They let me cook for them and photograph them for this project, and we had a lot of fun on cliff tops and by the beach. Their kids had a wonderful free spiritedness that showed in the way they embraced the outdoors. They photobombed me with cartwheels and gurning faces and I loved it.

I was also lucky enough to come into contact – via phone and internet – with some camper van people who I never actually got to meet. Why was this? Because they were out in the van, either for the hell of it or to attend a meet with other like-minded camper owners. It's the best excuse I can think of.

I also met up with a bunch of die-hard VW enthusiasts and life lovers who drive around Ireland each year for charity. They 'paid' for one overnight stop by offering to clean the beach they parked at. And they did a fine job of it, too. Over the years they have raised thousands for charity while raising hell (in the nicest possible way) at pubs, campsites and in fields all over Ireland.

Finally I met some extremely knowledgeable and clever people who share a passion for all things camper, camping and camper van. Despite working with campers all day every day, they still drive their own buses into the workshop at lunchtime to tinker with them. For them, the chance to keep people moving and keep the dreams alive is a dream job.

All these people share the same passion. And that's getting out and seeing the world, whether it's in a Daihatsu, a brand new motorhome or in a classic Bedford. It's what brings us all together and makes a project like this my dream job too.

So please, let the love that went into this book – from absolutely everyone involved – inspire you to turn the key one more time and head off on another great adventure. Happy camping.

WHY A CAMPER VAN?

This is a good question to kick off with, no?
On one level it's a relatively simple question to answer,
I think. It's because a camper makes getting out into the
world more convenient. But there is, of course, more to
it than simple convenience.

Throughout this book you'll find quotes from people in the camper
van world, people who own campers and people who dream of owning
a camper. Each and every one of them will try to define the essence of
what it means to them to own, live or travel in one. They will do their
best to answer the big question:

WHAT DOES IT MEAN TO YOU?

or

WHY?

What is it that brings us back, time and time again, to a little tin box on wheels?

Are we caught up in the whirlwind of hype? Have we been seduced by a promise of freedom? Have we fallen at the altar of iconoclasm? Are we misty eyed at romantic thoughts of living a simpler, more fulfilling life? Read on to find out.

As for me? I just like to go outside, which is the very best reason I can think of. Is that the same for everyone else too? Why do we love our camper vans so? Is it because we like being able to take the kitchen, diner, lounge and bedroom with us when we go away? The camper van is castle and keep, a home from home, a shelter and sanctuary. A place to call your own.

When I started sleeping in camper vans (in about 1986, well before the story overleaf) it was because I wanted to wake up next to the surf. This was in North Wales, and the place my friends and I camped was a campsite overlooking a beautiful reef where, under the right conditions, clean and crisp waves would thunder in towards the shore. The waves were always better around 2 hours after the tide so we wanted to be there when the moment came, no matter what time of the

Live

23

day it was. We wanted to turn out of bed into our wetsuits and then, at the end of the day we wanted to put out the driftwood fire and turn in again. And we wanted to do this all year round, come rain or shine. The camper van made it all possible. We tried tents and cars and sleeping under the stars but it just never quite cut it. When you have surfed in snow or hail you need to be able to find somewhere warm and dry to thaw out your bones. The camper van was the simplest answer.

Some days the surf wouldn't show. That meant we had to drive somewhere else to find our slice of golden sunset and cerulean. Once there we were home again, cocooned in warmth and comfort, no matter how far from our real home. Home, as they say, was wherever we parked it.

Camping, then as now, is one of the cheapest ways to holiday. And if you can camp wild, it's free. So the camper van offers a cheaper

WHAT does a CAMPER mean TO YOU?

'When my daughter Maggie was a baby, she was seriously ill with leukaemia. We spent six months by her side in hospital, 100 miles from home, willing her to keep on living. During that period, Jo and I hatched a plan to buy another camper (we were without at the time) and take off on a big adventure – if we got out intact. It was the promise of the open road that kept us going during those dark times. We needed something to live for beyond life itself. We needed a dream to chase. It was the very best antidote to the horror of the childhood cancer we were facing every day and became, for us, a symbol of a hopeful future. It meant not having to think about chemotherapy or blood counts or uncertainty. Maggie's sister, Charlotte, was born five months into treatment. Four weeks later – when Maggie was given the 'all clear' – we bought a Type 25 and, a few weeks after that, all four of us headed off to Ireland on a big, if cautious, adventure. Our dreams came true. We had everything. Our family. Our girls. Our hopes. A future. We survived.'
Martin Dorey *AUTHOR OF THIS BOOK*

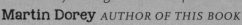

alternative to staying in hotels or guest houses – even if the cost of ownership of a classic is never going to go down.

What about the freedom? Is that just a myth? The camper van's long association with counterculture means that it has become a symbol of freedom, the open road, free choice and a life without barriers. So, whether you like it or not, you take that baggage with you every time you step into a camper van. It's not a bad bag to carry. Even if you don't have the freedom to go wherever you want or do whatever you want to do, you can still enjoy the association that it brings. Even if it isn't real freedom, it certainly feels like it.

The potential is always there... If only you didn't have to [insert what holds you back here] you could jam it into first gear, set a course for the location of your dreams and drive off into the sunset.

The camper van EXPLOSION

We're all going on a summer holiday.

You can't go anywhere these days without seeing an image of a VW camper on a cushion or wallpaper. Go into any seaside gift shop or trendy clothing retailer and you'll be confronted with the loveable, smiling face of an 'iconic' camper. It's a guaranteed sale. Everyone loves a camper, especially a VW camper. They love the shape, the funny headlights, the spare wheel-like-a-nose and the way it's always at the front of the queue.

It's not as if they were rare like other classic cars either! Between 1950 and 1967 around 1,470,000 Type 2 Split Screen VWs were made. After that, VW produced almost 3,300,000 'Bay Window' Type 2 vans, which ranks them among the most popular vehicles of all time.

Perhaps it is the sheer numbers that give us a clue as to the enduring quality of these vehicles' image. Because there were so many of them, there are so many of us who have memories of them from childhood. They were bread vans in Ireland (my wife remembers it well), fire trucks in Germany, ambulances in Australia and just about everything just about everywhere else. Thankfully, for the travelling classes, parts were available almost anywhere too – thanks to VW's extensive dealer network throughout the world – something that made long overland journeys easier than with vehicles for which parts were scarce.

Perhaps it's also because so many of them survive today that we love them so.

Other popular 'people's cars', like the Citroen 2 CV A series cars – of which 8.8 million were made – haven't endured the test of time so well. Having owned one I can say that it's possibly a good thing. But the Type 2 just keeps on going, clapping out, being restored and going again. And you just can't keep a good van down.

Perhaps it's the fact that the VW camper – and other makes of camper vans – found their place among the surfers, nomads and dropouts of 1960s California, that they became synonymous with counterculture.

Then, as is the way with all things non-mainstream, eventually the masses locked into it and wanted a little slice of it for themselves. And whaddayaknow, suddenly hundreds of thousands of like-minded people – inspired by the promise of a freewheeling, free-as-a-bird lifestyle – got the vehicle to take them there. Generations found they had the wherewithal to 'live the dream' for themselves. They set off around Europe – perhaps with you and your siblings in the back – and found a new way of living, away from the drabness of everyday existence. If you are like most of the people I know whose parents did exactly that, you'll remember those heady days of summer with a great fondness that will never leave you.

The European road trip was an adventure few of us will ever forget. My family did ours in an MGBGT, but the feeling was the same. Except perhaps we did it a little faster.

Even so, those open roads of France and beyond will forever be etched on your subconscious. And each and every time you see a camper van you'll feel a pang for a life less complicated, with no mortgage, no austerity and no gadgets.

Eventually your nostalgia will lead you to rent or buy one. And life will never be the same again.

WHAT does a CAMPER mean TO YOU?

'Owning a camper van was always a dream. After months of looking, she came to our attention. She was the colour we wanted and had the added bonus of 888 in the number plate. We were married on the 8th and had our first child on the 8th. We just had to go and view her! I fell in love straight away and just knew she was right, despite looking a bit tired and in need of some TLC. Four years on and we're still tinkering. Every year there's something needs doing that takes over the plan we had for her the year before! But it's a work in progress and as we don't plan on getting rid of her anytime soon, we have all the time in the world! Bit like the amount of time it takes to drive anywhere in her! She has a new oil leak, which is being fixed tomorrow, but once that's done, she'll be ready to start the summer camping trips and days out. Can't wait! It's corny, but she really is one of the family and I hope that she has created some magical memories for our children.'

Sally Smith CAMPER VAN OWNER

The CAMPING experience

We've been in love with recreational camping for well over 100 years. Thanks to the father of the scouting movement, Robert Baden-Powell (*Scouting for Boys* (1908) is still the world's second best-selling book of all time) and the father of modern camping, Thomas Hiram Holding (*The Camper's Handbook* (1908) is widely acknowledged to be the starting place of the recreational camping movement), the idea of sleeping under canvas for its own sake has become a part of our psyche. The year 1908 was a good year for being outside.

The Camping and Caravanning Club (as it is now known) began life as the Bicycle Touring Club when it was formed by Holding in 1878. In 1909 Captain Robert Falcon Scott became the president until his death, in Antarctica, in 1911. In 1919 Sir Robert Baden-Powell, who was by then famous the world over for starting the Scouting movement, became president.

Why tell you this? Because it's important to know where our love for the great outdoors comes from – and how much it is a part of our culture. That three such highly regarded and remarkable individuals should have been at the helm of the movement is testimony enough that camping is important to us.

I remain ever grateful to the Scouting movement for inspiring my grandfather to camp in the 1920s and to become a Scout leader in later years. His knowledge and guidance saw me through some rough weather, while his obsession with lightweight camping haunts me still. However, I am also extremely grateful to those who put camping on wheels in the name of the greater good (and greater comfort) at around the same time.

Why?

Because camper vans are better than tents.

'Camper vans are better than tents.' Discuss.

Why a camper van
is BETTER THAN A TENT

I have camped all my life. So I've seen it all, and have experience enough to make up my mind about the way I like to camp. And I choose a camper van.

My personal love of campers comes down to portability, which might seem odd in the face of the fact that a tent is the ultimate pop-up home. But bear with me. The fact remains that a camper van is a home that can be driven. That means you don't always have to make major alterations to move it. If you've got it right then you should be able to drive your camper away from your camping spot without having to do too much. Yes, so you might have to de-pop a pop top roof, pull the bed down and pack away a few clothes, but at least you don't have to dismantle it entirely to make a swift getaway.

But that's just the start of it. Here are some very good reasons why I choose camper van every time.

see also:
How do you camp? page 77 and The Secrets of Happy Camping page 124

Live

30

CAMPER VANS ARE BETTER THAN TENTS BECAUSE...

...they offer a level of protection a tent never could. They don't blow down in the night. They don't flap and flail and keep you awake. Rarely will you wake to the sound of ripping nylon or humming guy ropes – the sounds that signal disaster is close at hand.

...you can drive them. So, when the weather gets really bad, there is a threat of a flood or snow, wind and rain, you can always drive out of there.

...a few inches of flood water won't bother you in the least. In a tent it spells disaster.

...they don't leak if you touch the sides or allow the fly sheet to touch the inner part of the tent. Some do leak, yes, but not necessarily as part of their makeup. A well made camper is a waterproof camper.

...you don't sleep on the ground. You are on wheels above it. That means you won't get that creeping chill in the small of your back that you get when you sleep on the ground, even with a half decent insulated mattress.

...you can have them ready to go at a moment's notice. Sleeping bags, spare toothbrush, pots and pans and a few clothes – they can all be stored neatly in a camper, ready for the off.

...they do not have to be dried out after you use them (unless it's really bad). They also don't have to be stuffed back into a bag that never fits at the end of a trip.

...they have their own power source for running electrical items, radios and fridges. They can also be plugged in to mains electrics easily for charging mobiles, running DVD players, etc.

...the perfect camper has everything you need, right there, where you need it.

...you can still get a good night's sleep, even if you have to park on a slope. With clever use of a couple of levelling chocks you can sleep on the level. Who ever heard of a self-levelling tent?

...if absolutely necessary, you can sleep in a camper almost anywhere. Try pitching a tent outside the Dog and Duck and see what happens.

...creepy crawlies find it hard to find their way into a camper, unless they are of the flying variety.

...you can lock them from the inside, so keeping you safe from the threat of bears, lions, snakes and mad axe men.

WHAT IS A CAMPER VAN?

The camper van is many things. But mostly, according to 'official sources', it is the following:
According to Collins Dictionary, a camper van (or campervan) 'is a van equipped with beds and cooking equipment so that you can live, cook and sleep in it'.

It is also, according to Wikipedia, a 'self-propelled vehicle that provides both transport and sleeping accommodation'.

And a 'motor caravan' (which encompasses both motorhomes and camper vans), according to the UK Driver and Vehicle Licensing Agency, is a very specific type of vehicle. For a camper van to be registered as a motor caravan on its V5 log book, it must meet all of the following criteria:

- *It must have* a door that provides access to the living accommodation.
- *It must have* a bed with a minimum length of 1800mm (approximately 6ft). It can be converted from seats but must be permanently fixed within the body of the vehicle.
- *It must have* a water storage tank.
- *It must have* a seating and dining area permanently attached to the vehicle. The table may be detachable but must have some permanent means of attachment to the vehicle.
- *It must have* a permanently fixed means of storage.
- *It must have* a permanently fixed cooking facility.
- *It must have* at least one window on the side of the accommodation.

That settles it then. Well, not really. I know many camper vans that would meet few of the above criteria. Their owners still classify them as camper vans, but UK law does not.

So a camper van can be a motor caravan, a motorhome, a 'house home' and, if you read Australian camper van history, a 'home from home'.

It's also, for millions of people, a symbol of good times.

The CAMPER VAN around the world

Bonjour. Hallo. Guten Tag. G'day.

It's only natural that camper vans and motorhomes should be called different things in different languages and cultures. There's more about it in the section on camper van history (*see* page 38), but the base vehicle for the VW camper has always been known, officially, as the Transporter. It still is today.

Early models of the Transporter that were designed to carry people were known as the Kombi or Kombinationskraftwagen, and this name has stuck. In Australia and Brazil you'll hear the VW referred to as the Kombi, whereas in Mexico it is known as the Combi.

The Transporter was originally going to be called the Bulli, but it didn't quite happen because of a tractor manufacturer who produced a range of farm tractors called Bulldogs. Despite this, the Transporter is sometimes known as the Bulli in Germany and elsewhere. VW's concept car, a re-imagining of the Split Screen, is known as the Bulli Concept. In Germany the VW camper is also known as the VW bus. Motorhomes in Germany are known as Wohnmobil: literally, live mobile.

→ **Fi and Louisa set off on a round Ireland adventure** every year in the company of other camper van lovers to raise money for good causes. In 2015 it was their 10th year. Since it started the Eireball run has raised many thousands upon thousands of Euros.

74 C 962

In Holland the VW camper is known as the camperbusje. In Denmark and Portugal, the VW Transporter's shape gives rise (rise, geddit?) to the name Pão-de-Forma and Rugbrød, or 'bread load'. In Portugal and Spain the motorhome is known as an Auto-Caravana.

In France live-aboard vehicles – and that includes camper vans and motorhomes – are known as Camping Cars.

In Sweden the motorhome is known as the Husbil. One such vehicle that came out of Sweden was the Saab 92H a vehicle that's half car, half caravan. It has to be seen to be believed.

Across the water in the USA the VW is known as the Microbus, after one of its earliest incarnations in Germany, the Split Screen Microbus, or as a Combi. Or simply the Vee-dub. Misty eyed accounts from the 1960s might also call it a magic bus. Larger camper vans and motorhomes are known as RVs – recreational vehicles – in the US, which is a catch-all for live-in vehicles. Bus conversions with slide outs to create more space are known as the Class As (A-Class in the UK and Europe), while what we think of as campers (van-derived) are Class B campers. Class C campers are van derived but with a coach-built back.

Reputations south of the border have the Combi assuming a

different moniker altogether, with Peru apparently preferring to call it the Combi Asesina (murder bus, literally), due to the tenacity and recklessness of bus drivers in Lima.

In South Africa the VW camper is known as the Volksie bus while in Nigeria, where the Type 3 (Type 25) Transporter is often used for public transport, it is known as the Danfo.

House bus is the term used in New Zealand for that particular type of motorhome that's home built or made from converted buses.

Back in the UK, there is a clear distinction between camper vans and motorhomes. Camper vans are vehicles that retain their van shell, whereas a motorhome is generally used to refer to A-Class and coach-built motorhomes. You might also hear big motorhomes referred to as Winnebagos in a few countries. Winnebago Industries is an American company that manufactures all kinds of large RVs but the term is generally used to refer to big motorhomes. In the UK film industry Winnebago is the generic term for a portable (luxury) motorhome used on location for hair and makeup, or as a dressing room. However, as I have explained elsewhere, UK law refers to camper vans, motorhomes and Winnebagos under the one title: motor caravans.

So now you know. Bet you wish you hadn't asked now, don't you? You didn't ask? Oh well.

A POTTED HISTORY of the camper van

There has been much written about the history of the camper van. It often begins with Hitler's 'people's car' and ends in 2014, with the final Type 2 VW Transporters rolling off the production line in Brazil. But there is more to it than that.

The Volkswagen has become so ubiquitous that it's almost completely eclipsed the memory of those others that went before it or that have driven beside it (and continue to do so). Yet there were, and still are, other makes available. The reason the VW has endured is due to its amazing popularity, which is down, in part, to VW's strategy to create a global network of dealerships. This has meant that parts have been available all over the world since the 1960s, which is a major advantage over other 'domestic' vehicles when it comes to overlanding. The support has always been there.

Of course the VWs were always simply made, well built and easy to work on, and this has contributed to their success, there is no doubt. After all, how many other makes of vintage camper van did you see rolling by the last time you took to the highway last bank holiday? Not many, I'll wager.

BACK TO THE BEGINNING

And it starts, as with everything, with a basic need for people to sleep and live on the move. Whole mythologies have been built upon it. Indeed nations have been built on the notion of a generation hitching up their wagons and taking to the land on a great lifetime's adventure. Think of gypsy caravans, showmen's wagons and shepherd's huts. Think of the prairies, too, with all the hope and optimism of setting off in a covered wagon to look for the Promised Land. Sound familiar?

However, for our intents and purposes we're going to sidestep the horse drawn caravan or wagon (because that's another book entirely) and concentrate on the self-powered home on wheels. How did it happen?

In the early part of the 20th century, camping and touring by car became popular in the USA and the UK, with 'motorised vagabonds' taking to the road in large numbers. So really, it was inevitable that someone would forget his or her tent and kip in the car at some point. We've all done it. Thereafter, it's only a little leap to making it more comfortable, perhaps with a few modifications, a cooker and a washbasin. Or maybe an old shed, plonked directly on the chassis.

THE EARLIEST RV?

Big companies weren't slow to cash in on this new movement of people seeking solace in the green spaces. One of the very earliest 'production' self-powered camper vans that has earned its place in the RV Hall of Fame as 'the earliest RV' was the Pierce Arrow Touring Landau. It was a luxury camper with all mod cons, including a rear seat that folded into a bed, a sink 'behind the chauffeur' and a chamber pot. It also had a telephone connection between the passengers and chauffeur, so, as you can imagine, wasn't massively democratic or cheap. The Landau was unveiled by Pierce Arrow in 1910 at Madison Square Gardens in New York City. Production lasted until 1913.

ON THE ROAD DOWN UNDER

Meanwhile, in Australia, what is accepted as the country's first motorhome was built by GC 'Pop' Kaesler, an engineer from Nuriootpa. He decided he wanted to go walkabout, so in 1929 he built his 'home from home' on the chassis of a 1924 Dodge 4 motor truck. In the following years his family enjoyed the comfort of a 12 by 6ft interior with wireless, stove, beds, tables and wardrobes on trips across South Australia, Queensland, New South Wales and Victoria. It was bought by the mayor of Goolwa later in 1929 and languished there until it was restored in 2000. It now resides at the Goolwa National Trust Museum, having enjoyed a further restoration in 2008.

live

The
Kaesler

THE TILLY - THE FIRST KOMBIS

In the UK, it began in much the same way as it had in the USA, with
a company called Martin Walter, coach builders, that were based in
Folkestone, Kent. Their first forays into converting vehicles brought the
'Utilicon', an all-purpose vehicle made in 1935. The Utilicon could be
used as a working van during the week and then a family seven-seater
at the weekend. Is it beginning to sound familiar now? The Utilicon
was used extensively in the Second World War by all government
departments, and many thousands were made.

After the war, Martin Walter turned its attention to creating a
'bedroom on wheels', with a prototype Dormobile that was exhibited
at the Commercial Vehicle Show in 1952. This was after witnessing
traders throwing cushions into their daily work vans in order to take
the family away for the weekend. The Dormobile was an immediate
success. It seated seven for driving and converted to twin beds at night.
The Dormobile caravan, with elevating fibreglass roof, was introduced
in 1957. The first Dormobiles were based on the Bedford CA van,
with other conversions following on behind, including our beloved
VW Type 2. For a while there in the 1960s, Dormobile was the generic
term for 'camper van' (although don't let the Dormobile Owners' Club
hear you call it such). The Bedford CA, which is rare these days, was
Vauxhall's response to the need for a small and agile delivery van that
VW had tackled so well with the Type 2 Transporter.

THE VW STORY

And I think that brings us neatly to the story of the Volkswagen, which
begins a little earlier than 1952, with a man called Adolf Hitler and a
'people's car', the much loved and lovable Beetle. While production
of the Type 1 Volkswagen never really happened under Hitler, it was
resurrected by a legend in the VW world: a Major Ivan Hirst, a British
Army officer who was tasked with the job of overseeing the original
factory in Wolfsburgh after the war. He is the man responsible for
resurrecting the Type 1 and bringing the factory back into working order
(and in doing so, perhaps playing a major part in Germany's post-war
economic miracle).

The next stage comes with the 'Plattenwagen', a vehicle Hirst
designed to carry heavy parts around the factory. It was based on the
Kubelwagen, a vehicle produced in the factory during the war. Enter
Ben Pon, another VW legend, and a car dealer from Holland who was
looking to import the Beetle for sale in his showrooms. Having seen the

The
Plattenwagen

Plattenwagen – and understanding the need for a light, load-carrying vehicle – Ben Pon was inspired to draw the now famous sketch of the Type 2. Long story short, VW took on the idea and launched it at the Geneva Motor Show in November 1949, with the first Transporter panel vans rolling off the production line in March 1950.

There is a lot more to it than that but that's the basic crux of the story. However, we have yet to convert our T2 into a van that we can live in. That would have to wait until 1951, when, so the story goes, a British officer took his new VW T2 to a coach-building company called Westfalia. He asked it to make him a camping interior, which could be easily removed and wouldn't look out of place in his house. The result was the Camping Box, Westfalia's first VW conversion. The company saw the potential and went into production with it almost immediately. In 1958 the company was recognised by VW as the makers of the VW Westfalia camper van. It was the first to have official VW approval. In time, Westfalia offered all kinds of conversions with awnings and accessories.

The first Type 2s are generally known as 'Splittys' because of their split windscreen. They were superseded in 1968 by the Type 2 'Bay Window' camper. This was refined until 1979, when it was replaced by the air-cooled Type 3 (Type 25). This became water-cooled in 1981, with the last air-cooled VW being produced in Germany in 1982. A 4 x 4 version, the Syncro, was introduced in 1985. The T25 was replaced by

Of all the pictures of vans I have ever taken, this is one of my favourites. It's effortless, and embodies VW ownership to me. Rob Camber, the owner, is a great guy who cares deeply about his VWs. When he heard we were looking for a split for our cover shoot he got in touch and offered to drive down to Bristol from Gloucester.

above: T4, below: T25

the T4, a front engine version in 1990. In 2003 this was replaced by the T5, which was replaced by the T6 in late 2015*.

Westfalia conversions are the most sought after of all the conversions available on the market and continued to be produced until 2004, when the company was taken over by Mercedes Benz. After that, VW decided to produce its own coach-built camper van for the very first time, based on the T5 Transporter. This was the California. Of all the campers on the market it is one of the best designed and best built.

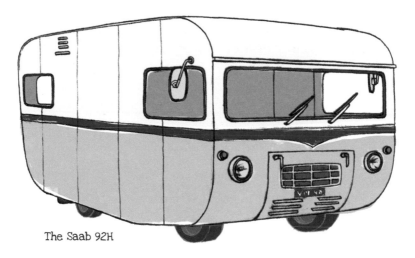

The Saab 92H

THE SWEDISH CONNECTION

We take a little detour now to look at an intriguing vehicle, the Saab 92H – one of the world's first 'A' Class motorhomes. It was created in Sweden by Torsten Johannesson, a man who figured you could marry a car and a caravan and make something that you could drive and camp in; basically, it's a caravan that drives itself!

Unfortunately the vehicle failed its inspection and was abandoned and then consigned to a slow death rotting away in a forest. Torsten then began work on the second generation, which was based on a Saab 95. Saab refused to recognise the project and it came to a halt. Several decades later the 95 was discovered in a forest clearing, after which it was discovered that there were two of these vehicles. They were both fully restored. They are truly remarkable vehicles and worth a Google.

---

* If you want to know more about the history of VW then seek out the books of Dave Eccles. His knowledge is encyclopaedic. Mike Harding's *The VW Camper Van: A biography* is also well worth a read for the way he has placed the VW in a social and historical context.

THE FATHER OF MODERN MOTORHOMING

But, for now, let's go back to the US of A, where we pick up with a gentleman by the name of Raymond Frank, the man who is credited with giving the 'motorhome' its moniker. In 1958 Frank built his first motorhome on a Dodge chassis, so that he could see a bit of the States. As with all good things, the idea captured the imagination of other campers and Frank received orders for more. By 1960 he had made and sold seven, so he decided to start Frank Motor Homes Inc. In 1961 the company changed its name to Dodge Motorhomes and so began the first mass-produced motorhomes.

In keeping with the trend for producing smaller, van-based conversions, Frank turned its attention to smaller vehicles in 1968, producing campers in smaller vehicles.

THE BRITISH CONVERTERS

But of course, on this side of the pond a number of converters were already doing that. In 1959 a chap called Calverley Trevelyan built a camper for his family from an Austin J2, so that he could take his family touring in France. On their return the vehicle was sold to Henley's of Bristol, who almost immediately ordered five more, and then another twelve. Soon after, the company Auto-Sleepers was created. It has survived crashes and fires and now makes some of the best – if the not the best – motorhomes and camper conversions in the UK market. It was also the first company to be given official approval as converters of the Volkswagen T4.

Meanwhile, other companies were also getting in on the act. The other big names in the VW conversion racket in the UK are Devon and Danbury. Devon Conversions are 'probably' the oldest converter in the UK. The founder, Jack White, like many converters, started out converting a Type 2

Transporter for his own use and then found there was demand for more. The company was formed in 1956 in Sidmouth and soon became one of VW's small number of approved converters. Its Moonraker model is one of the most sought-after VW conversions in the UK, with a full-length, side elevating roof that offers a huge amount of double bed space 'upstairs'.

1970S GROOVE, MODERN WHEELS

Danbury Motorcaravans was formed by Joy and George Dawson in 1967, also converting the VW Type 2 Transporter. It was an official VW converter, but lost the status in 1971, only to regain it in 1978. The company went out of business in the 1980s but the name was resurrected by Jason Jones and his brothers, who began importing VW Beetles from Brazil in 1997 and then Type 2 vans in 1998. They re-registered the name Danbury Motorcaravans in 2002.

← **Pretty in pink.**
The Danbury Type 2 is the way to own a classic shape without the classic issues. Imported from Brazil and converted by Danbury, these campers run off bio fuel as well as unleaded and are available with lots of options, including power steering and air con. Imagine that!

Today, they continue to convert and import VWs from Brazil, even though production ceased in 2014. Danbury Motorcaravans' current models include the T5 and T6 and Ford Transit. It also invented the innovative and space gaining T5 Doubleback, a strange hybrid camper with a pull-out rear section, and has been instrumental in bringing the 1970s groove back to campervanning – but without the hassle of actually having to drive a Type 2 from the 1970s.

Live

49

INTO THE FUTURE

The VW T5 is, as ever, a very popular choice for converting to a camper van. However, due to cost, availability and personal choice, almost every van make is now being converted by any number of skilled converters, such as Westward Leisure in North Devon. Its vans are high spec, high price, but offer all mod cons and state-of-the-art safety in a T5 (and soon to be T6).

Auto-Sleepers now converts Peugeot Boxers as well as makes its own coach-built motorhomes. It also converts Mercedes Vitos. Other companies are taking the same tack and converting all kinds of base vehicles. In recent years there has been a trend away from the big white box type motorhomes back towards motorhome-style van conversions in larger vans like the Boxer, Fiat Ducato and Mercedes Sprint. These vans offer the best of both worlds – comfort and space in a manageable base vehicle.

VW produced a concept car of the Bulli in recent years and the internet is constantly awash with stories about the original Type 2 Splitty being revived (in the same way it did with the Beetle). According to VW, it is currently languishing in a warehouse somewhere in the USA, so who knows what will happen to it. In the meantime, VW brought out a day van version with more seats and fewer bits and bobs, the California Beach. I like the look of it. But then there's nothing like driving a 1979 Type 2 Devon Moonraker.

Watch this space.

With thanks to:
Jason Jones,
DANBURY
MOTORHOMES
Andy Brand,
AUTO-SLEEPERS
Allan Horne,
DORMOBILE
OWNER'S CLUB

Live

50

What's YOURS called?*

Imagine the scenario.** You are staring at the embers of a fire. It's late at night and you are chatting with new friends you have met on the campsite. Brought together by your love of camper vans and camping, you share beers under the moonlight, the fire warming your faces as you look into the dying flames.

The conversation turns to the vans. You chat about engines, conversions, equipment. Then the talk turns to names. One of your new friends announces that his is called Monty.

The reason? He explains, 'It's short for Monte Carlo. It was where, after a blissful trip through the vineyards of northern France, a few climbs in the Massif Central and several unbelievable nights under the stars in the pine forests of Aquitaine, the van, on its maiden voyage, finally coughed and spluttered to a halt for the first time in our care.

'Of course it wasn't terminal, and after a quick call to the roadside

---

* Our old van was called Dave after St David's, where I broke down for the first time while making my TV show.
** This is a fictitious story, but it could happen.

assistance provider in the UK, parts were obtained, fixes made and the trip carried on, uneventful, save for another 1000 miles through the olive groves of Italy.'

It's magical. What a story.

Another new friend pipes up. 'Our van is called Tippy because we broke down in Tipperary for the first time after buying it. We bought it and headed off. It was a brilliant trip to the west coast of Ireland. What about your van? What's that called?'

You shuffle a little and kick an ember, as if you were kicking the tyre of a brand new van, just as you did shortly before you got to name your van. 'Well, it's a little embarrassing, really,' you reply, 'we had to get provisions.'

'So what's it called then?'

'Aldi'

'Oh.'

And with that everyone says their goodnights and darts off to bed.

Why did I tell you this story? Well it's because I believe that camper vans should be named after the first place you break down*. This means that they should only ever be used for going to good and exciting places and if you end up with a van named after a supermarket or a shop or somewhere rubbish, that's your fault. Don't let it happen. You have been warned.

WHAT does a CAMPER mean TO YOU? 'Chirpy is a 1999 T4 that we 'converted'. We have insulation and lining, an IKEA sofa bed, Aldi cool bag, suitcase stove and a washing up bowl. Don't need owt else. Had him just under a year and so far been to 25 different campsites. Me, hubby and Mya, the leggy lurcher babe. Black van, black dog, with me and him wearing black, too (so easy to pack, everything matches!) – we must look like The Munsters rolling up. Happy days, wish we'd done it years ago when our daughter was a bab.

P.S. Van named Chirpy as he chirps like a little bird, don't know why. We don't ask in case it's expensive to de-chirp him.'
Julie Gorman *CAMPER VAN OWNER*

---

* If you don't break down then you have the right to call your van anything you like, as long as it's something like Fred, Betsy, Wallop, Titch, Molly or Olive, or something equally cute.

BUYING A CAMPER VAN

H̲ave you got your heart set on a camper?
Congratulations. We look forward to waving to you
along the road somewhere. And we will. But first, before
you buy there are a lot of questions you need to ask
yourself. I have listed them in detail in the following
pages so that you'll know what to look for and what
kind of recommendations can be made.

New VERSUS old

I've owned four old campers now and we are about to embark
on another buying adventure, this time to buy something newer, but not
new. So we're going through the whole experience as if it was the first
time all over again. We are beyond excited.

New campers are wonderful, but cost. So if you have the moolah then
you're going to have a lot of fun choosing all the bits and pieces, options,
add-ons and gadgets and widgets. It's a bit like ordering a new car but
with two or three times the number of options. You want memory foam,
a heater and an underslung tank? We'll talk about all those things later.

The point is, there is no such thing as a standard camper. Even the
single model California SE from VW has so many options and add-ons
that you could never get them all on the same forecourt. The possibilities
are endless. So even if you 'cop out' and go for a new T5 or T6, you'll still
be driving something that is largely unique to you because you chose it.
Even going to a converter and choosing one of their models will lead you
down all kinds of roads of possibilities, as you'll have to choose a base
vehicle and all the bits and pieces that that comes with before you even
get on to your camping set-up.

WHAT does a CAMPER mean TO YOU?

'Having sold our previous caravan to fund a new business venture, we had promised ourselves that when we could we would get something, more us ... more quirky ... more individual. When the time came, I had my heart set on a camper van and after travelling many miles to look at quite a few ugly ducklings we found our van – a 78 VW Bay Window Devon conversion, special Jubilee edition. As we were travelling back home, ELO's 'Mr. Blue Sky' came on the radio and the name Mr Blue was born. Working for ourselves, being able to escape was always a challenge, but once we had Mr Blue all we had to do was climb inside and as soon as we had turned out of the drive we felt like we were already on holiday. He is the ultimate escape, whether for fish'n'chips near our local beach, a day trip on the ferry to the Isle of Wight, winding round the lanes or a full touring and camping trip. Our best ever was a mini tour of Britain we did in only two and a half weeks – no accommodation booked, not even a campsite; we just stopped wherever we liked, we found some amazing places, saw stunning scenery and met some fabulous people. I don't think we have ever travelled in Mr Blue without whole families waving at us in passing cars and flashing their headlights. I love the fact that my boys have grown up with him and I hope that one day one of them will want to take Mr Blue on.'

Lucy Jayne Grout *FOUNDER AND OWNER OF LUCY JAYNE VINTAGE CARAVANS*

Live

However, buying secondhand can also lead to all sorts of conundrums and choices, from the type of bed you choose to the type and age of the base vehicle.

My recommendation, if you want it, is to go to as many big dealers, motorhome retailers, VW festivals and conventions as you can. Nose about in as many vehicles as you can. Check out the layouts, seating arrangements and budget, and try to identify the vehicle that's perfect for you.

There will be one, all you have to do is find it.

TOP TIPS for searching for your PERFECT CAMPER

Go to a big motorhome show and see how the big boys do it. Warners Group publish the UK's biggest motorhome magazine, *MMM (Motorcaravan Motorhome Monthly)* as well as the UK's first dedicated camper van magazine, *Camper and Bus*. They also put on shows around the UK where you'll be able to see all kinds of models from the tiniest micro campers for one to deluxe Winnebagos for the whole tribe in one place. *See* **www.warnersgroup.co.uk** for info.

Rent before you buy. I think this is so important that I have given it a whole section later on. Some people find out very quickly that a camper van is not for them when they rent, so saving themselves thousands. Turn to page 109 to read it in full.

Read magazines and books, er, like this one. Read *MMM Magazine, Volksworld, Camper and Bus* and any other specialist magazine, and you'll soon find out what's available. Mind-boggling though it may be.

Live

56

Search the WWW. There are also lots of VW camper van buyers' guides on t'internet where it's possible to get all kinds of good advice.

Consider alternatives. The Classic Camper Club concerns itself with other makes than VWs, thankfully, although it's tough to get away from it. Take a peek. You may well fall in love yet. www.classiccamperclub.co.uk

Go to a VW meet-up and nose about. It's the very best way to see what VWs are around and available, what it's going to cost you, and what kind of a lifestyle and community you could be buying into. There are hundreds of them around the UK on almost every weekend of the year. Check them out at www.volksworld.com/events

Accost people and be nosy. I love showing people around my camper if they ask politely when I am out and about. So if you see one you like the look of, just ask. All they can say is no. But they might show you around and it may be up for sale...

Consider an import. VWs from hot countries like Australia and South Africa are often rust free (and RHD, right-hand drive). Plenty of companies import them to restore or drive as they are. Imports for the LHD lovers come from California and Mexico. *See* www.gdaykombis.co.uk

Go to a large dealership or converter. Here you'll get an opportunity to look at a lot of vans in one place. There are many to choose from but here are some that I know well.
 MARQUIS MOTORHOMES has dealerships in every corner of the UK, with hundreds of models to look at in each location. www.marquisleisure.co.uk
 DANBURY, importers of the Brazilian Type 2 until it stopped production in 2014, has a large showroom near Bristol, UK, with hundreds of camper vans to choose from, including used models. www.danburymotorcaravans.com
 VW KAMPERS, on the south coast of the UK, sells a vast stock of used Danbury Brazilian VW imports as well as those made in Germany, Australia and South Africa. www.vwkampers.com

Things to THINK ABOUT when buying your camper

A few things to think about when you buy a camper van. Actually I think the subtitle of this section is wrong: it should be 'a long list of the sorts of things you'll need to think about if you decide to buy a camper van'.

Why? Why indeed. Buying a camper isn't like buying a car. There are more things to think about than whether you go for the metallic paint or the GL rather than the GT. You'll need to think about your budget, your family (now and in the future), the amount of time and love you are prepared to invest, and what kind of camping you want to do.

Oh, and how fast you want to travel.

The first question I would like you to ask yourself is "WHY?"

There is no wrong or right answer to this question. Whatever you answer, I hope it will lead you to the right vehicle for you. In answering the 'why' question you set out your aims and dreams for the van you hope to own. You define its use and the way you see it. Are you looking for something to cherish, to bring back to life, to take you on the biggest adventures of your life, because you think it's cool, because you are too long in the tooth to camp in discomfort or just because you want to save a few quid? The following questions will help you to figure it out.

Question 1: *Why do you want or need a camper?* > *see* page 64

Question 2: *What's your budget?* > *see* page 65

Question 3: *How many do you need to sleep/carry?* > *see* pages 66–75

Question 4: *How do you camp?* > *see* pages 77–85

Question 5: *What do you need up top?* > *see* pages 86–91

Live

63

WHY DO YOU WANT OR NEED A CAMPER?

Is it to own a classic? > Yes? That's fine. Be prepared to lavish money and time on your new ride. Lots of it.

Is it to travel the world? > Great! You won't be the first and you'll be joining a long line of adventurers who have dropped everything to tour in a camper. Good luck.

Is it to get away every weekend? > The camper is the ideal getaway vehicle for weekends. *See* 'Camping Box' section on page 124.

Is it because everybody else does it? > Campers are cool. There's no denying it.

Is it because you want to save money on accommodation? > *See* later section on the costs of ownership (page 116). You may not save, unless you want to camp a lot more than you currently do.

Is it because you want to carry sports gear or equipment? > Make sure you choose wisely – some will carry and some won't.

Is it because you still want to camp but don't want to give up your comforts? > Then a camper will be perfect for you. Or perhaps think about a motorhome and go the whole hog.

Is it because you want to take your own space with you when you travel? > This is a very good reason to buy a van. It's a home from home.

Live

64

↙ **Big is beautiful.** Ado, Rachel, Jack and Meggy the Jack Russell have been known to rent out their house and spend their summers in this long wheelbase, home converted Mercedes Vito. It's a home from home with lots of space that doubles as work vehicle when at home in Cornwall. Living the dream.

WHAT'S YOUR BUDGET?

Sorry, but this is the nitty gritty. Once you set your budget you are well on your way to having some of your choices made for you. Your budget will decide everything, from the age to the interior to the condition, mileage and number of owners. It also comes back to the 'why' question.

It's easy to spend a small fortune on a camper, and you could do this just as easily with a modern camper as with a classic from the 1960s. It all depends on how far you want to go. It's worthwhile totting up the running costs, too. Keeping an old camper on the road can be just as costly as buying it in the first place. *See* page 116 for our section on running costs.

How much is it going to cost you?

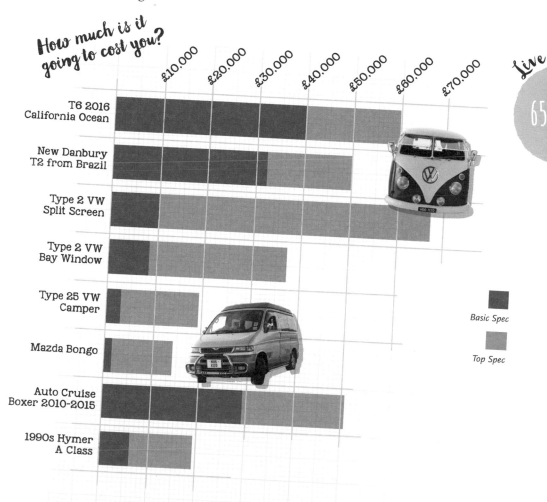

	£10,000	£20,000	£30,000	£40,000	£50,000	£60,000	£70,000

- T6 2016 California Ocean
- New Danbury T2 from Brazil
- Type 2 VW Split Screen
- Type 2 VW Bay Window
- Type 25 VW Camper
- Mazda Bongo
- Auto Cruise Boxer 2010-2015
- 1990s Hymer A Class

Basic Spec

Top Spec

Live

65

Another fundamental. If it's just you then it's easy. Life is so much simpler. You just throw it all in the back and enjoy living the way you want to. My friend Nick had a camper van made out of an old VW Beetle. It was just him, his surfboards, a stove for a brew and a few tins of tuna. Everyone was happy, except perhaps the tuna.

Two is easy, too, as you kind of hope there's an agreement of some sort between you that makes the sleeping arrangements amicable and comfortable. Most camper vans – except perhaps the micro campers – will sleep at least two. It just gets a little more difficult when you go beyond that.

The fact is that everyone is different and everyone's needs are different. And every family or group changes as time goes on. Kids don't stay kids forever. They have a tricky habit of growing up, getting bigger and growing out of bunk beds, hammocks and high-top sleeping platforms. Your little darlings might sleep in a Moses basket on the front seat for now, but it won't be too long until they need somewhere to stretch out, their own locker for clothes and their own space on the bike rack. That's life. Things change.

Live

66

I met **Paul Potgeiter** when he was camping solo in his Daihatsu Hijetta at the end of my road. I left a note on his windscreen saying I wanted to photograph it for my book. He called me back almost immediately and allowed me to lead him off to a lonely camping spot overlooking the sea, where he ended up setting up camp. A trusting chap and lovely van. Sleeps one.

Terry lives in his Hijet during the week, when he works away from home. However, come the weekend, Terry still gets out in it to enjoy the simple life that camping brings. Why would you want to stay in a house when you have got a Hijet?

Couples and kids

For two-berth camper vans it is possible to add hammocks that fit across the front seat and fasten to the A pillar and window pillars, or that slip over swivel seats. These have a weight restriction of around 50kg so are only really suitable for younger kids. They can also be used for storage, which can be useful when you want to fling off your clothes and dive into bed (and find all your clothes again the next morning).

Unless you intend to use a pup tent or sleep in an awning, then you'll need to look at four or more berth campers. That will mean looking at a pop top or high top, or a camper that has more sleeping space. The only VW that can sleep more than four currently is the Super Viking, which can sleep six. However, and this is something to watch for, the Super Viking only seats five. So who's the extra one?

This is a typical issue to be aware of. In vehicles manufactured after 2006 passengers must travel in designated travel seats. That means you can only travel with the same number of people as there are designated seats, irrespective of the number of berths. (There's more important information about seat belt law on page 364).

More than four

If you are looking at sleeping more than four, then you might well have to move into motorhome territory or consider a bespoke build. Some motorhomes will sleep six and have six designated passenger seats so you can all travel together.

If you can't find a suitable camper van to sleep in, then the next best thing will be to make sure you get something that will seat everyone safely. That's when a day van might be your best choice. It might not be the home on wheels with kitchen and cupboards you always dreamed of – and it will affect the way you camp – but at least you'll be getting out there.

↑ **OK, so you want the lifestyle** but without the cramped accommodation. We took this Swift Lifestyle 696 to the Lizard on a wet and windy weekend in November. It sleeps 6 so it's spacious enough for everyone. A Class awesomeness…

Sleeping layouts

By now you will know that different campers have different layouts. Of course! The layout will always affect the way you live and sleep in any camper, even in the most spacious of vans. Some work well, some are okay while the kids are small, some are perfect for two, awful with four.

↑ **Danbury Surf.** a ¾ width bedded 4 berth camper.

The three-quarter width rock and roll

This is the 'industry standard' nowadays. It's the layout that's lasted because it's the most practical, giving a healthy compromise between space to sleep and storage space. It applies as much to vintage campers as it does to modern campers and is the adopted style of the T5 California, among many others. Some r&r beds are safer than others (*see* page 300 for more).

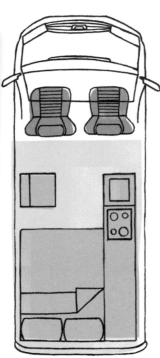

¾ width rock and roll

The full width rock and roll

If you need sleeping and chilling space, this is a good layout to go for. However, the compromise is storage space, as your units will be at the front. In older vans you have the option of having three seats with belts in the back, and the two inertia reel belts.

VW Type 2 with full width bed

Rear kitchen/shower

This is a popular layout for couples that like smaller campers but don't want to give up the indoor plumbing. In early models it allowed for a rear kitchen and in modern conversions it allows for a kitchen plus loo and even shower arrangement. Offers two single beds using the front swivel seats.

Rear kitchen/shower

Rear 'lounge'

This type of layout is only really possible in larger vans and van derived motorhomes that have space enough for two side facing bench seats in the back. These then turn into a big double bed. The greatest advantage of these is having good space and the ability to open the rear doors to the outside. However, having a galley kitchen and shower in the middle of the camper can compromise the living space.

Rear bunks with front double

Rear bunks are great if your van is wide enough to fit them in. However, unless you are driving something that's over 6ft wide, it might not be much good for grown-ups. However, kids will love them until they grow (as kids do) too lanky to fit anymore...

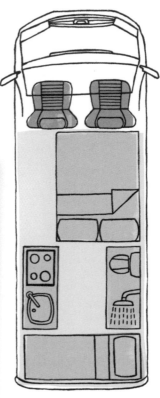

Rear bunks with front double

Over cab beds, Luton style

A-Class motorhomes and coach-built motorhomes often have over cab bunks. They are useful if you want extra storage as sleeping bags, pillows, etc. can then be slung upstairs out of the way during the day. It also leaves space for more beds downstairs.

Josh's Viking 'Nan the Van'

Viking Spacemaker

The Viking Spacemaker roof was launched in 1974 and represented something novel and innovative at the time, which was an overhanging roof that could sleep three or four adults in a circular ring of beds around the central roof opening. They are somewhat of a rarity today but much loved.

In cab hammocks

For kids and luggage, a neat solution to needing extra space might be to consider an over cab hammock. These are popular in VWs and will add an extra bed for little ones, although they are only capable of carrying a certain amount of weight.

For more information on interiors of VW campers over the years, I recommend getting into the books of David and Cee Eccles.

In roof hammocks

Again, in roof hammocks are great for little people or for storage, but not always the best solution for bigger people, as the elevating or pop tops can be a little low, and the getting in and out is undignified at best.

Live

4 HOW DO YOU CAMP?

We all camp the same don't we? We turn up, cook, hang out, sleep, wake and do it all again. Well yes, but no. Just as all camper vans are different, so are all camping experiences different. If you know the types of places you are going and the type of camping you intend to do then it can really help you to decide what type of van is going to be right for you.

There is a lot more about campsites and camping later on, but, for the moment let's discuss camping styles and how they might affect your choice of camper van.

Glamorous camping

This term came into being a little while ago and it's now become the new thing. But what does it mean? Glamping is a bastardisation of 'glamour' and 'camping', designed to attract those who like their comforts to something that perhaps isn't always such a glamorous activity.

What does your average glamper drive? Something glamorous, obviously, probably vintage, maybe even a little quirky. That means it needs to be some kind of a classic. Perhaps not a VW. Perhaps something bigger, with crochet and bunting for sure. And plenty of space.

- Space, for lounging around glamorously
- Shower and toilet, because, why else?
- Kitchen, for preparing glamorous snacks and Italian classics
- Retro looks and styling to make it ever so groovy
- Lots of comforts and space so it's not like camping at all

What you need: *A retrotastic 1980s A-Class? Maybe. Perhaps a Karmann Gypsy.*

Festival camping

I don't know what type of festivals you are used to, but those that I have been to tend to be mucky affairs, with madness outside and a lot of rain. So the perfect festival camper van needs to be a private space where you can get away from the chaos to reapply the lip gloss before venturing out again for more. It doesn't really have to be anything other than dry, comfortable and warm, perhaps with a fridge for keeping a few beers cool.

- Porta Potti, to save late night trips to the portaloos
- Fridge, for keeping a few beers on ice
- Cooker, for putting on a brew first thing in the morning
- A very comfortable bed, for crashing out
- Good curtains (or blackouts) for keeping out nosey neighbours

A VW classic will make you feel all cool and whatnot, but a 4WD Bongo might stand a better chance of getting you out of there once the fat lady has sung.

What you need: *A T25 Syncro to guarantee you'll get out of there? 4WD all the way.*

> **The Mazda Bongo Friendee** is a brilliant and cheaper alternative to the VW or other camper conversions. This one is owned by Ian Boyd, of Bude Surf Cabin.

Touring park camping

This is the kind of camping most of us will be used to. Touring parks are the kind of campsites that have a little of everything, so don't be surprised to find a few mobile homes, some caravans and an area for tents. You can also expect an electric hook-up, hardstanding pitches, clean toilets and showers (we hope) and all mod cons. There may also be a shop. Basically, it's a very safe way of camping, with everything laid on.

- Kitchenette
- Beds
- Electric unit (if you want to charge mobiles, tablets, etc.)
- Awning, if you need more space to spread out
- The kitchen sink for a good quality family holiday

What you need: *Any camper will do, to be honest. It all depends on the level of comfort you expect, the amount of space you need and the number of you. Most campsites will allow you to add to your space by putting up an awning or a pup tent.*

Small site camping

Small sites are the non-corporate sites where it can be a bit rough and ready. These are the types of sites that appeal to the independently minded camper. They may be in a farmer's field or just in a great spot. The French call it 'camping à la ferme' or 'camping au naturel' (which is not to be confused with naked). Again, any type of camper van might be perfect, although bigger vans and large 'units' might struggle a little if there is no hardstanding. If your van relies on having electric, then these kinds of sites might not always be right. They're often without electric, shops or much in the way of glamorous comfort. Best kind, IMHO.

- Capable of being independent of electric
- Kitchen and BBQ
- Fire pit (if allowed) for genuine 'out there' feeling
- Awning or pup tent (for leaving gear) if you go out and about

What you need: *Anything goes, although big motorhomes might not last too long if electric is an issue and access or hardstanding is unavailable.*

Live

81

Stealth camping

As the name suggests, stealth camping is the type of camping you do under the radar. Often in towns, pub car parks or at the side of the road, but done in such a way as to avoid detection. The stealth camper van needs to be unassuming, without accoutrements (on the outside) and, for all intents and purposes, look like a standard van.

- No windows or blacked out windows
- Whatever you need inside – no one can see in anyway
- No bikes, roof racks, or any kind of outside stuff
- No awnings

What you need: *This is when the 'white van man' type van comes into its own. Suits any home conversions without windows and converted tin top VWs without windows. Perfect for an ex-AA Type 4 or blacked out T5.*

Live

82

Wild camping

This is camping off-grid, out there, away from it all. Other camping books call it the 'holy grail' of camping. I just call it 'proper camping'. This is where the camper van comes into its own for my money. You've got everything you really need – heat, light, comfort – so there's no need for any of the extra glampy comforts like electricity or showers. Motorhomers who don't mind living without the hook-up will be best placed to enjoy comforts in the wild – especially if it's Scotland, Ireland or somewhere that can be wet, wild, swarming with midges and generally uncomfortable in anything but a roomier vehicle. If there's no loo you might have to take a spade or a Porta Potti.

Take everything you need:
Cooking gear
Porta Potti
Spade
Fire pit/BBQ
Solar shower

Aire camping

This is camping in designated spaces and particularly applies if you are camping in Europe. The rules of aire camping dictate that you must not spread out beyond your camper, which means that tables and chairs and hammocks cannot be put out. That requires you to be self-contained. If you carry a lot of kit, camping on aires can be difficult as everything needs to be packed away, even in night mode. With a family of four in a small camper, things can get tight.

- Perfect for bigger vans and motorhomes
- Need to be self-contained
- Some aires have toilets
- Some hook-ups available
- Stay for 24–48 hours maximum

What you need: *Again, lots of campers will be perfect for aire camping, although day vans might struggle if they rely on extra space to camp.*

Britstop/Passion camping

Passion sites are camping places available to self-contained motorhomes and campers at places like vineyards, farms, auberges and restaurants. Like aire camping, you need to be self-contained as many sites won't have toilets, taps or electricity. Britstops are the same but in the UK, and largely pubs and farm shops.

- Free but be prepared to spend on a meal or goods
- Must be self-contained
- Suitable for bigger motorhomes and self-contained campers

What you need: *Big motorhomes are fine for these sorts of stops but you need to be self-contained and containable. If you can camp without toilets, water or electricity then you'll love Passion sites and Britstops.*

↗ **The Royale.** Danbury's top-end 2 berth camper with rear loo.

5 WHAT DO YOU NEED UP TOP?

One of the first decisions you're going to face when you consider a camper is what sort of top it's got – or what sort of top you are going to need. There are various options to consider and each has advantages and drawbacks.

Rag top

When talking about rag tops on campers we are generally talking about VW Type 2s. The models everyone will think of with the most affection are the Samba and the Microbus. The Samba Deluxe was VW's most luxurious Split Screen and was originally advertised as being ideal for

WHAT does a CAMPER mean TO YOU?

'I lived in Custard for a year (Custard is my yellow Mazda E2000 van). I met her through the classified ads of the Sydney Morning Herald in 2002, and together we embarked on a journey that took us the length and breadth of Australia. My life changed direction on that trip. I met the man who later became my husband. I figured (correctly) that if we could live together happily for a year in the back of a van, then marriage would be a doddle. Van-life taught me to value simple things. Having left behind a crazy-paced career in television, I found myself taking real pleasure in stuff like waking up with nature and hearing the birds, washing up and cooking outdoors, watching the waves and noticing the weather...

I felt such a connection with that trusty rusty yellow van, that when the time came to return home, Custard came too. She carried us from the church on our wedding day and the precious cargo of our babies on their first camping trips. I chucked in my telly job and created a new career using the van as the focus for a column I write in a camping magazine. Custard remains the embodiment of happiness, freedom and family fun. Just inhaling that familiar, evocative smell of my van every time I climb behind the wheel is enough to remind me what really matters in life.'

Ali Ray *WRITER, COOK, CAMPER VAN OWNER*

Buzz Burrell's Retro Tourer is something completely different. Looking more like a snail on wheels than your average camper, it's a brand new concept in retro style camping. Except it's got a VW T5 as its base. If you want one of a kind, this is the one to go for.

Trading Vehicles
from £24,000

Motor Homes
from £33,500

touring the Alps, thanks to its sliding cloth roof and 21 or 23 window design. Bays were also made with factory fitted sunroofs as options.

Who wants a rag top? Rag top campers are kind of groovy (not to mention highly collectible and valuable if they are Sambas) if you want to feel the wind in your hair and you live in California, but not everybody wants that. And in countries where it rains more than it shines... I don't know... do they leak? Are they noisy at speed? Possibly. Do they give you any advantages for camping? Possibly not.

Besides, if you owned one of the 1950s Sambas you probably wouldn't want anyone's muddy boots in it anyway.

Tin top

This is a standard metal roof on any van or camper. In the case of a VW it'll be a van that still has its original roof. In the UK a classic VW with a tin top will be relatively rare as many vans have had their roofs chopped off to make more room with a high top or a pop top. However, in later models, such as T25s (T3) T4s and T5s, the tin top is more common, simply because there are more base vans around than converted campers. It's the same for other types of vans, such as transits (UK) and modern transporter style vans, although many manufacturers now offer high top options.

Who wants a tin top? Tin top campers are great for couples or singles and families who are happy to camp using a pup tent for kids or extra guests. In smaller vans, having a tin top usually means having just one double bed in the back. Tin tops are also useful for people who want to camp stealthily in a vehicle that looks more like a work van than a camper. With no windows and no discernible visible evidence that anyone is sleeping inside, the stealth camper offers the chance to avoid the 'knock in the night' if sleeping somewhere that camping may not be allowed.

What's so good about a tin top? The advantages of having a tin top are that it won't leak, they are more streamlined (and arguably more fuel efficient) and they retain the original lines of the original transporter.

Tin top campers are also favoured by campers looking for a classic 'day van' that they can use with a tent. However, the disadvantage is that it'll make standing up impossible. So everything will need to be done sitting down, cooking included.

A tin top van also offers potential, as it is possible to add a pop top later if you feel the need to add extra berths or require more space.

High top vans

When we are talking about VWs with high tops we're talking about vans that have had high roofs added on after manufacture by camper conversion companies, as well as those that came out of the factory with high roofs and that have subsequently been converted to campers.

Originally, Type 2 Split Screen high top vans would have been special

High top VW T25

models intended to be used as mobile shops or high topped delivery vans. Today they are rare and highly sought after. However, type 2 Bay Window campers with high tops were converted by conversion companies, so are more common.

Later models, the Type 25 (Type 3) and Type 4 and 5, as well as other makes, are also available with factory fitted high tops.

Who wants a high top? High tops have one major advantage over other conversions or vans: this is the ability to stand up, or, when it comes to pop tops, the ability to stand up without popping the top. It might not seem a significant addition but it can make a huge difference, especially when it comes to cooking.

High tops often have enough space in the roof for a secondary bed or 'upstairs' for small children or adults, something that instantly turns your two berth camper into a four berth vehicle.

It is possible to convert standard tin top vans to high tops. Some companies use fibreglass shells while other, more imaginative converters have been known to use boats and parts of cars.

What's so good about a high top? Apart from the standing up business, which is very important to some people (I hate cooking sitting down, although I am used to it), the high top roof offers space for storage and a means to stow bedding, clothes, kit and all the stuff you like to carry in the roof – leaving the 'downstairs' tidy as you drive. As a quality, this is not to be underestimated! If you travel as a family or with lots of kit then storage space is vital. The ability to fall into bed without having to move everything should never be underestimated either. When you have rearranged everything for 70 nights in a row (as we have) you'll begin to wish that you either didn't bring so much or had a high top van.

Why don't we all drive high tops? High tops can be tricky in side winds. They also produce more wind resistance than the more aerodynamic shapes, which can affect both speed and fuel consumption. Furthermore, they can be a problem at some beauty spots, supermarkets, car parks and places where there are height restrictions. A standard T2 with a pop top is likely to stand around 2m tall – and will fit under most height barriers – whereas a high top can be as tall as 2.6m and will not.

While being unable to access beauty spots is a problem, in my honest opinion being unable to access supermarkets and car parks isn't. Make your own mind up.

Live

89

Pop tops

The pop top is the way many camper van builders add extra sleeping space without compromising the lines too much. The original roof is cut out and replaced with a fibreglass roof that either pops up on struts, or hinges at one side. This then forms a roof tent with bellows made from cloth or vinyl and, in some cases, from solid panels.

Who wants a pop top? Me, for a start. Pop tops and side elevating roofs are fantastic for families as they double the sleeping capacity (more in the case of the Viking roof, which sleeps four 'upstairs') of an ordinary pop top van, adding options of either a double up top or bunks. They also offer standing room for cooking and living for people who want extra space when they park up.

What's so good about a pop top? Pop tops are great for adding space without adding height. They will alter the profile of the van but not significantly like a high top will. The lower profile means it won't affect speed or fuel efficiency too much either, something that makes it a no brainer for some. Pop tops can also be retro fitted to any non-converted van, such as a T5 or T4, which makes them perfect for the home conversion market – something that makes ownership more democratic. Pop tops will add to the value of a converted van.

Why wouldn't you want a pop top? The pop top, while creating space, only creates space when parked up with top popped. So they are great for turning a standard day van or tin top into a four berth camper van, but useless if you want to increase the luggage carrying capacity of your van. You still have to carry everything with you downstairs. And it has to live somewhere when the pop top isn't popped, in drive mode.

Pop tops won't always carry roof racks (although many will) so it's worth considering if you need to carry boards, bikes, top boxes or any of that stuff.

Some pop tops in older campers have hammocks,

which are extremely uncomfortable, even for kids, while solid sided versions like those made by Holdsworth or Auto-Sleeper have precious little head room.

The transition between night mode, camping mode and drive mode can sometimes be a big hassle, especially if you travel with lots of kit and don't have extra space such as awning or pup tents.

Day vans versus night vans

When is a camper van not a camper van? The answer, of course, is when it's a day van. What's the difference? A day van is a van that's used … er … primarily in the day time. So it's not a camper van then? Well, that's where it gets confusing. When I talk about a day van I actually mean a van that's primarily used for daytime activities (commuting, playing, transporting the kids around) but that also has sleeping and camping capabilities. So basically, it's a camper van without the kitchen, loo or shower.

This makes the van much more useful on a day to day basis, and with much more space than a standard camper since less room is taken up with cupboards, sinks, storage, etc. For people who want to camp occasionally but also need a vehicle that's practical for doing the school run, picking up flat packed furniture from IKEA or carrying bikes and boards, it's a really useful option and means that you don't have to live with equipment you hardly ever use. However the addition of the beds – and also an elevating roof with additional berths – makes it great if you camp occasionally, like to cook outdoors or just fancy a lie down on a day out!

Some companies make removable camping pods containing a sink/cooker/fridge so that there is space left in the van when you have pitched your tent. It means you have your own little portable camp kitchen that can be removed at any time.

Personally, I think day vans are the way to go if you camp and play on short hops and don't feel the need for lots of cupboard space or fancy gadgets. Keep all that stuff in your Camping Box for when Friday comes around.

Live

93

CARRYING gear/boards/ kayaks/TOYS

Why your toys should determine how your camper rolls

Did I ever mention that in writing this book I have made all the mistakes so you don't have to? Well I have. And one of the mistakes I made was not thinking hard enough about all the kit we like to take with us. Before I had kids I used to travel with a surfboard, a wetsuit, clothes, a skateboard, a guitar and occasionally a bike. Life was easy, and my old VW Type 25 (Type 3) could carry it all without any hassle. As I have said before I just sort of slung it in the back and got on with it.

Nowadays things are different. There are four of us. That means four wetsuits, four bikes, four boards and four lots of everything. It's a squeeze. Our Type 2 was a pop top and didn't have a roof rack or a bike rack that fits more than two bikes. We once spent ten weeks travelling round France and Spain with two bikes and three surfboards inside the van. With hindsight we'd have done it differently.

So, on the basis of the mistakes I have made, here is some sound advice: if you are like me then you will need to consider your toys in your choice of vehicle. In fact, I would say it really is one of the most important factors in your choice of vehicle. What you need to carry will dictate everything, especially if it's bikes and boards or kayaks.

BIKE RACKS

There are lots of bike racks on the market and there are a few ways of carrying them. Tow bar mounted racks can often carry four full sized bikes, while rear mounted racks depend on the shape of the vehicle. Roof mounted racks also depend on the ability to carry a roof rack or the ability to be able to get access to the roof (on bigger vans).

One of the main manufacturers of bike racks for camper vans

Roof mounting your bikes

This is pretty simple – if you can fit roof bars to your van. But some pop tops won't take roof bars unless you drill them because the profile of the pop top restricts access to the guttering. Also, consider the weight of the bikes on your pop top. And don't forget about them when you go under low bridges.

and motorhomes, Fiamma, makes a broad range of racks for all kinds of leisure vehicles. In fact, it is the only manufacturer that makes racks for specific VW models, such as the Type 2.

But, a lot of its racks will only take a limited number of bikes. So, if you are a family of four who are mad cyclists and want to buy a Type 2, you may have to reconsider, as the Fiamma rack only takes two bikes or a maximum weight of 35kg. It's the same for the Type 3 rack, which only takes three bikes and a maximum weight of 50kg. This is down to the fact that the racks sit on the rear tailgate so it can't carry too much weight. Moving up to the T4 and T5 models it gets easier, as their racks will take four bikes.

If a rear mounted carrier isn't an option then consider a tow bar mounted version. You'll need a tow bar for this, obviously, which is another consideration, as on most older vehicles they don't come fitted as standard.

SURF BOARDS/KAYAKS/SUPS/WINDSURFERS

Carrying surfboards is pretty straightforward if you can fit roof bars on your camper. The only potential issue is security, in which case you can invest in lockable straps or make sure your board is locked away in the van when you aren't with it.

Westfalia supplies special brackets to fit roof bars on its pop tops, while products like Camper Van Culture's Load Rings will allow you to strap boards down to pop tops without fitting specific roof bars.

If you are considering a high top then you may need to consider mounting J bars on the side of your roof to carry boards. Some of these will sit on the gutter and fix to the roof itself, while others will have to be adapted to bolt on to the roof.

You could always travel with bikes inside the van. But believe me, if there are more than two of you it is a pain. Trust me. I know.

TOP BOXES

A further option is to travel with a top box on roof bars. Now I've always been against top boxes as they represent something of a middle of the road attitude towards travel. But, I am assured by friends, that you can

fit a couple of short surfboards and wetsuits inside them. And they are lockable, too. So that's me told. I still don't like them. Oh yes. A top box on a Type 2 or Type 25? Not on my watch.

ROOFS AND THEIR CARRYING LIMITATIONS

Reimo make full length pop tops for all types of vans, including VWs. Their roofs will allow you to mount roof bars. Their Type 25 roofs, similar to Westfalia roofs, have a luggage pan for carrying extra suitcases and can be adapted to take roof bars.

Westfalia roofs hinge either from the front or the back, depending on the conversion. Like the Reimo they have a luggage pan – either at the back or front – that can carry smaller items like chairs, tables, suitcases and awnings etc.

Space roofs are the first company to manufacture new roofs for Split Screen and Bay Type 2 campers in a long time. Their 'turret' and three-quarter length roofs will allow you to fit an additional roof rack to the guttering of these vans for extra carrying space.

Viking and Devon Moonraker full length roofs will not allow you to fix roof bars to the guttering. To add roof bars or fixings you will have to customise. Three-quarter length roofs and concertina roofs will allow for forward roof racks.

Danbury roofs for their new Type 2 campers are three-quarter length, meaning you can add a roof rack over the cab. The Type 5 roofs will take roof racks and roof bars but have a weight limit so are suitable for kayaks, boards and bikes, but not necessarily heavy items.

Auto-Sleeper roofs on T25s and T4s are solid sided. Like Westfalia roofs, they have a luggage pan at the front.

Dormobile roofs are still available for Bay and Split Screen campers. They are shorter than the length of the van so will allow fitting of small roof racks at the front and rear.

live

BUYING ADVICE

PRELOVED: Don't go crazy. Keep your EYES OPEN.

Okay. So you know what you need. You have done your research. You know what kind of a camper you're going for. Your budget is set. Your heart is also set.

What's to stop you?

First, buying a camper is like buying a second hand car (unless you are lucky enough to buy new), so in the excitement you'll need to remember that things can go terribly wrong and that the world isn't always a kind place.

When you are buying a vehicle, the thing to keep at the back of your mind is 'buyer beware'. That means if it dies or falls apart or doesn't live up to expectations, the only person you can blame, in many cases, is yourself.

However, the law will protect you in some circumstances. If you buy from a dealer, then through sale of goods legislation (Sale of Goods Act 1979) you are entitled to expect that any goods you buy are of satisfactory quality. That means they must be of a reasonable quality that a reasonable person could expect, in relation to the way the goods were described, the price and the fact that they were second hand. So, is it fit for purpose? Is it of satisfactory appearance? Is it as described? If not, then you are entitled to a full refund (within a reasonable time of the sale), but you'll need to demonstrate the goods were not of satisfactory quality at the time of sale.

When you buy privately you don't have so many rights. You can still expect the vehicle to be as described and if it is not, you can sue for compensation. But the best advice to give here is to be fully aware of what you are buying. Check it over and check it over again. If things go dreadfully wrong, talk to the seller. I have bought four used camper vans in my life. I know how fraught it can be buying an old vehicle. I also know what it feels like to drive away knowing you have just committed

a huge amount of cash to something that, really, you don't know much about yet. You have to believe a little, but you also have to insure yourself against problems by being as cautious and questioning as you can.

I have also sold campers and have been at the wrong end of a catastrophic engine failure less than 24 hours after selling. As a genuine camper lover and honest seller I was distraught and faced a very difficult decision. In the end I bought a new engine for the buyer out of goodwill. I didn't have to but I didn't want it on my conscience.

Take a mechanic with you when you view

If you can, take someone with you who can give the vehicle a good going over when you view any vehicle for the first time. That means looking at it properly inside and out, underneath and on top. If you are looking at a classic or vintage camper, take a checklist and look at each item in turn carefully.

Follow your instinct

Look at the seller. Observe his or her body language. How does he or she seem to you? Honest? Above board? Are they willing to let you give the vehicle a good going over? Does it feel good? If it doesn't, don't let your excitement get the better of you. Take some time to think about it.

Live

100

Never assume it will be all right – assume the worst

Sometimes 'it'll be grand' isn't enough. Trusting to luck can leave you out of pocket and with a very red face if things go wrong.

Lower your expectations and be pleasantly surprised

You might want it to be perfect, but don't expect it to be so. Lower your expectations and you will or might be pleasantly surprised. If you think it's going to be a crock, then if it isn't you'll already be on to a winner.

Ask questions

Ask lots of questions about everything. Be relentless. Ask about history, cost of ownership, miles per gallon (mpg), anything you can think of. Get as much info as you can from the seller. And don't be afraid to call up if you think of anything else in the meantime.

Look at the log book and history

The history of a vehicle can tell you a lot about how it's been treated. If it has had lots of owners or if there are MOTs missing or bills showing what work has been done, then you'll find out more about it than the owner may be able or willing to tell you. No history doesn't always mean dodgy history, but it could be a sign of something.

Test everything

Turn on the gas. Fire up the fridge. Open the cupboards. Pull out the bed. Pop the top. Test everything to check whether it works. If things are broken or not working as they should, then you can either use it to negotiate a drop in price or as a reason not to buy. Don't ever feel pressured.

That's it. If it's not right, don't buy it, no matter how pretty it is.

'Bernie was such a bargain! Our first journey together was from Oxford to Glastonbury Festival and took 36 hours, including a night at the Solstice Park industrial estate. Our second took us across mid-Wales and ended abruptly somewhere called Creampots with a blown head gasket. He was so unreliable, every turn of the key felt like a step into the unknown. But that sense of adventure, the smell of the 1980s upholstery and all the associated happy memories turned Bernie into a powerful time machine, somewhere I could hide with a guitar and be transported to wherever I chose. I spent countless hours writing in his cosy faded interior and two [Stornoway] albums whizzed by. I've always been drawn to strong personalities, and Bernie was no exception. It's easier to swallow the garage bills if you're dealing with a family member... Although it also harder to say goodbye. RIP Bernie!'

Brian Briggs *THE SINGER WITH STORNOWAY, WHO USED TO OWN BERNIE, A RENAULT TRAFFIC CAMPER VAN*

live

101

Buying new: VISIT A DEALER

While I am not advocating wasting anyone's time. I think it's a good plan to visit a big camper dealership to see what's available, what things cost and what your money could buy you if it was no object, even if you are thinking of buying second hand. If you can also get a factory tour at the same time then you'll get a good insight into the way campers are put together, the work that goes into converting new (or old) campers and the possibilities when it comes to choosing layouts, accessories and your individual specifications.

BUYING OR CONVERTING 'NEW'

There are plenty of companies who can source used vans to convert or will convert new vans for you. Obviously this adds another level of complication to the buying process as you need to choose a base vehicle that's specced right from the off. The market leans towards the VW T5 (and now the T6) because they are so popular but, of course, other makes are also available.

Choosing the base vehicle can be just as important as choosing the conversion because some base models (the VW T5 Kombi) are more difficult to convert than other models, simply because of the way they are finished. Often the more basic the better, as it provides a blank canvas.

Advice: talk to the dealer about what you want, what base vehicle they recommend.

Choosing the basic conversion

We've been through reasons for choosing different conversions already, with considerations such as number of passengers, amount of storage, etc. being really important. However, when you get to see a dealer or converter you'll again have an awful lot more choice. Many dealers or converters have similar basic models, with each having different accessories and features, with the option of add-ons as you go. This is when the sky becomes the limit, with possibilities for DVD players, interior lighting options, showers, water tanks and heaters, interior heating, inverters, swivel seat bases and a whole lot more.

↘ **Lunchbreak at Danbury** and the lads in the workshop are still at it, fixing up one of their own. It is this love of the form that makes companies like Danbury among the best in class. It's a way of life more than a job.

Bespoke conversions

Every new conversion will be bespoke to a certain extent, even if the base conversion is the same as everyone else's. However, you may be offered a choice of furniture finishes as well as accessories that will make your camper unique.

At this point in the buying process – when everything has yet to happen – it's important to get a feel for the stages of creation of a camper and what has to happen at what point to bring it all together.

I visited Danbury Motorcaravans in Bristol for a full factory tour and to see how they put their campers together. It all takes time and everything has to happen in a certain order so that the process is as efficient as possible – so you might just find that your bespoke conversion won't happen overnight.

Bear in mind that things may happen in different orders at different converters and that motorhome/van conversions have a lot more plumbing, electrics and gadgetry than your standard van-derived campers. Having said that, there are lots of newer T5 sized camper van models that are including more and more of the type of furniture that you might expect from a larger camper conversion, including water and waste tanks, cassette toilets (as opposed to Porta Potties), showers, water heaters and ovens.

This isn't a guide to building your own camper van. However I hope it will give you an idea of the process that's involved in putting together a new camper conversion.

Live

104

You choose:
The exciting bit. You choose the finish, accessories, paint, conversion and anything else you think you may need.

Source and strip the base vehicle: To your spec, or your existing. Any lining, floors, etc. will need to be removed before the basics can happen, if they exist.

Upgrade mechanical: New Brazilian Type 2 campers may have additional aftermarket power steering or be converted to RHD for the UK market.

Paint: If the base vehicle isn't the right colour or your bumpers aren't colour coded (for example) it'll go to the paint shop to be repainted to your spec.

Live

105

Roof: Cutting the hole for the raising roof sounds like a big deal but it's not as dramatic as I thought it might be. The converter does it with a jigsaw to a preformed template, then adds in wood or metal mouldings to create the opening onto which the prefabricated and pre-colour matched roof is fixed.

WHAT does a CAMPER mean TO YOU?

'A camper van to me means freedom and impromptu adventures. It's more than just my daily transport, it's a realisation of my dreams. We often jump in our Danbury for unscheduled day trips to explore the great British countryside. If we like where we've ended up, we stay the night because we can. If we don't, we turn the key and move on... Further long-term trips are always fun, as you would expect, but having the flexibility to change or make plans/locations immediately without having to contact a hotel means we are always in control.

The kids often tell us the best holidays they've had are when we are in our camper van together. Always having a spare bedroom means we've used our camper at home when extra guests visit as well as when we go off to parties. Having your own bed, fridge, cooker and heating system wherever you go and great daily transport that's easy to drive and park should never be underestimated. Add the various shows, community spirit and the wave or flash of lights as you pass another camper on their adventures, and it always makes me smile!'

Jason Jones *DIRECTOR, DANBURY MOTORCARAVANS*

Windows: Panel vans don't have side windows, although Kombis do, so this is the point at which your windows will be cut and installed. 240v water fillers and vents for fridges etc. may also be cut at this point.

Camping wiring and electrics: This is a new and separate circuit that includes all camping electrics, 240v feeds and leisure battery. This will allow the van to be plugged into mains at campsites but also for the camping electrics to be used from the leisure battery. It will also include a battery charger and split relay to charge the leisure battery from mains as well as from the main vehicle battery when driving. The looms go in before any of the interior fitting.

Insulation lining floor: Once the electrical looms are in, the van can be insulated inside the panels and lined with carpet liner on all other surfaces, depending on the model and finish. The ply floor then goes in to provide a level surface from which to build.

Tanks and plumbing basics: If your vehicle has underslung tanks they have to be fitted, insulated and all the plumbing fixed.

Furniture: The carcases of the furniture are built outside the van, often from panels that have been pre-cut by a CNC cutter (computer-controlled cutting machine) to a specific van template. Cookers, water heaters and all accessories are included in this build, so the entire unit can be lifted into place, fixed and connected.

Upholstery: Seat and bed bases etc. are recovered, ready for fitting.

Final fixes: Furniture goes in, facilities are connected, plumbing connected.

Seats and rock and roll beds: Beds and captain seats are fixed with new upholstery etc. where necessary.

Final extras quality control (QC) and final polish: Any additional mechanical accessories (alloys, bespoke steering wheels, etc.) are fitted. Everything is tested to ensure that it works and is safe to use, and cleaned ready for the customer. If necessary, gas fittings are certified.

You drive away: And the dream comes true. See you on the road!

With grateful thanks to the team at Danbury for their help with this section.

RENTING A CAMPER

Rent before you buy. This is the sagest piece of advice I am ever going to give you if you are looking for a camper van. For some people the reality of life in a tin box doesn't live up to the hype. And, let's face it there has been a lot of hype – we've had 60 years of hype, as one generation after another finds its freedom at the wheel of a camper van. But it's not for everybody.

I hear from rental companies that occasionally they get camper vans returned before the due date by campers with tired eyes and mournful faces, who drop the keys back on the rental desk with a sigh, claiming it just wasn't for them.

It happens. Some people want more than what the camper van can offer. If you've known indoor plumbing and deeply filled hotel baths with pools and waiters and views overlooking the sea, you might be just a little disappointed with your campsite. It's understandable. When the rain lashes down and the neighbours are being bores, it can be tough living in a VW. I really hope it isn't like that for you because I believe that the good times are out there. It's just that there are times when it's hard to see through the mist and drizzle. But hey, better to find out when you are just a few hundred quid down than when you have just handed over your life savings.

What to do then? Do you turn around and ask for your money back? By that time it's too late and you've got that sinking feeling that maybe, just maybe it isn't going to go well. I've had that. I get it every time I buy a camper. Yes, so things will go wrong, whatever you drive. Just make sure you're fit to cope.

My advice? Rent a van for a week, a weekend, a night. It really doesn't matter. Once you've parked up, got the kettle on and settled down for the night you'll know. If, after a week you still love it, start saving.

How to AVOID a rental CAMPER VAN disaster

❦ Choose wisely. Rent with a company that is well established, with back-up plans if things go wrong. O'Connors Campers in Okehampton, Devon, is one of the most established firms and has in-house mechanics and spare vehicles.

❦ Don't get over excited. The more excited you are, the bigger the crash, if it comes. Keep steady. Hold your nerve. Enjoy the moment. Don't go potty.

❦ Go with a rental company that can provide you with a back-up vehicle if things go wrong. Ask questions. Make sure it will look after you properly. Does it have roadside assistance? What will happen if you break down?

❦ Get prices from lots of companies. Don't go for the cheapest quote (as with everything in life).

❦ Do not over pack. Camper vans are small. So take the least you think you can get away with. I hear that lots of customers take everything – and I mean everything – when they rent a camper for the first time. This will only end in misery as you will have to move everything each time you want to go to bed or make a brew. Take less, enjoy more.

❦ Make sure the rental has a bike rack or roof racks to carry bikes, boards and any of that stuff. Double check.

❦ When the sun shines, make hay. By this I mean stop and take a few minutes to smell the coffee. Park up. Put your feet up. Read a book. Enjoy the moment.

Rent and save

Penny at O'Connors Campers in Devon, UK, tells me that she has customers who love to travel and holiday in a VW camper van but just don't have the spare cash or time to lavish on a vehicle that gets used only a few times a year. So they rent and enjoy the experience without the problems and responsibility of ownership. It's a smart way to go if you are limited in funds or technical know-how. Rental isn't cheap but then buying a classic can be a lot more expensive.

↗ **Is it possible for a vehicle to save a marriage?** This one did. It's a Majestic 155 and we took it to The Lake District in February. We lasted the whole week and enjoyed the benefit of heating, hot water, a fixed bed and all manner of luxuries. It's a home from home for extreme conditions.

Never underestimate the power of a good brew in a tense situation. Get the kettle on.

Kick back and slack. Stop haring around. You won't hit 60 even if you try, so don't try. Learn to live at the pace of the van, not at the pace you're used to. Nothing wrong with underachieving. Achieve nothing.

Make a plan and stick to it – but don't be over ambitious. The moment you stray from your planned path is the moment things begin to go wrong. The freedom of the open road is all very well but a little planning goes a long way. Go and see stuff you have wanted to for ages. Driving around looking for inspiration rarely lives up to expectation.

Book into a really good campsite. Don't settle for anything less than something really special. Disappointing campsites can kill your expectations stone dead. If the weather is looking iffy, book into a campsite with a bar, indoor pool, sheltered BBQ area or restaurant.

If other people are the issue, find a good wild spot. Go somewhere you know, where it's certain you'll have a good time.

WHAT does a CAMPER mean TO YOU?

'Tents may be my first love, but for as long as I could remember, I had a hankering to own a VW camper van. Sadly, I never had the resources – financial or time – to make my dream a reality. My collection of camper-themed memorabilia was no consolation; in fact, every time someone added to it ('Ooh, a pair of camper van bookends. Lovely.'), it felt like they were mocking me. Then, at long last, I finally got to borrow a camper for a week. George (they always have names) turned out to be everything I hoped ... but at the same time everything I'd secretly feared. It looked great and was undeniably cool, but also ridiculously difficult to drive, ploddingly slow (being overtaken by a funeral cortege was a low point), mechanically unreliable and, worst of all, incredibly uncomfortable to live in. I was deflated. I returned the van a day early and sloped off to look at pictures of tents online. I've had my fix, now I'm sticking to canvas.'

Iain Duff, Editor *CAMPING MAGAZINE*

Rental companies

There are plenty of rental companies around, with new outfits springing up all the time. You only have to do a quick search on the web to realise that. As such, companies come and go, and, as often with these things, some may be better than others. So here are my limited recommendations. Purely personal and based on what I know, and therefore only in the UK I'm afraid. It doesn't mean others aren't also excellent, but I have no experience to back this up.

SOUTH

O'Connors Campers has a fleet of 15 camper vans, including relatively new VW T5 Californias. It is one of the UK's oldest rental companies and has a huge amount of experience, in-house mechanics and a really good way of working. Lovely folks, too. Perfect for trips west.

O'Connors Campers

Highlands, Old Road
High Street
Okehampton EX20 1SP
01837 659599

penny@oconnorscampers.co.uk
www.oconnorscampers.co.uk

Deeside Classic Campers

Crann Dearg
Drumhead Finzean
Aberdeenshire AB31 6PB
01330 850555

office@deesideclassiccampers.com
www.deesideclassiccampers.com

NORTH

Deeside Classic Campers is relatively new but its campers are a cut above. Claire, who owns the company, has big ideas and demands rigorous standards from her three campers. As such, they are immaculately decked out, beautifully prepared and well maintained. If you want to see the Highlands, this is the way.

Live

114

WHAT does a CAMPER mean TO YOU?

'**There are few vehicles** on the road today that raise the smiles than that of a VW camper van. DCC was created in 2014 to share our passion and love of this iconic vehicle and lifestyle. We have had customers of all ages who have thrown themselves into the 'VW classic camper adventure' for their own special holiday reason, be it on beaches, by lochs, over glens, or enjoying the great outdoors without gadgets! Waving is obligatory in a camper!

We love customers' reactions from the moment they collect their V-dub, to reluctantly returning them, eager to share with us their special adventure and photos. Customers have thanked us for enabling them to have the best holiday they have ever had, and we have shared their laughter and their tears when saying goodbye. It is an honour and a privilege to meet lovely people and to help make their dreams come true! As one customer said, 'To be honest, who wouldn't want to holiday in a funky camper van?!''

Claire Page *OWNER OF DEESIDE CLASSIC CAMPERS*

THE COST OF OWNERSHIP

Typical RUNNING costs

When I add up how much I have spent on my campers over the years, it's frightening. But it's important to know – in advance – how much your camper is likely to cost you if things go wrong. Rather than work out how much the van has cost me in total (which I have done anyway) I thought it'd be more interesting to work out the cost per night. Why do it this way? It's an interesting exercise, especially if you intend to own a camper to save money on holidays. It might help to reveal some uncomfortable truths. It may even serve as a really good sales patter if I ever decide to sell it.

When you compare the cost of my old classic Type 2 against a modern vehicle that requires far less maintenance and upkeep, and does at least twice the mpg, it's easy to see that buying classic really could be a labour of love – unless you can get one that needs no work whatsoever... It's up to you to decide what's for you.*

* Disclaimer: This comparison is based on the cost of ownership of one typical vehicle, Type 2, against a typical Type 5, assuming the cost of petrol to have been a constant £5 per gallon and insurance to be either £400 or £500 per year.

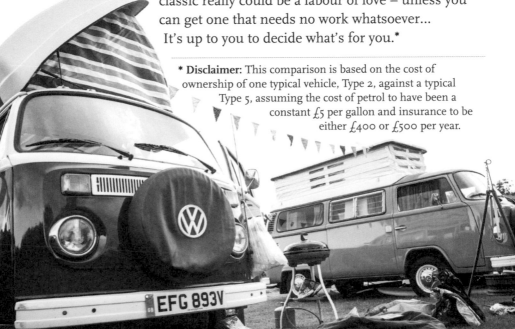

So here goes (take a deep breath):

VW Transporter Type 2 Devon Conversion 1979 2.0l	
Road tax	£1150
MOT	£275
Insurance	£2000
New engine 2012	£4000
Repairs to roof 2011	£1500
Interior 2013	£500
Heating 2013	£500
Re-spray 2014	£3000
Servicing	£2000
Tyres	£500
New seats	£175
SUBTOTAL	**£15,600**

Mileage based on 10k per year:	50,000
Fuel consumed (approx. 18mpg):	2700 gallons
Average cost per gallon @ £5:	£13,500
Total cost of ownership over 5 years:	£29,100
TOTAL COST OF OWNERSHIP PER YEAR:	**£5820**

Total number of nights spent camping:	
2010	50
2011	35
2012	65
2013	20
2014	20
TOTAL	**190**

Total cost per night*	**£153****

* Don't forget that this also includes the cost of getting there as well as the cost of the accommodation, but doesn't include camping fees. It's not too bad, considering. But really, we ought to get out more.
** This doesn't include the initial cost of buying the van. Even so, flipping heck.

Okay, so let's transpose these costs to owning a T5 California. Assuming you won't have any major mechanicals or need a rebuild and respray in the first five years of ownership, then it's a safe bet to compare, as I have done so below.

VW Transporter Type 5 California 2.5l diesel	
Road tax	£1150
MOT	£275
Insurance	£2500
Servicing	£2000
Tyres	£1000
SUBTOTAL	**£6925**

Mileage based on 10k per year	50,000
Fuel consumed (approx. 36mpg)	1388 gallons
Average cost per gallon @ £5	£6944
Total cost of ownership over 5 years	£13,869
Total cost per night*	**£73**

* Again this doesn't include the cost of buying the vehicle in the first place, which could well be £50K+. Again, flipping heck.

How to work out your mpg

It's funny, isn't it, how we buy fuel in litres yet we still use mpg to measure our car's efficiency? Anyhow. Working out your fuel consumption is easy.

1 Fill your tank.
2 Record the mileage.
3 When the time comes to fill up again, refill your tank to the same level again, keeping note of the litres you used.

4 Note your mileage since you first filled up.
5 Divide the mileage by the total litres used. Then multiply by 4.546 to get the mpg figure.

Live

118

THE ECO-CONSCIOUS CAMPER

OR WHY it's okay to drive an old banger (ahem, CLASSIC camper)

I have often wondered about the green implications of sticking with an old camper. According to fuel consumption data required by law from manufacturers, the engine will give an average of 23.9mpg at 58mph. So, as modern cars go, it's a gas guzzler. And, to be honest, that's optimistic as a figure.

So is it appropriate, knowing what we know about climate change, to continue to drive a classic car if it's got such a poor carbon footprint?

Well, there's good news. When it comes to the van's overall carbon footprint we can't just consider the amount of fuel it noshes on each run. We also have to consider the carbon footprint of the entire life cycle of the van. That includes energy used in manufacture and disposal.

Let's think about disposal first. At some point your van may give up the ghost and discontinue its existence. At that point it will cease to be more than the sum of its parts. However, it will still have value for its parts. That means much of the vehicle may be recycled and reused, so giving it another life and reducing the need for new parts (complete with their own carbon footprint). Those parts may also keep another vehicle going, so reducing further the need for new vehicles to be manufactured.

Now let's think about manufacture. My old van was only made once, so its total footprint over its lifetime will only ever be the manufacturing costs plus the running costs plus the disposal costs. That means that the total life carbon emissions of keeping one older vehicle on the road may well add up to a lot less than buying a new car every five years for the life of the van. Five years is the average time before sale for new cars in the UK. When I sold my van it was 35 years old, so, if I had had it from new, I would have saved the carbon emissions of buying on average seven new cars in the same period of time. The percentage of a vehicle's life carbon emissions that is created in manufacture is estimated to be anywhere between 12 and 35 per cent of the total. The longer it stays on the road, the less that percentage becomes. But with modern cars, which have an average life span of 13 years before being scrapped, the percentage of embedded carbon (from manufacture) is greater. Even if the emissions of those seven new cars were twice as good as my old van and the carbon footprint of manufacture half that of my old van, I am still winning. So, yeah. It's ok to drive an old banger.

Driving an OLD BANGER: Getting more BANG for your BUCK

We're all a bit concerned about the environment. It's facing tough times. And while we have already established that driving a classic camper (or a newer one for that matter) may not have such a devastating carbon footprint as we feared, it still burns petrol. So it's only right that we should do all we can to use as little fuel as possible. And that will help us to keep our running costs down.

Maintenance
This is your first stop on fuel saving. A vehicle that is poorly serviced will use more fuel than one that is serviced regularly. Old vehicles have shorter service intervals than modern cars so make sure you service whenever it is needed. Use the correct oil too, as this will make your engine run more efficiently.

Tyres
Another important factor. Always drive with your tyres at the correct pressure. Driving with them too soft can lower your mpg.

Watch your speed
The faster you drive, the more fuel you use. Figures. According to the AA, driving at 70mph uses up to 9 per cent more fuel than at 60mph and up to 15 per cent more than at 50mph. Cruising at 80mph can use up to 25 per cent more fuel than at 70mph. But you can't do that can you?

Be smooth

Driving smoothly into junctions and out of them again will help to improve your fuel efficiency. So try to keep moving, rather than stopping and starting a lot. Driving defensively – making sure you keep enough space between you and the car in front, and driving slowly but steadily in queues – will help in stop-start situations.

Change gear earlier

Don't rev the engine too much. Let it work at its most comfortable rate and it'll reward you with better efficiency. No more revving or red lining.

Turn off everything!

Well, don't if you need it. But keeping your heater blower (or air con if you have it) on will contribute to your mpg in a negative way, by placing more demand on your engine to replace the battery power it's using. If you don't need it turn it off.

Switch off if it's more than 10 seconds

If you are sitting in traffic or waiting in line then it can pay to switch off. As long as it starts again, you could make savings on long waits.

To coast or not to coast?

All the advice points to the safety aspect of coasting down hills to try and save fuel. If you run a carburettor then you'll save money by coasting out of gear but is it worth it? When you coast you are effectively out of control. Better to be safer. Keep in gear, be in control.

Ditch the top box

I knew it! Top boxes will add to your vehicle's drag, as will racks, open windows, surfboards and kayaks. The rule is, if you're not using it, get rid of it.

Lose some weight

The lighter your vehicle, the less fuel you'll burn. So it pays to get rid of things you don't need and travel as light as possible. The same applies to camping in general. Less is more.

live

123

THE SECRETS OF HAPPY CAMPING

Find a PLACE for YOUR everything

One of the secrets of good camper van living (and living in general) is to find a place for everything and then to make sure everything is in its place. It might seem to be a bit bleedin' obvious but you should try telling that to my children. In unscientific tests my family spent 50 per cent longer packing away their stuff when no one knew where to put anything. Anyway, if it's got a place then you will know where to put it back after you have finished using it. If you know where it is supposed to be you can also find it pretty darn easily when the time comes to use it. Yeah. It's the secret to happy camping. You better believe it.

BEING READY at a moment's notice: the CAMPING BOX Mk2

Here's an idea. I stole it from Westfalia. On page 41 you'll read about the Westfalia Camping Box as being the massively significant piece of van furniture that started the camper van ball rolling. The idea was to have a removable piece of furniture that could be fitted neatly into a Type 2 VW Transporter, which would contain everything necessary for camping. It also had to look okay in the home once removed from the van.

Well, my idea is similar but not quite so significant, worth a lot less money to a collector and probably won't look great in your home. But the idea is the same: to make camping easier.

The Camping Box Mk2 will appeal to you if you are an impulsive sort of a person and like to feel that you are free to take off at any time. However, if you are anything like most of us, you'll probably be held in place from Monday to Friday by schools, jobs, work, mortgages and such like. It's boring I know, but that's why you have a camper van. And it's why the Camping Box Mk2 is a brilliant idea that will remind you of the weekend to come as you trip over it every morning on your way to work.

The Camping Box Mk2 is simply a box (hence the title) that sits by the front door (or somewhere equally visible but convenient, where you won't trip over it) and reminds you of the fact that you cannot wait to get out and get camping.

Take more tea towels than you need

When you hit the road you are going to find that everything rattles: the pots and pans, the grill pan, the cooker lid and so on and so forth. If you have spare tea towels you can use them to dampen the sound of the grill rack in the grill pan and all those other annoying sounds that come from a typical camper van.

WHAT does a CAMPER mean TO YOU?

'For Alison and me, the van has become our escape capsule, reassuringly ready and waiting to go. A means to break free from everyday pressures, even if only for an afternoon or the odd night away, not too far from home; and for longer trips to foreign shores with the opportunity to explore and absorb continental ways. But always with the comforting familiarity of our VW.

We weren't looking for a van when we came across our scruffy, tired T25, but like a stray dog or cat in need of a home, it sort of chose us, and so began a relationship that has given so much pleasure. There are few better sounds after a night's sleep than the click and rumble of the sliding door opening onto a new day. Add a hot drink, fresh morning air and a chance to be still and enjoy the moment. Inspirational magical moments.'

Geoff Campbell *CAMPER VAN OWNER*

WHAT'S IN THE CAMPING BOX?

Basically, everything, from toothbrushes and toothpaste to sleeping bags, cutlery, plates and even some basic, long-life staples. All you really need for a swift get away and all the basics to sleep out under the stars (in your camper) are here, ready to go. It's perfect for the day van camper and for those who don't like leaving stuff in the camper for long periods.

The idea, as I have said, is simple. When it's time to go you can top up on the essentials, slip the box into the back of the van and go. No need to pack and repack every time. Why waste time faffing about at home on a Friday night when you could be out there? The Camping Box solves it. Include the following:

live

127

- Toothbrushes
- Toothpaste
- Water container (if not on board)
- Single ring gas cooker and spare gas
- Sleeping bags
- Loo roll
- Cutlery
- Chopping board
- Plates, bowl, mugs
- Frying pan and pots
- Tea bags
- Sugar
- Dine Box with seasoning, oil and basic spices
- Pasta
- Tins of tuna (or other tinned favourites)
- UHT milk for emergencies

The Camping Box

Everything else – pillows, clothes, surfboards and perishables – can be grabbed as you dash out of the door. (*See* page 164 for more on removable cookers and cooking pods).

ESSENTIAL camping KIT

Accessories that will make camping easier

Some bits of camping gear are, in my humble opinion, essential. These are the bits that make life easier, will give you a good night's sleep or will make your space go further.

There is a lot of camping gadgetry out there. It's like any other massive industry in the respect that there are always innovations and new products for you to splurge your hard earned cash on. Some of them, inevitably, will be a bit gimmicky, like a musical pillow or a blow-up gadget chair, but others will be 'essential' in that they should form the basis of your keep-on-board camping gear. The list, inevitably, is short, because your van should provide you with basic cooking, washing, dining and sleeping facilities. Anything else is just being greedy.

An axe

This will make chopping wood easy. As if anything else would! If you intend to make kindling, chop logs or generally make any kind of fire, you're going to need one of these. I have a favourite, a lightweight, double edged billhook that's fantastic for making kindling, if a bit light for dropping trees. Not that I'd want to be. It's more than adequate and can be stored easily.

Fire steel

Sometimes you lose your matches. Sometimes they get soggy. Sometimes you can't get a lighter to work. A fire steel is difficult to lose, easy to use and very difficult to get wrong. It's in the glove box constantly.

Electric hook-up

Does anyone ever travel without an electronic device? Doubtful. That means you need power to be able to charge it up. And electric hook-up – whether it's a 16 amp C-form cable or a complete hook-up kit – means you can connect to campsite electrics and enjoy mains lighting, recharging and running any on-board items like fridges and cookers (some people have them) off the mains.

TV aerial

16 amp C-form hook-up

If you are travelling outside your home country, don't forget to check the local current, voltage and plug type, and take an appropriate adaptor.

Levelling chocks

And possibly a spirit level. With a decent pair of levelling chocks you won't have to sleep on a slope. There's an art to getting it right and appreciation in a job well done. Your reward for using the spirit level? A great night's sleep.

Water hose

If you have an on-board water tank you'll need to be able to fill it up. Even if you have a portable water container, it can be a pain to fill if you don't have at least a short length of hose. Include universal attachments to fit any tap.

Head torch

Useful for cooking in the dark, walking to the pub, finding the loo or late night hiking (AKA being lost on a walk). Small enough to pack away tidily in the corner of a cupboard.

Map

I don't go big on sat nav technology as it always goes wrong. Better to learn how to use a map and then buy the most detailed one you can. Maps tell you everything you need to know about an area. They are wonderful sources of fascination and information. Map reading is a skill and a joy. I would urge everyone to learn how.

Live

131

Swiss Army knife

The only tool you'll ever need. Get a good one and you'll be able to do almost anything (almost). Don't bother with the one with two blades and a bottle opener. Go for the big one, with everything. It is a thing to cherish and use, and if it ever goes missing you will be bereft. Know where it is at all times.

Water storage

Some larger vans and motorhomes will have a tank on board. Other campers will need to arrange their own. Foldable and collapsible are all very well but little can replace a solid jerry can type water container with a tap attachment. They won't puncture, are easy to carry and the tap makes it easy to pour.

Fresh tank filler

Easy-to-put-on shoes

I'm thinking of your comfort and ease here. Slip-ons (such as Crocs) are a godsend to the camper as they are easy to put on for middle of the night and early morning wee visits, are light to carry and are comfortable to wear around the campsite. Although, what the fashion police might say is another matter. In winter, wellies are essential for early morning walks through long and wet grass.

Decent weatherproof clothes

Don't scrimp on the waterproofs. And don't leave them at home. Better to leave them in the van so you'll always have them to hand if the heavens open. Getting cold and wet is the first step to misery and is difficult to recover from. It can actually be dangerous, too.

Loo paper and folding spade

The spade is non-essential but could be useful. The loo paper is, of course, vital to a happy trip. And there's nothing like walking across a muddy field with a roll of it early in the morning. Everyone knows where you are off to. No one minds.

First aid kit

People hurt themselves camping. It's being out of the comfortable zone where nothing exciting ever happens that does it; we relax, let down our

Live

132

guard, enjoy a few glasses of Prosecco and then strips, slips and falls catch us out. With any luck the worst it'll be is a few cuts, stings and bruises. But if it's not, make sure you have enough first aid supplies to deal with it – at least until you can get help.

- Plasters
- Scissors
- Bandages
- Gauze and lint for dressing wounds
- Antiseptic cream for cuts and grazes
- Antihistamine cream for bites and stings
- Sudocrem for sore skin and grazes
- Steri-strips for larger cuts
- Antibacterial handwash
- Insect repellent
- Sun cream

AWNINGS AND PUP TENTS

For some, an awning is an essential, either for sleeping, cooking or for sheltering in unseasonal weather. If you want to leave stuff and go off for the day, then a drive-away awning is essential. It enables you to have a storage space to leave gear, bikes, etc. instead of packing everything up. When you get back all you have to do is clip it back on (or use whatever method yours employs) and, hey presto, you have another room to your van.

Fixed wind out awning

The fixed awning is the type that bolts to your roof and then winds out to provide you with shade. They are available with sides if it's windy and can be pegged out to avoid gusty disasters. However you dress them up and set them up they remain fixed to the van, so everything still needs to go inside. But they are useful for cooking under and don't need to be packed away and fighting for space along with everything else.

Drive-away awning

This is where you can go crazy. Drive-away awnings come in all shapes and sizes and can be one finger operation, multi-poled or even

inflatable. We have camped with all kinds of awnings and they are great for storage, adding extra space and sleeping in.

They can also be bulky, heavy and take up valuable luggage room in a small camper. Also, no good for camping wild or using on aires. So, for us, the smaller and easier to carry, the better.

Awnings fix to vans in different ways. If a van has a gutter then a clip-on figure-of-eight piece can be used that runs the length of the sliding door. A cord section of the awning entrance then feeds into one part of the figure-of-eight and the gutter sits in the other. Otherwise a pole and clamps make a good, secure method of fixing that's easy to dismantle when you want to drive off. Just don't forget it's attached before you do so.

For vans with no guttering there are a couple of methods to fix to the van. One is to have straps that go over the van and secure to the ground. The other is to use suction mounts that stick to paintwork.

Drive-away awnings are very good for developing your accurate driving skills, if you wish to make sure that the connection piece is

taut. An inch of reversing either way and you could end up with a slack, water gathering join that is too tempting to tip on your fellow passengers. You have been warned.

Awning skirts

There is one thing about awnings that is annoying and that is the fact that wind blows under the van and into the awning, making everyone cold and making it billow. The way to avoid this is to use an awning skirt that connects between the two wheels of the van and blocks out any moving air, although a surfboard will work just as well!

Live

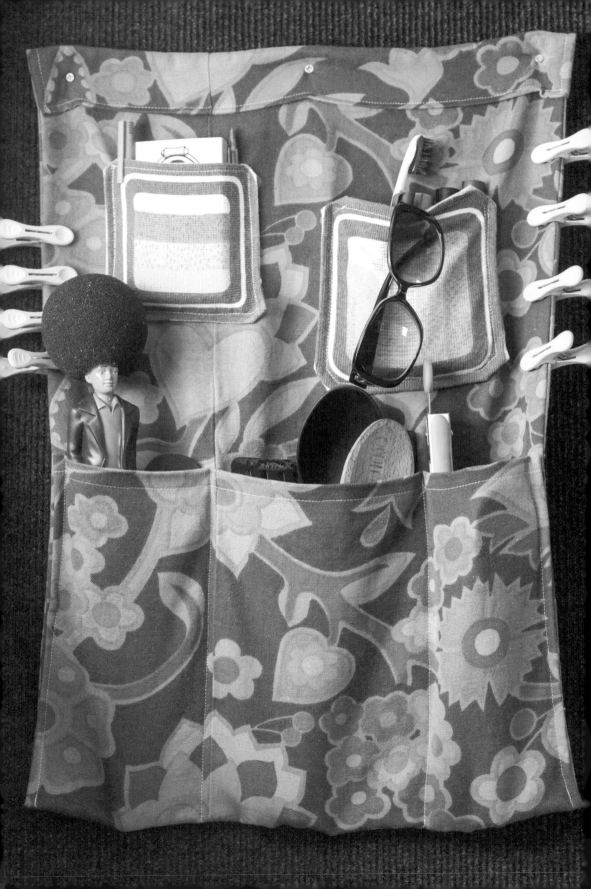

TOILET AND SHOWER TENTS

Aka the latrine. These are pretty useful if you have a Porta Potti and don't want it in the van while you sleep; handily small and packawayable for midnight visits when the loo block is just a stroll too far away or for when you're out in the wilds. They even come in pop-up form so you can wrestle them away when you've done your business. Now that's glamping.

Make your own shower curtain sunshade

Using a standard shower curtain is a really quick and easy way to make a funky looking sunshade/awning for your camper. It's cheap too, and if you have spare tent poles and guy ropes knocking about, will cost you very little. If you currently use an awning you can mix and match the fixings and poles for your sunshade if you don't want to use the awning.

1 Buy a shower curtain. This is the most important bit. Make sure it is the type that has eyes at one end, and that the eyes aren't huge, and that it's made of material rather than just plastic sheet. If the eyes are too big then your tent poles will simply fall through them.
2 You'll need a way of fixing the awning to your van above the sliding door. If you have a gutter on your van then it's reasonably easy with a pole and clamps. If you don't have a gutter then suction cups and a pole will do it.
3 Sew a pocket into the opposite edge to the eyelets to take a tent pole. This will give your sunshade its rigidity at the door end. Push a tent pole into the pocket and then attach it to the van above the sliding door as you would a standard awning.
4 At the opposite end, use tent poles with spigots to sit in the eyelet holes of the shower curtain. You should then be able to use guy ropes to peg out the poles and so create a great sunshade ... easy!

Live

139

RAN 81U

Toilets

We carry a Porta Potti in our van. It lives in our 'buddy box' and gets used in 'emergencies only'. That means nothing serious happens in it. We carry it because it's handy to have and it means we can wild camp if necessary. It also means we can stay on Passion sites and aires where there are no loos, if we feel the need. It's not necessarily because we don't want to use public loos, because we are quite happy to.

Porta Potties and chemiloos

Porta Potties are self-contained camping toilets that have their own mini water reservoir for flushing and a container for the waste. They come apart and can be separated for ease of handling and cleaning. Chemicals are added to the flushing reservoir (often known as pink chemicals) as well as the waste container (blue or green chemicals) to aid cleaning and waste breakdown.

Porta Potties

When buying chemicals for your Porta Potti you can choose eco friendly products or non-eco friendly, which are products that may be more effective but that can be harmful outside the contained usage of the loo. Some campsites will specify the use of eco-friendly chemicals only.

The advantage of a Porta Potti is that it can travel, even when used, so you don't have to worry about emptying it immediately after use. But don't leave it any longer than a day or two.

Bucket and chuck it toilets

Really? Yes. There are very simple products available that are nothing more than a bucket with a seat. You go, then you pour it away, but you wouldn't really want to be too far from an emptying point, as it's not going to travel well. And you really can't empty it anywhere (see the section below).

Toilet powders

There are some products available that use powders to gelify waste in a biodegradable plastic bag. These are then put into a standard bin or compost. The advantage of such a system is that all the components pack neatly down and contain no water. It's all dry.

Spade and straddle

I bought Mrs D a folding spade for Christmas. It didn't go down too well, but it was an improvement on the old diving flipper she used to have to use to dig a hole; hell hath no fury like a woman walking back from the dunes I can tell you. Anyway, if you must dig a hole (and you must dig a hole rather than not dig a hole), do it at least 100m from any water courses, rivers, streams, paths or the sea, cover it up properly and restore the ground to how it was before you got there.

Cassette toilets

Some camper vans (usually the larger ones) will have cassette toilets. Some may also have electric flushes and all kinds of luxury. These combine with an integral loo inside the vehicle. The cassette refers to a removable cassette (watertight container or tank that holds the waste) that can be removed from the vehicle for emptying from a hatch outside the motorhome. The flush tank (which is separate from the fresh water tank) and waste tank will take chemicals, like the Porta Potti.

EMPTYING YOUR TANKS

This is where it gets fun. On campsites all over Europe, at around 8 a.m. you'll find a steady stream of grim faced men between the ages of 35 and 85 (it's always the men) strolling over to the 'slophopper'. Once there, they will make weak jokes about the day only getting better from here while they slop out the tanks with a stoic smile. There's a knack to avoiding unpleasant splashback, with some tanks having an air release valve to make for a better flow.

Anyway, the rules are that you do not empty your tanks into anywhere there is fresh water because it is a toxic mélange that must go into the sewage system and be treated properly. It must not be emptied into drains, overflows or rivers. Some campsites will have special areas for out swilling. Use them.

Loo paper

It is recommended that you use special 'quick dissolve' toilet paper in chemical loos. This is because it will break down quicker and lead to less clogging. It's not the cheapest option but it does work. Alternatively use thin, cheap paper.

Keeping clean

Sometimes keeping clean can present a challenge when you are out and about in a camper van. Not all camper vans will have on-board facilities, which means making do with what you have got. For those who dare, washing in rivers and lakes is okay as long as you don't use detergents that will kill fish and damage the natural environment you have worked so hard to enjoy.

Personally I am in favour of this 'leave it nicer' idea, where our camping and camper vanning has a positive impact on the environment (I will bang on about this later). So that means being as considerate with waste and detergents as you would with all your other waste, like bottles, cans and plastics.

FOR CAMPERS AND MOTORHOMES WITH ON-BOARD FACILITIES

As I have said before, I am not your mother so I am not going to tell you how often or how to wash in your own little on-board bathroom. Lucky old you. However, I do want to talk about one aspect of your ablutions that I think it's worth discussing. Goodness knows how many forums and online discussions I have read about this and everybody has an opinion on it. It is the emptying of grey water tanks.

● **Grey water tanks** contain food particles and the residue of your washing up and washing and showering. Unless you use 100 per cent environmentally friendly detergents, soaps and tooth-pastes (which are particularly bad), your grey water can be harmful to the environment, water courses and wild life.

● **Food particles in grey water** can help to attract rodents and scavengers if it is dumped at the side of the road, on a pitch or over someone's hedge.

● **Dumping your grey water tank** on your pitch, everyone agrees, is unsociable and leads to bad smells and unhealthy patches. So, don't do it.

● **Dumping grey water while driving** along is considered bad practice and unsociable. Whoever you believe, it may also lead you to a prosecution for polluting. It also gives us all a bad name.

● **Dumping grey water down a drain** at the side of the road isn't good practice. Unless you can guarantee that a roadside drain flows into the mains sewerage plant or into the mains drainage, it could pollute and cause harm to wildlife. Therefore it's not good practice.

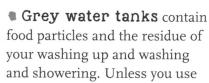

Dealing with grey water: best practice
🍂 Use a motorhome service point if there is one available.

🍂 If there isn't one available, consider emptying your grey water into a container and disposing of it in approved drains or sinks.

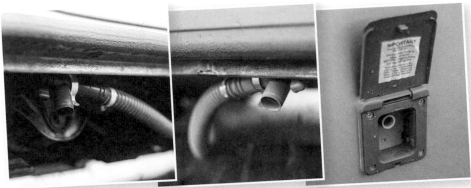

Drain for fresh water   Drain for grey water   Filler for fresh tanks

FOR CAMPERVANNERS AND MOTORHOMERS WITHOUT ON-BOARD FACILITIES

Again, I'm not your mother so I'm not going to tell you how to clean yourself or remind you to wash behind your ears. But I would like to propagate some ideas about the way we wash and brush up when we are in the wilds (or even just on a campsite).

Baby wipes
Tempting though it might be, don't freshen up with baby wipes. Unless they are made from biodegradable materials (not plastics) they contain plastics that will not disintegrate like toilet paper. If you flush them they cause blockages in the sewer system. And when you leave them in a hedge they will not rot down. No gold stars. You are better off using a washable cotton flannel.

Solar showers
Showering in the wild using a solar shower – great in Europe or on hot days – can be a bit of a laugh (I would recommend taking a bit of rope to hang the solar shower from an appropriate branch or tree). But if you must, try to avoid using soaps or shampoos unless they are 100 per cent biodegradable. Even then, don't. When you consider what some of the chemicals we put on our bodies can do to watercourses or plants, it's a wonder we use them in the first place.

Use a dry wash

These products are useful if you can't get to water. They will cleanse and then evaporate so can be a useful stop-gap until you get to a decent bathroom. Available as body washes and shampoos.

Be dirty

There are some 48-hour deodorants on the market that will keep you free from pongs and unsociable odours for more than a day or so. Try them if you can't get to a tap...

Take a dip in the pool

If you want to go wild, then a swimming pool can be a great way to wash off the muck and grime. Some leisure centres will even allow you to pay for just a shower, which is perfect. We have done this on many occasions and, as a result, found the very best showers in the world ever, at the Bridge Centre in Stornoway on the Isle of Lewis. When you're up that way, try them.

One day on, one day off

Camping wild is great but sometimes you need to freshen up in a proper shower. When we camp wild we tend to do a couple of days then check in to a campsite – if we can't use the solar shower. Once there you can do all your laundry, wash and brush up, have a good clean up and use all the toiletries you like, knowing they will be treated properly.

EAT

I wish I was a hamburger all covered in cheese.
To be a Big Mac would be such a wheeze.
And when they put the bread on
I'd give a little scream (aaaaaah!).
I wish I was a hamburger,
I have a hamburger dream.

I wish you were a hamburger too,
Big Mac or Whopper, it's up to you.
Or even a cheese burger,
I really don't mind,
Just as long as I can take you home at tea-time.

© Martin Dorey

INTRODUCTION

Camping breaks life down into the essentials, and nothing more. You eat, sleep and play without distractions and interruptions, living simply, away from the vapid trappings of our everyday existence. No mortgage, no bills, no telly (for most of us), no shopping, no grooming regime, no crowds, no pressure, no crap. It's the very best opportunity we'll ever get to take pleasure in the small things. For once we can stop rushing, forget fast food, quit sitting in traffic and give up giving up stuff. We can enjoy the important things: family, friends, fun, nature, sky, sea, clean air, freedom.

And, of course, food. It doesn't have to be complicated or flashy, as long as it tastes good, is cooked with love and gets to be appreciated. On the campsite it becomes a part of the basic ritual of life. Everything stops and we gather to eat as one, in the open air.

But.

And it's a big but. There's no need to make a big song and dance about it. The way I see it, camping and camper van cooking should be simple, easy and done with as little fuss as possible. Of course it's nice to do showy feasts from time to time, but even they don't have to be over fiddly and take hours. No one has to prove anything. All we want to do is eat well and live well.

So, if you can, remember the golden rule: if it takes longer to wash up than it does to eat you've gone wrong somewhere. Camping is supposed to be fun. If you're flinging yourself on the old Camping Gaz stove in an act of selfless martyrdom to feed your guests with the best meal they've ever tasted, the chances are you aren't enjoying it. Relax. Take it easy. Grab a beer from the cool box and go back to basics.

WHAT does a CAMPER mean TO YOU?

'**In many ways,** our camper van is part of the family. She's a Type 2 Viking Super Six conversion, registered in 1979. We call her 'Nan the Van'. I bought her with the money my grandmother left me when she passed away just one week short of her 100th birthday. I keep a log of every single litre of petrol and drop of oil I've poured into her 2l engine, noting the mileage at each top-up. I also have a fold-out roadmap of Britain, on which I have marked every single mile we've travelled together, from the Shetland Islands to South Devon. It's an honour and a privilege to own a classic VW. I love the smiles Nan the Van generates as we drive through towns and villages, but best of all I love the sound of the solid 'clunk' as I slide the side door closed. It always marks the beginning of another adventure.'

Josh Sutton *AKA THE GUYROPE GOURMET*

The RECIPES in this section

I love my food. And I love to cook for and with my family. It's always from scratch and always using the freshest ingredients we can get our hands on. We don't coddle, engastrate or flash freeze with nitrogen on our camping trips and neither should you. Life is too short.

We don't do cheffy shizz.

The recipes in this section reflect this simplicity. You might even be surprised to see that there are a few old faves included. And why not? I have been cooking spag bol for over 30 years and I think I've got it pretty much nailed the way I like it. So why the heck shouldn't I share it?

This section also includes a bunch of ideas for cooking outdoors, whether it's a breakfast, on the open fire or in one pot. It's all good stuff and it's all got a reason for being in here.

And that is because we absolutely love it.

MY CULINARY JOURNEY SO FAR...

I burned my first sausages aged 16 on a disastrous camping trip with my friend Olly Wilson. It was a miracle that we managed to cook at all as I had made myself responsible for all camping kit and, consequently, had left most of it behind. Some of the most vital elements had been forgotten, and these included our tent pegs.

In light of this disaster, and with no other means of either putting our tent up or getting to a camping shop, we used our cutlery to peg out the tent. I'm not joking either. It meant we had to take the tent down each time we needed to eat, which as it turned out, wasn't as often as it should have been. With no shop, no transport and no clue we ate in the pub most days. To our shame, on the other days we were fed by our kindly neighbours. They lent us cutlery to eat it, too.

From these humble beginnings – it would never get as bad again – I learned the hard way, ruining plenty of meals in the name of passable gastronomy. There's nothing wrong with that, as long as you can work out what went wrong and why so you can avoid it next time. Since then we've had all kinds of delicious – and some not so delicious – meals on camping trips. We've experimented and we've been lazy. We've fallen back on much-loved favourites and chased ingredients and dishes for new tastes we've liked the look of. These are the *Fabada*, the *pimentos de Padron*, the *tortilla*, the *crêpes*. All dishes with great memories.

Some things we cook time and time again because we know they will see us through a lack of inspiration. Those are the stalwarts, the can-dos, the fall-backs and the crowd pleasers. Sometimes they have a 'twist', sometimes they don't need it.

Either way we would never be without them.

WHAT YOU NEED

Keep it SIMPLE

Eat

154

Like all things camper van, cooking in the wilds should be about simplicity. The less you take and the more you work within the limits the happier you'll be. You don't need flashy gadgets. You don't need hundreds of pans. You don't need electrical gizmos.

All you need, really, is fire and a very sharp knife. The rest is all about improvisation.

The recipes in this book have been compiled based on very strict principles. It has to be simple.

Ideally, your ingredients will be bought fresh and locally, too. The idea isn't for you to stock up at your big local supermarket and take it all with you. For me, that's defeating the object of going somewhere. All you are doing is importing food and packaging and giving your money to a big, faceless corporation. Camping frees us from the tyranny of the supermarket. If you can, enjoy it.

Besides, if you stock up on a few staples before you set off then you'll always have enough in your store cupboard for a few emergency dishes if there's nothing open when you get there. If you carry onions, risotto rice, wine and butter you can make a fantastic meal with just about anything. Buying local on your travels means you get to meet people, find out a little about the place you are visiting, contribute to the local economy and eat fresh. Your shopping makes a positive contribution, small though it may seem. Besides, if you go to the seaside, for example, why would you want to eat seafood from thousands of miles away when it's merely hours out of the sea just down the road?

Of course it's difficult to give up the convenience of doing your shop all at once in one place. But camping will give you the gift of time, so how about using it to stomp off to the local shops to get your provisions? Swish a stick in the hedgerows, put on a rucksack (no plastic bags, please), buy what's local and fresh and give yourself a break from the trolley pushing. Good luck!

KIT you need

As we know, cooking can be as simple or as complicated as you want to make it. I prefer it to be fuss-free, with lots of laughter, people poking their noses in (back seat cookery is a regular happening in our van), too much wine and kids running everywhere – spoiling it for all the killjoys. So when it comes to kit, I'd always prefer to cook with a few well chosen items than with lots of gadgetry and gizmos. There's not enough space for even the kitchen sink in a lot of campers, so loading up with stuff won't add anything to the experience.

Often it's a compromise between portability and space when camping. It may also be a matter of cost. But buying cheap or lightweight camping kit won't always help when you are cooking. We aren't yomping over Dartmoor here. We are travelling in relative luxury, so, if you are going to put your foot down anywhere and demand quality, put it down in the camper van kitchen.

So. Here it is. What we travel with.

Kit you need

Pans and pots

The first thing to think of here is the size of your cooker rather than the size of your cupboard. If you use tall or small pans on a big ring the heat will go up the sides of the pans and heat up the handles rather than the food. And vice versa. So, while it might seem useful to make everything micro so you can carry more, or macro so you can cook more, it may well work against you.

Also, if your pans are too big then you may not be able to fit two on your cooker at one time. This is particularly relevant when it comes to in-van cookers that have enclosed heat shields. If you have a frying pan that's so big you can't fit the kettle on the stove at the same time, then breakfast can be a nightmare.

Lightweight pans might seem like a good idea but they can burn more easily than those with heavy bottoms. The heat, even when it's low, can often be too intense. A heavy bottom will make the heat more even.

Knives

You can't cook without decent knives. And the sharper the better. Just because you are camping it doesn't mean you should settle for some rubbish serrated knife from a garage. Bring your best knives, keep them sharp and slice with impunity. If in doubt, test them out on a ripe tomato.

- **Large kitchen knife**
- **Small veg knife**
- **Bread knife**

Knife sharpener

See above. A sharp knife is a happy knife.

Chopping boards

I don't think you need all the colour-coded boards that health and safety would ask of you. But I wouldn't want to travel with just one. We travel with a couple of lightweight plastic boards. One for meat, one for veg.

Veg peeler

You could use a knife, but why bother?

Heavy duty steamer

Steaming veg is easier than boiling and the steaming baskets double up as strainers and colanders. If you were desperate you could even forsake the kettle in favour of this.

Heavy duty skillet/frying pan

Again, essential to have a decent frying pan for steaks and breakfasts. Doesn't have to be non-stick, although non-stick is good for pancakes and eggy bread.

Sieve

Not just useful for sieving and draining veg. Can also be used to mash vegetables for soups.

A rolling pin

You might argue that you could use a bottle for rolling out pastry and it's true, you can. But a rolling pin can also be used as a rudimentary pestle for pounding ingredients – like those in my pasta with pesto and tomatoes, for example (*see* page 258).

Mixing bowls

We usually travel with a few lightweight Tupperware bowls of different sizes. Useful for washing, salads, serving and all kinds of other useful business in the cooking department, such as mixing and egg whisking. And they stack to save space...

Knives and forks not sporks

The spork (a spoon and fork together as one) is good for nothing other than saving space on micro camping adventures. They are of precious little use to anyone to be honest because you need to to be able to control anything on your plate. And then you are back to square one... So carry proper cutlery. It's camping, not the dark ages.

Plates and bowls

I like melamine because it won't break or scratch and is light. It also washes more easily than plastic. You can buy melamine picnic sets that are squared off. Might seem obvious but when you are stuck for cupboard space, square plates and bowls can save a fair bit of space.

BBQ thermometer

If you worry about having burgers that are cooked right through, you'll need one of these. Prod it with the spike and eat without worry. Temperatures of more than 75°C will ensure all bugs are killed by the cooking process; 65°C will be enough if you are cooking for at least 10 minutes.

Pestle and mortar

I will get stick for this, but what the hell. I like to have crushed pepper and to occasionally crush garlic and herbs with a pestle. Making pesto is easier this way too. Do you need it? No, but the alternative is to carry a pepper grinder, which is just a pepper grinder and has no other uses.

Eat

157

Kit you need continued...

Cooking sundries

- BBQ tongs
- Metal fish slice
- Spatula
- Wooden spoons
- Serving spoon or two
- Ladle
- Whisk
- Masher (useful for soups as well as spuds)
- Washing-up bowl
- Metal or bamboo skewers
- Grater
- Scales, if you have space or a funky Tala Retro Cook's Measure – a very useful piece of kit.

Kitchen essentials

Don't forget the basic 'consumables': essentials for a happy and clean camper van kitchen:

- Dish cloths
- Washing-up scourer sponges
- Tea towels
- Washing-up liquid (eco if you are going to have to chuck it in a hedge)
- Antibacterial spray for cleaning
- Fire extinguisher
- Fire blanket
- Kitchen foil

Marshmallow toasting fork

If you listen to my kids you'll know this is essential. Otherwise you'll be roasting on sticks or getting your fingers burned with standard forks. No campfire is complete without toasting marshmallows.

OTHER STUFF IT'S NICE TO HAVE

Paella pan

Get one as big as will fit into your cupboard. That might go against all I said above but if you cook over a fire it'll be really useful for cooking a big brekkie for everyone – not to mention my fantastic paella that's on page 230. That one is a real treat.

Plancha

This is a flat, non-stick hot plate that can go over any heat. It's great for cooking kebabs and breakfasts as well as searing steaks and veg. Also, as it's flat it doesn't take up too much space. Ours is aluminium and is light, too.

Zester

Come on! It hardly takes up any space and is useful for zesting ... yes. Live with it.

HERBS **and spices**

The spice cupboard is a pretty important part of your kitchen equipment. Put together with care and topped up regularly, it'll see you through any number of culinary adventures.

I put mine in the kind of old plastic bin that you'd find at a plumbing merchants. It's exactly the right size to fit standard spice jars and means you can pull it out of the shelves all at once – rather than looking through each and every jar to find the one you need – like you do at home. I also have a little tin for garlic, stock cubes, bay leaves, chillis and larger spice items like star anise.

Yes, it does smell amazing.

- **Fennel seeds.** Amazing with pork or fish.
- **Smoked paprika.** Hot or sweet, great for flavouring meat and fish.
- **Dried rosemary/basil/thyme/mint.** Better fresh but handy to have.
- **Herbes de Provence.** A mix that's useful for BBQs and scrambled eggs.
- **Turmeric/coriander/cumin.** For curries.
- **Cinnamon.** For sweet and savoury dishes.
- **Nutmeg.** For sweet treats and Dauphinoise potatoes.
- **Garam masala.** Another fave for curries.

THE DINEBOX

A little while ago I discovered (was sent) a Dinebox Travel Pantry. It's a tin box full of herbs, already packaged up and sorted out, along with olive oil, cider vinegar, sea salt and ground black pepper. It also contains a tea towel (with a couple of recipes on it) and a few useful bits and pieces for camping. It's a very simple idea – as all the best ideas are – and does all the hard work for you in sourcing and packing up all the spices you might need. I don't do recommendations, as that's not the kind of book this is, but if I did I'd say that I have one, have used it on lots of camping trips and think it's a fine idea.

Get yours at **www.dinebox.co.uk**.

CONDIMENTS and cooking OILS

The only thing you really need to carry is some kind of cooking oil. However, I like to use olive oil as well as a vegetable oil. Veg oil doesn't break down under a high heat so is better for cooking curries and for griddles that rely on a lot of heat.

Decanting oil into lightweight screw top bottles can help to ensure you won't have spillages if bottles fall over in transit. Small drinks bottles can be useful as they won't break and will seal well.

Some campers I know collect sachets from restaurants to have in their vans, which is a good idea if you want convenience. However, in the name of the planet I'd say best avoid those single use plastic pouches if you can. Buy in bulk and decant at home if you have the time.

Obviously what condiments and cooking oil you carry is up to you but here's our list:

- Olive oil
- Vegetable oil
- Garlic
- Chillies
- Ginger
- Tomato ketchup for the kids
- English mustard powder /wholegrain
- White wine vinegar
- Soy sauce (Kikkomans is best but their jars fall over and don't have stoppers; annoying, so decant)

DRY staples

We almost always carry a store of dry staples. The reason for this is that it means we can cook something if all else fails, we can't find a shop or we just fancy something simple like pasta and pesto (emergency jar of pesto guaranteed to put a smile on any child's face), it's no drama. They last for ages so won't go off.

- **Rice noodles:** Buy them dry from a Chinese supermarket (not those ready cooked ones – yuk) if yours doesn't stock them. Place in boiling water and leave for about 10 minutes before using. Easy and quick. And good for you.
- **Sushi rice:** There are very good reasons for making sushi while camping on page 202.
- **Risotto rice:** Risotto is so easy and very versatile. Make it with just about anything for a super filling meal.
- **Linguine:** Flat spaghetti; easy and quick, good with anything.
- **Chorizo:** Lasts for ages.
- **Lentils:** Last for a while, great for bulking up soups and stews.
- **White flour:** Useful for making pittas and thickening my special recipe Coq au Van (*see* page 240).

Tins

Tins are heavy so you may not want to stock up with too many. But a few will give you the basis for a lot of great dishes.

- Tomatoes
- Coconut milk
- Chickpeas
- Butter beans

WASHING UP

No one likes **washing up.** I hate washing up with a passion but, of course, even though I don't want to do it myself, I want it done properly. This is because I was once a kitchen porter. While it was a miserable time in my life, I learned how to wash up properly, how to make the most of the suds and how to tackle pots and pans. If you already know how to do this (many of you will) and are the kind of person who will write scathing reviews on Amazon (some of you may be), you may want to look away now.

- Remember that washing up is not a punishment.
- If it takes you longer to wash up than to eat you have gone wrong somewhere.
- If you intend chucking your dirty water away in the wild, use eco washing-up liquid. DO NOT USE STANDARD DETERGENT.
- Washing up on a campsite should be social.
- It's okay to ask for a squirt from other campers if you are short.
- Washing-up bowls are rarely big enough for washing up.
- Large plastic buckets with handles (trug buckets) are great for washing up – and easy to carry, too.
- Soak difficult dishes and dirt engrained pans first while you wash the rest.
- Wash glasses first.
- Wash cups and mugs second.
- Wash plates third or swill out and fill up again with fresh water and suds.
- Wash pans last.
- Dry up as you go.
- Leave the washing area tidy.
- Con someone else into doing it.

WHAT does a CAMPER mean TO YOU?

'The early years of my childhood were spent travelling in a camper van with my dad through England, Ireland and France. He is a surfer, so most of our travelling was to search for waves, be that along the wet, windy and jagged Irish coastline, or the vast beaches of south-west France. Whatever the scenery, we were always having a good time, living simply and freely. Life was spent outside playing, all day every day; on a skateboard or a bike, running, fishing, making log cabins on the beach or collecting driftwood so we had wood for a barbecue in the evening, or cooking in the van, reading or relaxing when it was too grim outside. No internet, computer, phone or TV. Looking back on those years now, I am forever grateful.'

Nico Chapman *CAMPER VAN DWELLER*

COOKING METHODS AND HEAT SOURCES

Equipment

ROADII FIREGRILL

The principle of the Roadii is, like all good things, very simple. You take a time-honoured way of hanging stuff from a fire, a tripod, and add it to a not so time-honoured way of containing fire, an old wheel. Then you add them together, add some little flourishes that make it more versatile and hey presto, you have something that's completely new but actually feels like you've seen it all before (*see below*).

For me that means it fits perfectly into any campsite.

The Roadii is a barbecue, campfire and fire pit all rolled into one. It's pit, the old wheel, sits off the ground so can be used in fire-sensitive areas (within reason and always with permission, of course). The clever bit comes with the tripod and grill, which hangs from each of the tripod legs on chains. These are fully adjustable so that the grill can be raised or lowered quickly to allow for more or less heat. I have used it a lot and really enjoy having control over it. As the fire dies you can lower the grill to adjust the temperature. That's what makes it great for dishes like paella that require a little finesse. It can also be used with a chain to hang a cookpot (Dutch oven), which makes it all the more versatile.

costs: *around £200*

CADAC CARRI CHEF

The Cadac is a versatile piece of cooking kit that comes from South Africa. It's basically a single burner that runs straight from a gas canister with lots of interchangeable bits and pieces like a griddle, grill plate and the brilliant and very useful Skottel, a dish shaped hot plate that's like a flattened wok (*see right*). It's great for stir frys and breakfast. You can also cook with it like an oven by placing the lid on it.

The Cadac can also be used as a BBQ in areas where you can't have fires. The BBQ plate on the Carri Chef, is a whopping 24in across so it's big enough for bangers for everyone. I use it in cooking demos a lot as it's easy to assemble and cleans and breaks down just as easily.

The only drawback is that it isn't compact so won't stow away that easily into a corner of the camper. But it is useful and will do something as banal as boil a kettle – although the pot stand is probably its weakest point. On a positive note the canisters are refillable so there is no packaging waste.

costs: *around £200*

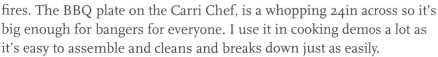

CAMPING GAZ CAMP STOVE

These little portable stoves make a great addition to any camp kitchen. They are small and light, stable enough to use anywhere and give a really good controllable heat, although they can be affected by wind. I use them all the time on cooking demos and for when I want to cook away from the van or with bigger pans. They are cheap to buy and come in small briefcase-like boxes, making them easy to store and pack away when not needed.

The only drawback is that the gas – isobutane – comes in disposable canisters and isn't cheap. The canisters don't last a long time – about an hour max – so you'll need to carry spares. A bit wasteful, especially if not recycled.

costs: *Around £20 + gas at around £3 per can*

GHILLIE KETTLE/ KELLY KETTLE

These little stoves are wonderful if you have the space and are looking to make boiling water in a hurry (*see left*). They use virtually any dry fuel, and very little of it, and will boil water in just a few minutes. All it needs is a few dry twigs and bits and pieces, so it's massively efficient. You can also cook on them if you need to with a range of accessories that turn the base into a basic cooker. For cups of tea on a walk, very useful.

costs: *Around £35*

KOTLICH

The Kotlich is a traditional Hungarian enamelled pot and tripod kit (*see right*). Invented for cooking goulash over wood fires – and subsequently for cooking all kinds of dishes – they are versatile bits of kit, with all kinds of accessories and bits and pieces to hang from the tripod or serve in. A hanging grill is available, along with a paella pan. The fire pit is particularly useful for enjoying open fires in places where lighting one on the ground would be inappropriate.

costs: *From around £75 for a pot and tripod*

MICRO STOVES

Unless you are really stuck for space, a micro stove might not be of much use to you. However, it's handy to keep one in your van. I do. When out on a walk and feeling thirsty, the appearance of a swiftly boiled pot for a refreshing cuppa can work wonders. Some teeny-weeny cookers can weigh in at as little as 50g or so. Mine is collapsible and stashes away somewhere small, ready for a hike in the hills.

costs: *around £30*

ROCKET STOVES

Rocket stoves work on the same principle as Kelly (or Ghillie) Kettles. They use little fuel but burn it with lots of oxygen to make a fierce flame that burns bright and hot for as long as it gets fed. They squeeze a lot of heat out of a few twigs and therefore are particularly useful if there isn't much fuel in the way of dry logs to be had. They can be lit with leaves and paper then fed with kindling or twigs. Useful but not that small.

costs: *around £75*

COBB

The Cobb is a miracle, so they say. It's compact and neat, and packs down small enough for most camping trips (*see below*). It'll also do all kinds of great stuff, such as the legendary beer can chicken, which is what everyone did on it when they first came out. As time has gone on they have become more and more versatile and now come in a gas version as well as the original cobble-stone version. When I first encountered them I felt they were limited because of the 2 hour cooking time of the cobblestones, which meant making a cup of tea was out of the question (and that's my first criteria for camping, let's face it). However, these days you can buy just about every kind of accessory for it, including smokers, so they are becoming easier to use. One thing to note is that they should not be used in a tent or in a vehicle, despite the fact that the outside remains cool when cooking.

costs: *around £140 for a basic model*

FRONTIER STOVE

This has to be the ultimate in outdoor cooking facilities.
I say that in the way that invites something better to
come along and take its place. But it's unlikely.

I first came across the Frontier Stove as part of my
everyday work. I discovered it when it had just been
developed as an idea for third world countries to cook
and heat their homes using a stove that does both.
Light, portable and about ten times more efficient
than cooking over an open fire, it's got a flue to
remove unwanted smoke from your eyes
when cooking and can be packed down
and carried away (*see right*). Two pots
fit comfortably on the top for
easy, two ring cooking with
an authentic twist.
Seriously flash too, for
the average camper...

costs: *around £160*

THERMOMIX

A friend recently introduced me
to the Thermomix. It's nothing
new, apparently, but it was to
me. It was also news to me that
this device is used and loved
by campers, motorhomers and caravanners
all over Europe. It's easy to see why. As long as you
have electricity the Thermomix will do everything for you. It weighs,
steams, stirs, cooks, whizzes, chops, preheats and all kinds of stuff
you never thought a food processor could do. It'll even guide you
through pre-designed recipes from start to finish with some pretty
smart technology. People I know who use them claim they take a
lot of the chore out of cooking on campsites and can be set to cook
soups and stews for when you get back from a walk or day on the
beach. Amazing! All it won't do is rock you to sleep. Oh, it will?
Bloody marvellous.

costs: *around £1000 (eek)*

YOUR IN-VAN STOVE

To be honest you don't really need anything else. If you have a standard one it might have two rings and a grill. Otherwise you might just have two rings, or even just one. Don't worry, you can cope. Just make sure you get pans that fit. There is little that is more frustrating that trying to boil a kettle and cook a breakfast at the same time when the pans are too big and will not fit on the stove at the same time.

costs: *around £200 from* **www.camperworks.com**

FUEL for COOKING (and heating)

Isobutane/butane

This is the gas that comes in your standard blue Camping Gaz containers. It is available universally throughout Europe, burns well, provides a good heat and produces an easily adjustable flame.

When bought in refillable canisters (*see right*) it can be reasonably cost effective, but if bought in disposable canisters it can be extremely wasteful, simply because of the single-use containers. Also, it doesn't burn well at temperatures below 4°C and stops vaporising at −1°C, so not good for cold weather camping. If your van has a Propex heater you might just be stuffed when you need it most – as the gas gets less powerful the colder it gets.

Propane/LPG

Propane gas or LPG is often the option for motorhomes – especially those that are used for cold weather camping. It usually comes in red containers, or grey and green for patio gas. It won't stop vaporising until around −27°C so it's going to be much more useful in colder climes. The flame is easily adjustable but not as intense as butane, although most of us wouldn't notice.

Propane comes in refillable tanks. Some motorhomes have on-board LPG tanks so that you can refill at a petrol station instead of having to change tanks.

SOLID FUEL
Cobblestones

These are specially made briquettes made for Cobb BBQs, from coconut husk. They are 'eco' and cost around £2 each. They will light within a few minutes thanks to their built in firelighter, and will burn hotter than standard briquettes, cooking for up to 2 hours, although shorter burning versions are available if all you want to do is boil a kettle. Ready to cook after about 5 minutes.

BBQ briquettes

These are the pre-formed BBQ briquettes. They are harder to light than charcoal but will burn for longer and hotter, so a good option for big BBQs.

Charcoal

Standard BBQ fuel, charcoal is the classic BBQ fuel. Unpredictable and often difficult to light, it's always a pleasure and challenge to cook well over a decent charcoal pit.

Wood

I like cooking with wood, although it can be the most difficult of all fuels to use, simply because different types will burn in different ways and with different heats. Hard woods burn hottest and for longest but might need a bit of chopping into thinner logs to ensure they light properly. Soft woods are easier to light (if dry) but will burn quicker and cooler than hard woods (*see right*).

WHAT does a CAMPER mean TO YOU?

'**In the early days** we made regular trips to Devon, Cornwall and The Lakes with boards or bikes, not stopping for long; eager to try somewhere else and following the brighter patches of sky. The camper van was the obvious choice for our honeymoon and South Uist in the Outer Hebrides was our goal. Driving north with memories of a fun-filled wedding and gifts of Champagne, homemade biscotti and china plates from Rev Murphy for our motor caravan. We journeyed through Scotland where, as we rose over Rannoch Moor, a loud banging persisted. At Morar, a garage tinkered long enough for us to continue and long enough to enjoy Silver Sands. Through Skye to Uist, even in the grey, the beaches were beautiful but when the sun came out truly unimaginable. Forever memories.

As our sons have grown up we have initiated them as babies and to them the camper van is part of our family – a regular ferry trip to Spain or a journey through France each summer would not be missed.'

Cath Knight *OWNER OF THE VAN, A 1979 VW TYPE 2, FOR THE LAST 18 YEARS*

Gas SAFETY

Gas is flammable, obviously. It is also highly combustible. That means it will and can blow up if it is allowed to leak and then meet a spark or naked flame. So you will need to observe some safety rules when using it.

● **Do not cook in your van** unless you have adequate ventilation, like the door open or all the windows open.

● **Turn your gas supply off** at the cylinder (regulator) before you travel.

● **If you suspect a leak,** don't look for it with a naked flame! If you do, kaboom.

● **Gas has smell added** to it so you can begin to detect where it is coming from using smell. After that, if you suspect a pipe or joint is leaking, use a washing-up liquid and water solution on it. Gas will bubble through it.

● **Get your gas equipment checked** regularly by a qualified gas fitter.

● **Don't smoke** when you change the bottle! D'oh.

● **Change cylinders** in the open air, or at least, with the doors wide open.

● **If you have vents** in the compartment where your gas is stored, make sure they are unobstructed. If you don't, get some fitted.

● **Carry a fire extinguisher.**

'*Our Discovery* is the perfect solution for short weekend breaks away with the family. No camping clutter or lengthy packing procedures, we just hop in and go out to a favourite camping spot to get away from it all.
    Running a busy VW camper hire business means time is always short, with summers taken up ensuring our customers get to enjoy the delights of a classic VW. The downside to this is we never have a camper available for ourselves as they're always out on hire. Step in the Discovery! It's a capable seven-seater family car, has a tow bar for our bike rack and with the roof-mounted tent, enables my wife and I plus two kids the chance to enjoy the great outdoors.'

Rod Monteiro OWNER, RETROCAMPERVAN HIRE

Eat

175

ALTERNATIVE kitchens

THE COOKING POD

The idea of a removable pod that can be taken out of a Transporter is nothing new. As we've already read on page 124, the Camping Box was the first VW camper conversion. So it's not such an alien concept to imagine making a removable pod that contains all your camping gear that can be removed when you want to use the van for everyday van things, such as going to work, doing the school run and all the other bits and pieces that vans get up to when they aren't being used for camping.

There are plenty of camper conversion companies making cooking pods for campers. After all, it makes a lot of really good sense. Some, like Cambee's lift out camper kitchen, the Picnic Pod they use in their 'Go' conversion, is like a glorified buddy box with extra bits, a removable stove, and space to stash the cutlery and bits and pieces. It can be lifted out of the boot and used on a picnic, under the awning or just in the van itself. Moving on from there is a removable pod with all the knobs and whistles of a standard camper, except that you can remove it.

There are other approaches to the same problem, which sit under the back seat and pull out to use, or can be completely removable to use in an awning, like the removable Cooking Pod from Slidepods. I like this idea very much as it allows you to cook under the tailgate when it's raining and saves a lot of space in the front of the van. The pod itself has sink, waste water tank (integrated), two hob burners linked to integrated gas system, storage and is linked into our 50l under-van clean water tank. Very handy if you wanted to add an extra row of seats in an LWB T5 or Kombi to house a large family but still want to camp with a fully functional kitchen.

↗ **Got a good idea?** Go with it. Jonny Ashworth's Slidepods are clever and simple and enable any VW Kombi owner to turn their van into a fully fitted camper in a few easy steps...

Fire, fire, BURNING bright

Having a fire is an essential part of camping. It's the rules. Why? Because a real fire takes us back to our pre-comfort days when fire was essential for warmth and for preserving life. We feel good sitting in front of a real fire, staring into the embers, passing the time, telling stories, being the social creatures we are.

Unfortunately we exist in a time when there are rules about lighting fires. Fortunately we also exist in a time when we are considerate to the natural world. Both of these facts conspire to mean that we can't always light fires wherever we like, for fear of it getting out of control and causing major damage.

Some campsites do allow fires but these are few and far between. Often in Europe, where fire danger poses a real risk to dry forest and habitats, BBQs are banned in all but the most controlled places. **www.campfiresburning.org** has a list of sites in the UK where

FIRE PITS

There are times when fire pits may be allowed, but lighting a fire on the ground is not. This is where your Roadii or Kotlich is going to come in useful as they can double as fire pits. Some campsites will rent them to you in order to preserve the grass on their fields.

Washing machine drum fire pit

If you have a friend with a welder and don't mind extracting a washing machine drum from its outer casing then these are fantastic containers for flames at the campsite, if bulky to stash in your van. The way the tubs are made makes them ideal for fires as they draw plenty of air and let out a lot of heat. Plus, if your friend the welder did it right it will sit off the ground and won't burn grass (or anything else). Ideal for cooking marshmallows, if little else.

TOP FIRE LIGHTING TIPS

As with many things, preparation is everything. Make sure you have enough tinder, kindling and fuel that is dry, and that you have enough matches and/or a lighter that works. Also make sure you have a method of controlling your fire if it were to get out of hand. A fire blanket, extinguisher or, at the very least, a bucket of water will do it.

Don't be tempted to pour petrol, WD40, oil or any flammable substance on your fire to encourage it. If you value your eyebrows, that is (and other more valid reasons).

- **Tinder** is what you use to start the fire; it could be rolled up newspaper, firelighters (no it's not cheating), dry grass or cotton wool.
- **Kindling** is the smaller twigs and finely chopped wood that is used to get the fire going once the tinder is lit.
- **Big kindling** is useful as a halfway house for logs if you are using them complete.
- **Chopping logs** in half makes them easier to light.

* **Digging a fire pit** and then encircling it with rocks will create a good pit in which to light your fire. It will also help to contain it should it get out of control.
* **DO NOT light your fire** anywhere near flammable items such as dry grass, fences, trees or peaty soil.
* **Keep a bucket of water** handy at all times in case your fire gets out of hand.
* **If you are thinking** of lighting a fire on grass, don't, as it will kill it. If you must, at least dig out a sod of turf, light the fire in the hole and replace the sod afterwards, once the fire is fully out.
* **Beware of lighting fires** on stones or flint that may chip and explode with heat.
* **Put the tinder** at the bottom, place a few bits of light kindling on top and light the tinder. Add kindling as it catches either in a square shape, narrowing as it piles up, or in a pyramid shape, and make sure there is adequate airflow. Don't add too much or you may smother the flames.
* **NEVER LEAVE YOUR FIRE** to burn out. If you have to depart, make sure it is put out completely and that the environment is put back exactly as it was. DO NOT leave mess, nails from old wood or litter.

WHAT does a CAMPER mean TO YOU?

'Our van is our freedom, we use it constantly and are always looking towards the next trip, be it heading to our local break at Highcliffe on the south coast for a couple of hours in the surf, or a camping trip away with friends. It's a 2012 Toffee Brown T5.1 102, with a self-build interior that is ever evolving. The latest addition is a pumped shower fitted in the tailgate, which we use for wetsuit washdowns and a quick rinse off after surfing or kayaking. After previously owning a 75ft Devon bay called Sunny and a 1998 T4 (called most things under the sun), this had to be the next step for a daily driver (reliable, quick and economical). It doesn't really have a name, but I often refer to it as 'Shed' because it's brown and frequently full of tools or junk. Having owned a camper van for so long, I can't now imagine a time where we would choose to be without one.'

Ant Penny *CAMPER VAN OWNER*

COOLING

Keeping food cool is essential for food safety. Food that is 'likely to support the growth of pathogenic micro-organisms and toxins should be kept at a temperature of less than 8°' (Food Standards Agency, *Guidance on Temperature Control Legislation in the UK*).That's the official line from UK authorities on the subject. Those food types include dairy, fresh and cured meats, fish, prepared and cooked foods and pastry or dough. The reason for this is that any toxins or pathogens in food are inactive below 8°C. Leave 'at risk' foods (poultry, seafood and pork) above 8°C for any long period and you could risk your health.

Of course food stays fresher, lasts longer and tastes better when cooled, not to mention the vital cooling of wine and beers for evening cocktails. Your cool box and fridge are vital pieces of equipment.

Camping FRIDGES

Camper vans and camper van owners have the choice between three different cooling methods for their fridges. Then, following that, they have a further choice of how their fridge is powered, either by 12v from the battery or solar, by gas or by 240v from a mains hook up. Often it will be a matter of size and price as to what your camper will take. Both types of in-built fridges (absorption and compression) can be bought to replace existing older style fridges typically found in older camper vans.

Absorption fridges

This is the method that many camper van fridges work on. It relies on a concentrated ammonia solution being heated by a boiler, giving off a vapour that is then condensed and evaporated. The process draws heat out of the storage container (fridge), so cooling it.

Advantages
- Can be run on LPG or butane gas
- Can be run on 12v or 240v mains
- Silent in operation
- Cheaper than compressor fridges
- Available in a range of 'standard' camper van sizes

Disadvantages
- Can only be run on 12v for short periods or when the vehicle is moving (and therefore charging the leisure battery)
- Will drain a leisure battery (and kill it) in a matter of hours
- Must be vented externally to allow dangerous gas fumes from the boiler to escape

Information for this section very kindly supplied by O'Briens Camping. **www.obrienscamping.co.uk**

Compressor fridges

Compressor fridges work by pushing a coolant, either as a gas or liquid, through a series of pipes that widen or narrow. The cooling works as the coolant is pumped around the system and warms up by pulling warmth out of the cooling compartment, then giving it out again as pipes narrow at the back of the fridge. It's all science and physics, and it's very clever. But for the likes of us it means that there is a motor that runs all or most of the time and that it can only be powered by electricity.

Advantages
- More efficient cooling, with the possibility of ice boxes
- Can be run on solar power
- Easier to install
- No need for external ventilation, as there are no fumes
- Pull much less battery power than an absorption fridge
- Modern designs make them much more efficient than older camper van fridges

Disadvantages
- Can be noisy
- More expensive than absorption fridges

Portable thermoelectric coolers

Thermoelectric cooling relies on electricity to power elements that give off heat and cooling energy. They are then enhanced by heat exchangers and air fans to drop the temperature of a cool box to below the ambient temperature.

Some cool boxes can be used with gas as well as 12v and 240v, so combining absorption and compression features. These cannot be used inside a camper on gas as they will not be sufficiently vented.

Advantages	Disadvantages
• Portable and can be run on 12v or 240v • Can be light and easy to carry • Low-cost solution	• Only cool to around 30°C below ambient temperature. In very hot climates this may not be sufficient. • Cannot be used on gas power inside

Cool boxes

For campers without fridges, cool boxes are the next best thing. Depending on the amount of insulation they contain, the ambient outside temperature and how often they are opened and closed, a cool box can remain cool for up to 24 hours or so.

A few years ago I undertook a cool box test to see how well my cool box, a Coleman steel belted cooler, would hold its temperature using a couple of freezer packs. I recorded the temperature of the cool box at various time intervals after placing the freezer packs in it. I only opened the cool box to take the temperature. While it wasn't scientifically controlled or calibrated in any way, it gives you an idea of how long it might be safe to leave food in a cool box. Sort of. The results are as follows:

Ambient room temperature	19.4°C
Ice pack temp (from freezer)	−22°C
Cool box after 4 hours	7.6°C
Cool box after 15 hours	7.7°C
Cool box after 24 hours	16.5°C

The crucial point of this test is to make sure you don't rely on your cool box for more than 24 hours unless you are able to top up your freezer packs.

WHAT does a CAMPER mean TO YOU?

'Basically the story of my VW campers is the story of my adult life, from my first trip round Europe in a 74 Devon at 21, our knackered 73 Dormi which was our wedding present and took 8 hours to get to the Lakes from London for our honeymoon, to our most 'recent' van, a 77, which we've now had for 20 years and which my son, now 18, has grown up with or in... back in the day family holidays, now music festivals and playing guitar together overlooking Woolacombe beach. It's the camper that has kept me young, introduced me to many friends, not to mention strangers, and continues to give me road trips that are the reason to earn money the rest of the time.'

Martin Friend *CAMPER VAN OWNER*

Chillin' TIPS

● **Some campsites have freezers** where you can put your freezer packs overnight. Before you do, mark them with indelible pen to prove they are yours.

● **If your campsite doesn't have** a freezer, you can always bury freezer packs in the freezer department of the local supermarket and then come back for them later. It's a risk but worth it. Bury them deep though, in less popular foods, like frozen gooseberries.

● **If you are short of space,** freeze bottles of water (or milk) before you go and place them in the fridge or cool box. They will help to bring down the temperature more quickly, so putting less demand on the fridge. If you use milk it'll help it to keep longer.

● **If your fridge isn't working** or too full, cool your wine in a river or rock pool. Just remember not to let it drift away...

RECIPES

Top ten tips for camper van cooking

1 Put butter in jam jars to stop it melting or getting messy.
2 Take a spare portable gas burner if you want fish and don't want to cook it in the van.
3 Take melamine plates. They won't break if you hit a speed bump.
4 Take basics you can't get anywhere but home: tea bags ... Marmite ... Worcestershire sauce.
5 Consider off-the-ground grills-cum-fire pits for campsites where you can't light fires but want to cook on an open flame.

6 Don't forget the marsh-mallows if you're travelling with kids. It's the rules!
7 Use a tea towel on your legs if you're using tin plates! They will burn your knees if your dinner is hot and you wear shorts.
8 Don't over pack your cupboards or you'll have to take everything out to find anything.
9 If you can't think of anything to cook, don't panic. That's what hot smoked paprika is for.
10 Check you have enough gas before you start a stew.

Breakfast tip

If camping with kids it will save washing up – and a load of hassle – if you buy a multipack of those little individually portioned cereals. Open the packet up, pour in the milk and hey presto! Brekkie on the run for busy kids.

BREKKIE

First meal of the day. Up time. One up, all up. Must be accompanied by a cuppa, a reasonable view (from the slider) and time to plan the day ahead.

Breakfast is massively important. It really is. It's your get up and go, your starting handle, your va va voom and your chilli up the backside before the whistle blows. Your day depends on it. The tone of your breakfast will set the tone for the rest of the day, so get that kettle on – for goodness' sake – and get cooking.

Perfectly perfick oeufs

Some time ago I received a scathing review on a well-known internet bookseller's website because I had written about making the perfect cuppa. What's wrong with the pursuit of a fine cup of tea? It's vital to a good camping experience and a good day ahead. The whistling kettle is music to the camper.

During my research for that article I found George Orwell's rules for the very same thing: how to make the perfect cup of tea. I also looked back on years of tea making (I used to be a runner on film sets, a job that involved making hundreds, if not thousands of cups of tea every week) and thought of some of the worst cups of tea I have ever had the misfortune to taste. There is an art to making a decent cuppa and it has to be done right (bag in, boiling water on, stir and squeeze then add milk, if you must know). It's the same with eggs. I am not the kind of person who will send poached eggs back in a hotel because they are too hard (although I have met some who will) but I do like them a certain way.

So, dear reviewer, if you feel the same way about perfect eggs as you do about being told how to make a cup of tea and find it all a bit basic, please do as you said you did with my last book and send this one off to the charity shop as well.

Make my day.

The eggs you choose

All eggs used in the making of this section were farm eggs from the side of the road, hence the yellow yolks. They are always the best tasting and biggest and worth chasing. If you can't get side-of-the-road eggs, get large free range organics. Cost more but so what? Treat yourself. You've got a day's camping to get through.

DIPPY eggs

The reason your boiled eggs crack and the yolks go hard is because the difference in the temperature between the egg and boiling water is too great. The air pocket inside the egg expands too quickly and the shell can't cope. The result? Eggs ruined. The way around it – and to get runny yolks and perfectly cooked whites – is to follow these rules:

● **Don't keep eggs in the fridge** before using. Keep them at room temperature.

● **Boil your water.** When the water has boiled, lower the heat a little and move the pan half off the heat so one half boils gently and the other is calm. This is important.

● **Drop your eggs gently** into the side of the pan that is off the heat. You'll notice that bubbles will start streaming from one end of each egg. This is the air escaping slowly through the porous shell.

● **Start counting** when the eggs go in. Five minutes please.

● **When this has almost passed** (about a minute or so, maybe a little less) slide the whole pan back on to the heat and allow it to boil again until 5 minutes is up.

● **Take the eggs out** and crack them all straight away (they will keep on cooking and spoil if you don't). You should have eggs with firm whites and runny yolks. If they are a tad too runny (if they are huge) then pop the lids back on for a minute or so.

● **Dip with soldiers.** As usual, white bread with salted butter.

POACHED eggs

These are a little more tricky. But I like to use a deep frying
pan filled with water that boils gently. I have experimented with the
vortex swirl method (okay, but not perfect) and with vinegar (tastes
of vinegar), and also that horrible cling film method (works well but
the way they look? Ewww). So, after much deliberation I resort to
the aforementioned non-stick pan full of gently boiling water.

- The eggs must be cracked carefully and dropped very gently – from
no height – into the water so the boiling doesn't break up the whites.
- Then they must be left alone for 2–3 minutes.
- Before removing the eggs with a slotted spoon use a fish slice
to gently make sure they haven't stuck to the bottom of the pan.
- Once safely out, dry them off in kitchen paper before serving
on crusty bread spread with lashings of bright yellow salted butter.
- The paper bit is actually very important here as watery eggs is a
proper sin at the breakfast table. No one wants half a pan of water
sloshing about on their plate. You have been warned.

SCRAMBLED eggs

Everyone likes their scrambled done differently. So if you
like eggs as hard as bullets leaking thin tasteless juices on your toast,
I can recommend you leave us now and go and stay in a Travel Inn
or Premier Lodge or something. I make no apologies for liking
scrambled eggs done runny. Here's how.

- Break three eggs into a non-stick frying pan.
- Add a splash of water (not milk – makes them too rich for my liking).
- With a fork, over a gentle heat, break the eggs and scramble. Don't
whisk them or mix them too well.
- Add freshly ground black pepper.
- Add a pinch of Herbes de Provence (typically rosemary, thyme,
marjoram, oregano).
- Fork the eggs over again and keep them moving gently until they
begin to harden.
- At this point it's up to you how hard you go. But generally, I would
remove them from the heat when they are *almost* ready enough for you.
Chuck them on to a couple of pieces of thickly buttered toast and eat
straight away. They will firm up as you serve them.

FRIED eggs

This is where you're starting to think it's getting silly, right? But bear with me. The secret to getting perfect fried eggs lies in the implements you use to flip them and the pan you cook in. I use a fish slice I picked up in a charity shop years ago. It has a wide but thin, flexible blade that will slip under a fried egg without breaking it (most of the time).

💧 Use olive oil or bacon fat. Bacon fat is best, as long as you haven't crucified the pan in the process of cooking it. If you have, the sharp blade of the fish slice may well save your bacon when it comes to getting eggs out of the pan.

💧 Anyway, if you go for the flip method, do it just before you serve and once the eggs are off the heat. Flip, count to two and then flip them to serve. The still hot pan will be enough to firm up the whites just enough to stop the kids moaning.

💧 Planchas are great for cooking eggs on a campsite as you can get the fish slice under them dead flat, unlike with a high sided frying pan.

God I'm particular aren't I?
But I bet you'll enjoy your breakfast.

EGGY BREAD with maple syrup and BACON

Eggy bread is a camping must. It's one of those essentials. It's so easy and so tasty and anyone – even the kids – can master it. This particular version is Maggie's favourite. We cooked it in a camper on the west coast of the Isle of Arran in Scotland, with the doors open to the beach and just the sound of the gulls and the lapping of the waves on the shore for company. It was the best we'd ever had it and the best start to a very fabulous trip.

For 2
4 slices of thick **white bread**
2 free range **eggs**
4 rashers of **smoked bacon,**
    chopped into lardons
2 tbsp **maple syrup**
Black pepper and salt to taste

Method

Fry the bacon in a pan until it is crispy. While that's doing, whisk up the eggs with a little black pepper in a bowl large enough to take a slice of bread at the bottom. When the bacon is ready, tip it out and put aside but leave the fat in the pan. Dunk a slice of bread in the egg mixture both sides and fry in the bacon fat on both sides until it's done to your liking. Repeat with all four slices. Serve with the bacon between two slices and a drizzle of maple syrup.

Authentic BRETON CRÊPES (pancakes) with GOAT'S CHEESE and honey

You can't drive past a crêperie in Brittany. It's against the rules to drive through the region without sampling at least one of their fantastic crêpes. I usually go savoury but the kids go sweet. This breakfast version is a mix of the two... Breton crêpes are made with two-thirds buckwheat flour (an inexpensive type of non-wheat flour that grows well in Brittany) and one-third normal flour. As buckwheat is gluten free, normal flour is added to add a little elasticity to the mix.

For approx. 6-8 (depending on thickness)

75g buckwheat flour
25g plain white flour
Half a pint of **milk**
1 large free range egg
Knob of butter
A pinch of salt
Goat's cheese
Honey

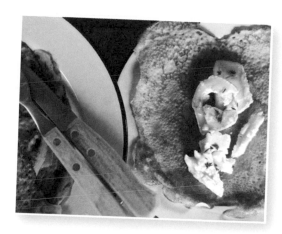

Method

Mix the flour in a bowl, then add the lightly whisked egg and a little of the milk and whisk into a batter. Then add the rest of the milk bit by bit and whisk until there are no lumps or bumps and it is the consistency of double cream. Leave for at least half an hour in a cool place, preferably more if you can wait.

Heat up a heavy bottomed frying pan over a medium/high heat. Add a knob of butter and drop half a ladle full of the mix. Swill the pan around to get a thin coating all over the pan. After a couple of minutes flip the pancake and cook for a further few minutes. Serve on a plate, add some crumbled goat's cheese and a few drizzles of honey (also a little thyme if you fancy) then roll it up.

(Note: Getting the pan temperature right can take a few attempts. Too hot and it will bubble and burn, too cool and it'll cook too slowly and become rubbery.)

PORRIDGE with maple syrup, hazelnut and figs

Whatever you like your porridge with, it doesn't really matter. This just happens to be a favourite of ours. The most important thing is that your porridge is salted, like a good porridge should be. The figs add fruitiness, without being too fruity. Make it with water and add the richness of milk and/or cream afterwards.

For

1 cup **porridge** oats
2 cups **water**
2 fresh ripe **figs**
A handful of crushed **hazelnuts**
A squirt of runny **honey**
A pinch of **salt**
Fresh **full fat milk**

Method

Add the oats to the water and chuck in the pinch of salt. Bring to the boil slowly, and once boiling, simmer for a few minutes. While that's doing, prepare the figs and bash the hazelnuts. Dish the porridge out into two bowls, throw in the figs and hazelnuts, drizzle with honey and then add a dash of milk.

SAUSAGE and marmalade SARNIE

This one comes from my friend and neighbour Bish, a man with taste. Apparently. So the story goes, he attempted to woo his good missus with this weird combo some time ago. It must work otherwise she wouldn't still be there now. There's something… well… something about it. Love it or hate it, it's got staying power. Try it.

For 2 (of course)

4 proper butcher's **pork sausages**
4 slices of thick cut **granary bread**
Orange **marmalade**
A few leaves of little **gem lettuce**
Butter

Method

Fry, grill or BBQ the sausages to your liking. Butter the bread. Split the sausages down the middle and put on one slice. Slap on a big dollop of marmalade and a couple of leaves of lettuce for a little bit of colour. Close it up and get stuck in…

SNACKS AND INBETWEENERS

I f the time between lunch and dinner seems like a vast chasm that cannot be filled in any other way, reach for the inbetweeners. Call it a late lunch or a light lunch or a brunch or dinner, I really don't care. Get it on and stop that rumbling tum. Just don't fill up on crisps.

The recipes here aren't your usual boring old snack-a-doodle and might well be useful as a gourmet pick-me-up come late afternoon, when dinner is within reach but still a grumble away. Smoked oysters at sunset? You bet.

Thai style
FISH CAKES

Spicy and with a taste of Thailand (ish) these fish cakes are delicious and pretty quick. The method of whipping the egg whites and combining makes for very light cakes that are delightful as a starter or as a snack.

For 2-4 as a snack
7 tbsp (100ml) **milk**
100g self-raising flour
1 tsp baking powder
2 salmon steaks, chopped
1 chilli, finely chopped
A bunch of coriander, chopped
Small knob of ginger, grated
2 large eggs, yolks and whites separated
1 tbsp fish sauce
5 spring onions, chopped
Sesame oil for frying (or veg oil if none available)
Salt and pepper for seasoning

Method

Whisk the milk and egg yolks in a medium bowl, to combine. Add the flour and baking powder, whisk in. Next stir in the salmon, chilli, coriander, ginger, spring onions and some seasoning.

In a clean bowl whisk the egg whites to soft peaks and gently fold into the mixture.

Heat two tablespoons of oil in a frying pan till sizzling. Using a couple of tablespoon's worth of mixture for each fish cake, dollop a couple in the hot oil at a time and allow them to sizzle for a few minutes on each side.

Serve with a sweet chilli dip or, for a more substantial meal, with a green salad and balsamic vinegar.

The practically perfect
MACKEREL SANDWICH

What's the secret to making the perfect mackerel sandwich? Heaven knows, honestly. I thought I had it when I presented it to my friends one evening. But no, apparently the mackerel sandwich is only practically perfect. That's fine by me.

However, we did discuss what would make it perfect and the feeling was that perhaps it'd be beetroot. Interesting, but perhaps a taste too far! Let me know. Either way, I am pretty happy with it the way it is.

Makes 1 practically perfect sandwich

A glug of oil
A knob of butter
A little plain **flour** for dusting
A pinch of chilli flakes
2 fresh mackerel fillets, deboned
2 slices of very fresh white bread (doorstep style)
1 tomato, thinly sliced
A handful of **watercress**
1 tsp creamed horseradish
3 cornichons, sliced
Black pepper

Method

Melt the butter in a frying pan, add the olive oil and heat over a medium heat. Mix the chilli flakes with the flour in a bowl and add a few grinds of black pepper. Coat the mackerel fillets and then cook them (skin side down first) for about 4 or 5 minutes each side (or until they are cooked and a bit crispy). Meanwhile, butter the bread, add the sliced tomatoes, and watercress. Then top with the fillets, horseradish and cornichons. Scoff.

Now tell me that isn't almost perfect.

SMOKED OYSTERS
with chilli and lime dip

I have talked about smoking before. But it really is such a great way of cooking shellfish that it's hard to ignore. And while it might sound a bit 'posh', it really isn't. Oysters, while expensive, are a working man's food sent as compensation by the gods for being working men and women. Splash out, splash a dash on and enjoy this most heavenly of *amuse-bouches*.

The art of smoking really isn't that difficult to get your head around. Hot smoking needs a smoking tin, a heat source and some smoking chips. I use a Camerons smoker, available from **www.hotsmoked.co.uk**. To make it work, add a spoonful of smoking dust (oak is good) to the bottom of the pan, place the drip tray and grill on top, place the oysters on top, close the lid and put on a hot flame for 8–10 minutes. Job done.

For 2-4

6 oysters
1 tsp soy sauce
Olive oil
Half a chilli, finely chopped
Juice of 1 lime
½ tsp brown sugar
Twist of black pepper

Method

Smoke the oysters. While they are doing, mix up all the other ingredients well in a cup to make a rich, sweet and sour dip. When the oysters are ready (they should have opened – if any don't, discard them), drizzle a little dip on each. Use a fork to eat them straight from the shell. Delicious, no?

Beery WELSH RAREBIT

Look. It's snack time. There's not much on and you can hardly be bothered to make anything, but you don't want to eat something dullard. You have a little beer and a good strong cheddar cheese in the fridge. There's not much else for it other than to whip up a decent Welsh rarebit.

For 2

Strong cheddar cheese, grated
A knob of butter
A glug of Guinness or stout
1 tsp English mustard powder
4 thick slices of white bread
1 tsp Worcestershire sauce
Black pepper

Method

Mix the cheese in a pan with the knob of butter, Guinness and mustard powder. Heat gently if it's a bit thick, but not so much that the cheese melt completely, until you have a thick, cheesy mess. Toast the bread on one side, then spread the mixture on the untoasted side and slam it back in under the grill. Once it's bubbling nicely, remove from the grill and splash on the Worcestershire sauce. Grate black pepper over the lot and devour before it gets too cool.

SUSHI rolls

Sushi isn't suitable for camper vans! I know what
you are thinking. However, I have some news. Sushi is very
suitable for camper vans. The reason is that the majority
of the ingredients – rice, seaweed, seasoning, wasabi,
soy sauce and ginger – can be stored for a long time.

So it's perfectly good to have it on standby in case you are lucky
enough to grab some fresh-from-the-sea fish or fresh-from-the-river
salmon, or simply fancy a fresh snack with a few simple pieces of
cucumber and avocado.

Rolling mats also take up very little space and you'll have a sharp
knife on you anyway... so there's nothing to stop you.

For 2

250g sushi rice
330ml water
3 tbsp seasoned
 sushi rice vinegar
2 sheets of nori
2in of cucumber, sliced
Sushi ginger
Wasabi paste

Method

Making sushi rice is the
fiddliest thing here. It needs to
be rinsed three or four times
and then put into a pan with
around 330ml of water. Bring to the boil then cover, lower the heat
down to a simmer and leave for 10 minutes, keeping the lid on the
whole time. After 10 minutes leave it to cool but leave the lid on.
When it's cold fold in 3 tbsp of seasoned sushi rice vinegar.

The next bit is the fun bit. Get your sushi rolling mat, place a sheet
of nori on it and cover with a thin layer of rice, except for about 2cm
at top and bottom. Place a line of cucumber at the bottom of the mat,
about 4cm up from the bottom. Then, roll up the mat and compress
the sushi so it makes a roll... hey presto!

Serve with pickled ginger and wasabi. Then, when you have got
it right, time to start playing.

TORTILLA deluxe

You might know the humble tortilla as the Spanish omelette. It's a classic dish that's just perfick for cooking in a camper because it requires very simple ingredients and can be cooked by anyone, to accompany anything.

In this version we have souped it up a bit by adding asparagus and Parma ham (hence the deluxe bit) but you could easily add sweet red peppers or chorizo (cook it first) or even just some herbs. Anything goes in tortilla land.

For 4
Handful of waxy potatoes
A good glug of olive oil
1 large white onion
Young asparagus
4 eggs
Seasoning
6 slices of Parma ham

Method

Slice the potatoes and onion thinly. And when I say thin, I mean about 3–4mm, no thicker. In a non-stick pan, add the olive oil and cook the spuds for about 10 minutes, covered, being careful not to burn them. Then add the onion and the asparagus and cook until the potato is cooked. Meanwhile, whisk up the eggs with seasoning in a bowl. Add the potato mix to this (take them out of the pan with a slotted spoon if you can, to leave a little oil in the pan) and add the Parma ham, torn into little pieces. Next, heat up the remaining oil until it is quite hot. Pour in the mix and allow it to cook a little around the edges (about a minute or so – you don't want to burn it) before turning down the heat and cooking for around 6–7 minutes.

Now, run a spatula around the edges of the tortilla to release it from the pan. Put a plate on top of the pan and turn the two upside down to release the tortilla. When it's safely out, slide it back into the pan so that it's cooked side up. Cook for another 6 minutes or so. Serve.

P.S. if you are afraid of doing the turning bit, do the top under the grill, but it's risky and fun to do it the proper way...

BURGERS, BAPS, BUNS AND PITTAS

I'd feel robbed if I went camping and there was nothing between two pieces of bread, bun or pitta. Honestly I would. Why? Because it's the perfect on-the-hoof food, for when there's nowhere to sit, when balancing a plate on your knee is impossible and when there's more stuff to do than sit around scoffing.

Bend over slightly to avoid getting any drips on your new tee and enjoy a hearty, wholesome burger wrapped in the cosy comfort of a bap, bun or bloomer. Nowt wrong with that.

Dolcelatte filled
LAMB BURGERS

I cooked this recipe in preparation for a cook-off at Camper Jam, one of the year's biggest VW festivals. I wanted it to be bold and exciting and to stand out from the normal burger offering.

With a burst of Italian blue cheese surpriseyness. It worked. I thought it was absolutely delicious and was very proud of it. Sadly, the jury, made up of punters from the crowd, voted for the other lamb burger (which was, ironically, from my other book).

This one came last. But that doesn't mean it isn't worth a look.

For 4

½ **tsp cumin**
½ **tsp turmeric**
½ **tsp ground ginger**
½ **kg fresh lamb mince**
1 red **onion, finely chopped**
Small handful of finely chopped **coriander**

1 large free range **egg**
100g **Dolcelatte cheese**
4 fresh white **bread rolls**
1 **tomato, thinly sliced**
Handful of fresh rocket
Black pepper and sea salt

Method

Mix the spices in a bowl, together with the mince, finely chopped onion, coriander and the egg. Split the mixture into four, then carefully roll into four balls. Take a blunt knife and create a pocket in each ball, then put a quarter of the cheese into each pocket. Seal them up with your hands and then flatten into burger shapes, making sure they stay together. Don't overwork or the cheese may fall out.

Cook over a hot griddle, BBQ or plancha for about 7–8 minutes each side.

Cut the bread rolls in half and toast them over the BBQ a little then serve each burger with tomato and rocket. Take a big bite and feel the cheese ooze from the middle among all that glorious, Moroccan-style spiciness.

Winner? I hope so.

Just a minute
SPICY BEAN BURGERS

Many moons ago there used to be a fast food joint on the M6 at the Hilton Park Service area, just past the M54 as you go north. It was called Just a Minute, and they served awful burgers. It almost always took longer than a minute to get your food cooked for you, too. However, their spicy bean burger was a thing to die for.

I'm not sure the Just a Minute burger is even a thing anymore, but this is for the good people who served me many a bean burger anyway. And it's an homage to the only bean burger ever in the history of the world for which it was deemed good enough to pull off the M6.

Makes 4 generous burgers

1 x 215g tin of **chickpeas**
1 x 215g tin of **kidney** beans
1 x 400g tin of **butter** beans
1 red **onion**, chopped
1 sweet **red pepper**
Small bunch of coriander, chopped
1 tsp **cumin**
1 red **chilli**, finely chopped
1 **carrot**, grated
1 **egg**
100g polenta
Olive oil
Seasoning

Method

Mash up the beans in a bowl. When you have a rough but mashed consistency (don't go mad), add the chopped onion, red pepper, coriander, cumin, chilli, carrot and season. Mix in the egg and then shape into four generous patties. Leave to bind for half an hour or so.

Before cooking, sprinkle polenta over them to form a polenta coating. Splash a dash of olive oil in a frying pan on a medium high heat. When the oil is sizzling hot, put the burgers in the pan and cook for about 8 minutes each side, or until they start to turn golden brown.

Serve with tomato, sour cream and mixed leaves on a bun.

KOFTA KEBABS
with tzatziki in pittas

These are super easy to make and taste just lovely, especially when you make the pittas yourself on the BBQ. It might seem like a faff to make pittas yourself but it's always worth a go – and it enables you to claim bragging rights over those who bought them, no matter how they turn out.

For the pittas
(4 large or 8 small)

1 **sachet of active dry yeast**
1 **cup warm water**
2½–3 **cups all-purpose flour**
2 **tsp salt**
1–2 **tsp olive oil**

Method

Mix the yeast in the cup of warm water, and then tip into a mixing bowl. Add the flour, salt and oil and mix well until you get a slightly wet dough. Remove from the bowl and knead a little on a floured surface. Meanwhile, clean the bowl then add a dash of olive oil to it. Cover the entire surface of the inside of the bowl with olive oil and then replace the dough ball, rolling it around to cover it in oil. Cover with a tea towel and leave to prove for 1–2 hours.

Cut into either four or eight pieces, depending on how hungry you are or how many of you there are, and roll into balls. Roll flat and cook on each side for 5 or so minutes on the BBQ or griddle, or until they begin to puff up or brown nicely.

For the kebabs
(4 large or 8 small)

500g **lean lamb mince**
1 **tsp cumin**
1 **tsp ground coriander**
1 **tsp paprika**
Lemon thyme (or thyme)
2 **tsp sumac (if you have it)**
Salt and pepper

Method

Mix the lamb with the cumin, coriander, paprika, thyme, sumac and seasoning. Divide into four and shape into four large, long, thin sausages (or eight smaller ones) around skewers. Before cooking, drizzle a little olive oil and lemon over the kebabs. Cook them on the BBQ, griddle or on a plancha for at least 10 minutes each side, turning often to get them a nice even brown.

When ready, slide off the skewers into the pittas.

For the tzatziki

200g **Greek yoghurt**
Cucumber, chopped
Fresh mint leaves
Juice of half a lemon

Method

Meanwhile mix up the yogurt, cucumber, mint and lemon juice to make your lovely dippy sauce.

Put it all together with chopped up little gem lettuce and chomp it like it's 4 a.m. and you're on the way home from a great night out … only this is better…

BARBIES, BARE GRILLS
AND FIRE PIT THRILLS

I love barbies. But I hate the throwaway kind. They produce barely enough heat to scare a sausage, are good for just a few minutes and are really wasteful. Plus you can't control the heat AND they encourage people to throw them away where they use them. Bad all round. Better buy a bucket BBQ and use it a few times if you want to be compact and portable.

So, on to cooking. My favourite thing is fish. It's always fish. And the fresher and simpler the better. I'm a bad fisherman, so all I ever catch is mackerel when they arrive in their hordes over the summer, so that's the fish I cook with most. It's perfect for the barbie because it's robust enough to take some chargrilling just as it is. It's also perfect for using the time-honoured 'five sheets of wet newspaper' trick.

FIVE SHEETS to the wind with caramelised baby veg: HOW TO BBQ A FISH

Gut and clean the fish. Fill the stomach cavity with fresh herbs (tarragon, parsley or thyme), a slice of lemon, a drizzle of olive oil and some sea salt and crushed black pepper. Wrap it up in five sheets of newspaper (broadsheet, obviously), wetting down each sheet well as you go. Then place over a fire or BBQ, turning once after a few minutes. Then leave until the paper dries out and catches fire. That's how you know it's done. Open it up and you should have perfectly steamed fish. Eat with your fingers while it's still hot!

CARAMELISED BABY VEG

So you like BBQ veg but you don't want to crucify them? That's okay. This is a great way of grilling baby veg (you can always use grown-up veg cut into batons if you can't get baby veg) that makes them sweet and crispy and ever so slightly lovely. It's easy, too, of course. Serve as a side to accompany a piece of fish or steak, or simply enjoy as they are.

For 2
A dash of olive oil
Juice of half a lemon
Baby carrots
Baby courgettes
Baby asparagus
Baby sweetcorn
Aubergine (cut into strips)
Sea salt and black pepper
100g brown sugar

Method

In a bowl, mix a dash of olive oil with the lemon juice. Prepare the vegetables and place them in the bowl, turning them with your hands so that every surface is coated with the oil and lemon. Drain away any excess liquid. Sprinkle the brown sugar over the veg and turn again, making sure that there is some on every bit of veg.

Fire up the BBQ or grill (or splash a dash of olive oil in a heavy duty skillet or frying pan on a medium-high heat) and get it hot. Put the veg on and allow to cook for 5–10 minutes, without burning the sugar (it's okay for it to caramelise). Turn the veg and cook for a further 5 or 10 minutes until it is all nicely browned.

MONKFISH PARCELS
with lemon thyme

Some fish, like sardines or mackerel, can cope well with the direct heat from a fire. Monkfish isn't one of those, and you risk all (it's not cheap either) by drying it out when you cook it. Having said that, it is a firm fish that can take a bit of cooking, and won't flake like cod or pollack.

Wrapping monkfish in pancetta or Parma ham is the perfect way to keep it moist and seal in the flavours. Parma ham adds a lovely salty crispiness when well cooked. Lemon thyme adds a citrus and herb flavour that complements both fish and pork.

For 4

1 large **monkfish tail**
Seasoning
A bunch of lemon thyme (or thyme if none available)
1 clove **garlic, finely** chopped
Olive oil
8 slices **Parma ham**
The zest of a lime

Method

First, cut the monkfish from the bone by slicing it away to leave the two sides. Cut these in two to give you four even pieces. Now open them out by slicing halfway through. Season, add the lemon thyme and garlic and a drizzle of olive oil, then roll up in the Parma ham. Barbecue (or griddle) until the Parma ham is crispy and the monkfish is cooked – about 5–10 minutes. Serve with lime zest on top.

SLOW COOKED RIBS with lemon, honey and paprika

Some food takes patience. This is one of those dishes. But I can assure you it will be worth it. In the meantime you get to play about with the fire, stoking it up and poking it with a stick to your heart's content while the ribs cook away in their sweet juices. At the end of the cooking time you get to unwrap them, before giving them a good roasting to make them super crackly and lovely.

For 2

Side of pork ribs
2 tbsp sweet smoked
    paprika
Juice of 1 large lemon
A large glug of olive oil
1 tbsp honey
1 tsp fennel seeds
2 tbsp cumin
A few sprigs of fresh
    thyme and rosemary

Method

Place the rack of ribs on a large enough piece of tin foil to wrap them completely. Mix the paprika, lemon juice, olive oil, honey, fennel seeds and cumin, and rub all over the ribs. Then place a few sprigs of each of the herbs on the rack before wrapping it up, and placing in a baking tray over the fire (it may be a good idea to double wrap it). Don't put it too close to the most intense part of the fire – you don't want it to burn.

Let the rack stew away for at least an hour – the longer the better. Keep an eye on it, turning it every 15 minutes or so, and be careful not to let it burn. When you are satisfied that the meat is tender and cooked right through, remove the ribs from the foil, keeping the juices aside and warm, and chargrill the ribs to make them crisp up nicely. Then, when serving, pour the juice over the ribs ... OMG ... or something.

Serve with grapefruit and fennel salad (*see* page 264) and minted potato salad (*see* page 266).

MOJO ROJO with grilled sardines

Once upon a time a mild mannered sardine got himself grilled. He was happy with how he was, as one of the world's finest grilled fishes available. But somehow he just wasn't complete. Then, just when he wasn't expecting it, he got laced with a drizzle of red Mojo, the fiery temptress. With the power to transform any shy fish, the Mojo got to work straight away, boosting the sardine's confidence and making it feel like ... like ... like ... a full flavoured beast of a dish.

The Mojo Rojo is the hot version of the Canarian Green Mojo sauce, which makes it perfect for enlivening little fishes with only a little bite.

For 2

4 fresh whole gutted **sardines**
Seasoning
3 red **chillies**, chopped and deseeded
½ tsp **salt**
½ tsp ground **cumin**
1 tsp hot smoked **paprika**
1 tsp sweet **pepper**
½ tsp brown **sugar**
200ml olive **oil**
150ml white wine **vinegar**

Method

Season the sardines with salt and black pepper and whack them on the grill (BBQ) until they are crispy and gorgeous. While that's going on, chop the chillies and pound them in your mortar. Add the salt, cumin, paprika, sweet pepper and sugar. Add a little of the oil at a time and continue to mix the sauce. Finally, add the vinegar to make it a drizzlable consistency.

When the fish are perfectly cooked, drizzle a little of the Mojo on them and serve with fresh salad leaves.

Moroccan-style
COUSCOUS WITH SPICY PORK

Couscous is a great go-to staple for camping.
It requires nothing other than boiling water to cook it
and makes a great base for all kinds of treats because
you can add almost anything to it and it'll taste great.

This is a relatively quick dinner that's easy to cook and has all
kinds of interesting flavours going on – a little spice, fruit and curry.
If you didn't fancy the pork then the couscous will go well with any
kind of BBQ meat or veg.

For 2

3 tbsp dried **apricots, chopped**
3 tbsp dates, chopped
250g couscous
Olive oil
Boiling water
3 tbsp sultanas
3 tbsp chopped **almonds**
1 bunch fresh **coriander**

FOR THE PORK
1 tsp paprika
1 tsp ground **cumin**
1 tsp curry powder
Juice of 1 lemon
1 tbsp olive oil
3 lean boned **pork** chops, diced
Crème fraîche

Method

Put the kettle on. While it's boiling, chop the apricots and dates.

Pour the couscous into a bowl. Drizzle a little olive oil into it and
then mix to coat each grain. This will help it to not stick. Next, pour
enough boiling water over the couscous so it's covered with water.
Cover with a tea towel and leave for about 10 minutes.

Now on to the pork chops. Mix the spices with the lemon juice and
oil in a pan. Add the pork and coat it all over. If you fancy getting a
BBQ on the go, leave the pork to marinade for about half an hour before
cooking. If not, fry the pork in a dash of oil. It should bubble away in
the juice of the lemon and olive oil. Once the pork is cooked (about
5 minutes) remove the pan from the heat and stir in the crème fraîche
to the pan to create a rich curried sauce.

Finally, fluff up the couscous with a fork and mix in the dried fruits,
nuts and coriander. Serve together with the pork.

SOMETHING FISHY'S GOING ON AROUND HERE

I love fish, and you'll find a lot of it in here. You'll find there's a lot of it throughout, in fact. It's partly a reflection of the way I like to camp and eat, or the place I live, which is by the sea.

Going to the fishmonger is always a treat, wherever I am and it's always nice to see different things in different places. From shellfish to deep-sea fish, there is such a lot of choice. However, we should always be careful to talk to the fishmonger about where it comes from, how sustainable it is and whether or not it is right to eat. If we turn away from endangered fish then the fishermen will be less likely to target it.

Take a look at **www.fishonline.org** and then vote with your feet.

FISHY BITS with homemade tartare sauce

Fish counters are wonderful places, especially in Spain. There is something wonderful about seeing the way the fish are dressed to sell and made to look delicious and inviting.

Sadly, in my experience, fish at Spanish fish counters also come in a different language, which means you have to point to order. That can mean you get a few bits and pieces you weren't expecting. But that's okay. That's when you need this recipe. It's frightfully *fácil* and will serve you well, whatever it is you end up buying. Each fish has a slightly different taste so will taste deliciously different, even with the tartare sauce.

Buenos. Or is it *bueno*? I'll have the fish.

For 4

Half a cup of plain **flour**
Ground black **pepper**
Sea salt
1 tsp ground cumin
½ tsp paprika
Pieces of scallop
10 king prawns
Fillet of bass, chopped into slices
2 x fillets of mackerel, chopped into slices
Hake, skinned, deboned and cut into pieces
Olive oil
A knob of butter

FOR THE TARTARE SAUCE
2 big tbsp mayonnaise
1 tsp capers, chopped
1 shallot, finely chopped
Juice and zest of 1 lemon
4 small pickles, chopped
Bunch of fresh parsley, chopped
Ground black **pepper**

Eat
223

Method

Mix the flour together with the pepper, salt, cumin and paprika in a bowl. Dust each of the pieces of fish/shellfish with the flour-spice mix and pan fry in the olive oil and butter until done. Vary cooking times for each fish, with scallops taking the least amount of time (about a minute each side).

Next, add the mayonnaise to the bowl and mix in the rest of the ingredients. Kazam. It's that easy.

Serve with salad and chunks of lemon.

Smoked mackerel
FISH CAKES

I first had fish cakes made with smoked mackerel when judging a 'cooking in a camper' contest at a VW show. Adding the mackerel, in my opinion, was the stroke of genius that won the day. It's not subtle in its flavour – but subtlety isn't what's needed here. What we're after is a hearty go-to dish that's adaptable and delicious and will fill you with smoky, salty, fishy loveliness.

To make this easier, it helps if you have a steamer with a big enough base to boil the spuds in, but if you don't, use a colander on top of the pan with a plate over it to steam the haddock.

Makes 4 generous
fish cakes

2 large peeled Maris Pipers
(or other fluffy spuds)
2 fillets haddock (unsmoked)
1 tbsp horseradish sauce
2 fillets smoked mackerel
Fresh chives, chopped

1 tbsp capers
1 large egg
Salt and pepper
1 tsp chilli flakes
Plain flour (for coating
and dusting)
Olive oil, for frying

Method

Wash, peel and chop the potatoes. Then boil until cooked but not
falling apart. While boiling, steam the haddock on the top of the pan
until cooked (a couple of minutes), if you can. If not, steam it separately.

Drain and mash the spuds until fluffy, then mix in the horseradish
sauce. Flake the haddock and mackerel and remove any skin or bones,
then mix in, along with the chives and capers.

Shape the mixture into four fish cakes using floured hands (a cling
film-lined ramekin can help here if you don't want to get messy hands).
Beat the egg in a bowl and
then coat each cake with
egg before dusting with
a mixture of salt, pepper,
chilli flakes and plain flour.

Fry in the oil until
crispy then serve with a
green salad or green veg,
such as steamed fresh
asparagus.

COCKLES IN CIDER
with linguine

This is really easy and light on washing up. But remember the rules of shellfish: purge them of grit and sand by soaking in cold, salted water, discard any that float and don't eat any that don't open. If you haven't got linguine, use spaghetti.

For 4

About 100g linguine per person
Olive oil
1 onion, finely chopped
1 clove garlic, finely chopped
1 chilli, chopped, or a few chilli flakes
150ml cider
1–2kg fresh cockles (can be bought at most fishmongers)
Seasoning
1 tbsp chopped parsley (for colour)

Method

Put the linguine on to boil. Add a dash of olive oil to the water – it will help to stop it sticking. In a deep frying pan with a lid, heat up some olive oil. Add the onion and cook for a few minutes until it begins to soften. Add the garlic and chilli. After a couple of minutes add the cider and allow it to bubble away for a few moments. Next add the cockles, stir in the juices, replace the lid and leave for 2–4 minutes (or until the shells open). Remove from the heat. Add the parsley, season to taste and stir to make sure every cockle has some juice on it. If you like creamy sauces you can add a little cream at this point.

Drain the linguine, add some olive oil (or butter) and dish out into bowls. Serve the cockles, with plenty of the sauce, on the top.

TEN-MINUTE NOODLES with king prawns and peanuts

This is another really quick dish that's so great for camper van living. It's loosely based on an Asian dish, Phad Thai, and has lots of flavours: sweet, chilli and lime, and a depth that only fish sauce can add.

Rice noodles are fantastic because they don't need cooking on the hob. All you have to do is soak them in boiling water for a few minutes until they soften enough to add to your dish. Also, they're cheap and will store for ages. If you can't find them at your local supermarket, try an Asian supermarket.

For 4

1 pack rice noodles (around 300–400g)
Splash of toasted sesame oil (optional)
2 tbsp cooking oil
A bunch of spring onions (5–7), roughly chopped
1 red chilli, finely chopped
2 cloves garlic, chopped or crushed
400g of peeled and cooked king prawns
1 tsp brown sugar
2 tbsp fish sauce
2 tbsp soy sauce
A bunch of fresh coriander, chopped coarsely
2 large eggs
Juice of 1 lime
A large handful of ready salted peanuts, crushed

Eat

227

Method

Boil a pan full of water. When boiling, remove from the heat and add the noodles. Make sure they are all covered. Leave them to soak while you cook the rest of the dish, but be careful not to leave them in for more than about 5 minutes. When they feel that they are almost done, drain and then rinse in cold water. Then, if you have it – although not essential – pour on a little toasted sesame oil and stir into the noodles. This will help to stop them sticking and becoming claggy. Leave until you are ready to use them.

In a large frying pan or wok (if you have one aboard), heat up the cooking oil on a medium/high flame and cook the spring onion, along

continued overleaf

with the chilli and garlic for just a couple of minutes.

Add the prawns and cook for a minute or so, then add the sugar, fish sauce, soy sauce and stir, before adding the cooked noodles and the coriander. Mix around gently once.

Next, move everything to one side of the pan and break the two eggs into the empty half. Scramble the eggs quickly and mix in with the noodles. Remove from the heat.

Squeeze lime juice all over and then serve in bowls. As a final garnish, sprinkle over each bowl with half of the peanuts.

BASS FILLET with lemon and fennel RISOTTO

Risotto is a life-saver, at home and away. It's easy to make and can be as versatile as you are, with almost anything making it into a super supper. I like it this way with a little of the fabulous aniseed flavour of the fennel, together with the freshness of the lemon.

Risotto goes with just about anything, especially fish when it's made tangy and fresh like this recipe. Don't forget to get your sea bass line caught (not trawled) and check with the Marine Conservation Society's Good Fish Guide (**www.fishonline.org**) if you fancy anything else.

For 4

1 chicken stock cube
1l boiling water
Bay leaf
50g butter
1 medium **onion**, finely chopped
2 large cloves **garlic**, finely
   chopped
1 bulb **fennel**, finely sliced

4 **bass** fillets
Olive oil
Large glass of white **wine**
300g of risotto **rice**
Fresh flat leaf **parsley**,
   chopped
1 lemon, juice and zest
Parmesan cheese

Method

Firstly make a stock by dissolving the stock cube in 1 litre of boiling water. Add a bay leaf. In a large pan, melt the butter and soften the onions over a medium heat. When softened, add the chopped garlic and the fennel. Cook for a further couple of minutes. Add the risotto rice into the pan and stir it into the butter so every grain gets coated. Add the white wine and allow to bubble for a few moments.

Then add the stock a ladle at a time. When the rice has absorbed it, add some more until the stock is all gone. Simmer the rice for about 15 minutes, stirring regularly. Meanwhile, season well and pan fry the bass skin side first in a little butter and olive oil, turning after a few minutes.

When the rice is still a little firm but nicely creamy, add the chopped parsley and squeeze the lemon into the risotto and stir. Serve with Parmesan shavings, parsley and a squeeze of lemon and zest on the sea bass.

CELEBRATION PAELLA
with prawns and moules

Paella is one of those dishes that can't be done quietly. It's not a quiet night in. It's a fiesta, a celebration, a feast. And when it's cooked over an open fire it's even better. This one's all about the shellfish (and other bits).

Even if you haven't got anything to celebrate, make something up when you have this, even if it's celebrating being away from the telly for a few days.

It's a treat. And it's a treat to make.

This can be cooked in a large frying pan (or two smaller ones) so there's no need to carry a paella dish with you on your travels. However, they don't take up much space and come in various sizes so you can find one that fits the cupboard. The bigger the better.

For 4

1l chicken stock
1 tbsp **boiling water**
1 tbsp oil
1 **chorizo** stick,
    chopped
1 **onion,** finely
    chopped
1 **clove garlic,** finely
    chopped
1 red **pepper,** deseeded
    and chopped
300g paella **rice**
2 pinches of **saffron**
½ tsp hot smoked
    paprika
8 large raw **prawns**
2 handfuls of cleaned
    mussels
Chopped parsley and
    lemon wedges

Method

Make your stock with boiling water and a chicken stock cube
… keep it to one side.

In a paella pan (or large frying pan), brown the chorizo over a
medium heat. You shouldn't need any fat as chorizo has plenty of
its own. Remove from the pan. In the chorizo fat, fry the onion for
5 minutes, until browned. Add the garlic and red pepper and cook,
stirring, for a couple of minutes. Tip the rice into the pan along with
the saffron and its liquid, the paprika and the chorizo. Season and stir.
Next, add stock until the rice is submerged – it won't require all of it.
Bring to a simmer and then leave for around 10 minutes. If it starts to
dry out, add more stock.

After 10 minutes, add the prawns and mussels, pushing them into
the rice. Again, add more stock if necessary and simmer for another
10 minutes to ensure all the stock is absorbed (but not that it's too dry).
Check the prawns have cooked and that the mussels have opened
(don't eat any that don't). Garnish with torn parsley and make it pretty
with lemon wedges.

Maggie's MOULES

This is a dish that Maggie and I cooked with wild mussels from Galicia. It's really easy to make and is similar to a *moules marinière*. It is, of course, delicious and takes just a few minutes.

As a final recipe for this series it's fitting, as it was perfect for cooking in the van with something we found along the way and using up all we had to go with it – a bit of cream, an onion and some bacon!

For 4

4kg fresh mussels
Pack of smoked bacon, chopped
1 white onion, finely chopped
2 cloves garlic, finely sliced
A glass of rosé
Around 150ml cream
A handful of chopped parsley

Method

Firstly, prep the mussels by de-bearding and cleaning them. Some people advocate leaving them overnight in fresh water with oats but I usually just rinse them in fresh water and leave them for about half an hour. If any float, discard them.

Cook the bacon until crispy in a large pan then remove and put aside. Fry off the onion until soft in the bacon fat. Then add the garlic. After a minute or so add the rosé, and then, when it's bubbling, add the mussels to the pan and cover with a lid. Steam the mussels for about 4–5 minutes until they open, shaking the pan every so often. Finally, put the bacon back into the pan, remove from the heat, then add the cream and the chopped parsley and stir. Serve with crusty white bread and butter.

SOUPS AND STEWS AND HEADY BREWS

You can't have burgers every day, can you? Although some in your party might be happy with a handheld something for every meal, your army needs to march on more substantial fodder.

For me, these recipes are the basis of every successful trip. From a traditional spag bol that tastes like it's been brewing for a week (the very best kind) to a warming Asturian Fabada, the following recipes will warm the cockles of anyone's heart. On cold winter days. On chilly autumn evenings. On bright summer nights. Wherever, whenever.

Good ol' SPAG BOL

Some people like their spag bol cooked light, with lots of tomatoes and basil. Well that's fine. But I like mine cooked dark and mean, with lots of deep flavours – like it's a couple of days older than it is (you know how it always tastes better on day two).

It's a version that I have been working on for over 30 years (probably more, actually) and I think I've got it just about spot on for the way I like it. So it's not your average. Heck, it doesn't even use spaghetti. That's because I prefer the way linguine holds more sauce. Eh? Just try it.

For 4

1 large **onion**, finely chopped
1 **red pepper**
Olive oil
4 cloves **garlic**, roughly chopped
500g lean minced **beef**
Ground black pepper
½ tsp brown sugar
1 beef **stock cube**
A dash of Henderson's **relish** (or Worcestershire sauce, if you can't get relish)

1 tbsp tomato **purée**
1 tsp rosemary, chopped
1 tsp thyme, chopped
1 tsp oregano, chopped
150g button **mushrooms**
1 x 400g tin chopped tomatoes
4 anchovies
500g linguine

Method

Soften the onion and pepper in a splash of olive oil. Add the garlic and cook for a couple of minutes. Add the mince and cook, stirring until the meat is browned. Add ground black pepper, the sugar, the stock cube, the Henderson's relish and the tomato purée, as well as the herbs. Stir to mix, then add the tomatoes and stir again. If the sauce is too thick, add half a can of water (200ml) and stir in. Add the anchovies and simmer for 10 minutes.

Put the linguine into boiling water with a little olive oil and salt. Continue to simmer for a further 15 minutes until the linguine is cooked. Season to taste and serve.

Slow cooked SHIN OF BEEF with coriander and star anise

This recipe is for those with lots of time on their hands, plenty of wood and a Dutch oven (or Kotlich) and tripod. It's easy to prep but does take some cooking time. It'll all be well worth the effort though, once your guests tuck in.

The rich flavours will remind you of Thai and Asian dishes. Serve with sticky Thai rice for an extra authentic touch. If you can't light a fire, then you can always cook this over a very low heat.

For 4

Vegetable oil
4 beef shin joints
1 large **onion, chopped**
2 large cloves **garlic, chopped**
2 fresh red **chillies, chopped**
1in fresh root **ginger, chopped**
2 whole **star anise**
600ml (about a pint) **beef stock**
1 tbsp soy sauce
1 tbsp mirin
A large bunch of coriander,
    chopped
A few baby carrots (or carrot
    batons)
Small pack of mange tout

Method

Heat the Dutch oven over the fire until water sizzles in it. Then add a few drizzles of vegetable oil and seal the beef shin pieces. Remove and put aside. Then remove the pan from the heat a little and add the onion, garlic, chilli and ginger. Allow it to soften for a couple of minutes before adding the star anise, stock, soy sauce, mirin and the chopped coriander. Bring to a simmer and then add the beef, making sure it is covered with the stock. Simmer for 2 hours. About 5 or 6 minutes before serving check for seasoning then add the carrots, then the mange tout about three minutes later.

Kampervan KORMA

In the 1980s I used to hang out in a field in North Wales with a bunch of reprobates from the North West Surf Club. Not one weekend would go down without someone whipping up a curry of some sort. The smell alone was invitation enough to invade their van with a meagre offering of a couple of cans of Carlsberg and a hopeful look.

It's the same on campsites all over the UK, as it seems that every camper van trip must have a curry – partly for the taste, but also partly to lure everyone else into your van with the heavenly aromas.

And this is why I am declaring curry as Britain's number 1 favourite camper van food. It's long been the nation's favourite takeaway, so why not extend things a bit more? That's right. Get your Kombi around this little beauty, a classic korma-esque cuzza made from scratch, that's easy to make and just as easy to scoff.

For 4

Vegetable oil
1 large **onion**, chopped
1 red **chilli**, finely chopped
1 large knob of fresh
    ginger (thumb sized),
    grated
2 cloves of **garlic**, chopped
1 tsp **turmeric**
1 tsp **ground coriander**
1 tsp **garam masala**
½ tsp **cayenne pepper**
    (more if you like it
    spicy)
1 tbsp **grated coconut**
1 tbsp **tomato purée**
1 x **440ml** tin **coconut** milk
8 boneless **chicken** thighs
A large handful of closed
    cup **mushrooms**,
    chopped
Half a pack of fine green
    beans
Bunch of coriander
1 tbsp **chopped almonds**
250g basmati **rice**
2–3 tbsp of Greek **yogurt**
Mango chutney to serve

Method

In your cook pot (or Kotlich) heat up a little oil. Add your onions, chilli and ginger and allow to sweat for a few minutes. Add the garlic and sweat a little more before adding all the spices. Mix them into a paste, then add the grated coconut and the tomato purée. This should make a nice korma paste.

Allow this to heat up and sizzle a little, mixing well, before tipping in the coconut milk and mixing well again. Once the coconut milk has begun to warm through and mix, add the chicken thighs and the mushrooms. If necessary, add a little water to ensure everything is covered. Leave to bubble away for 10–15 minutes, then add the beans and put the rice on. Simmer for another 10 minutes or until the chicken is cooked through (the longer the better really).

When you're happy that all is cooked properly, remove from the heat, tear up the coriander and add it, along with the chopped almonds and stir in. Prepare and wash the rice. Finally, add the yogurt and stir in for an extra creamy dollop of freshness. Serve with mango chutney and enjoy.

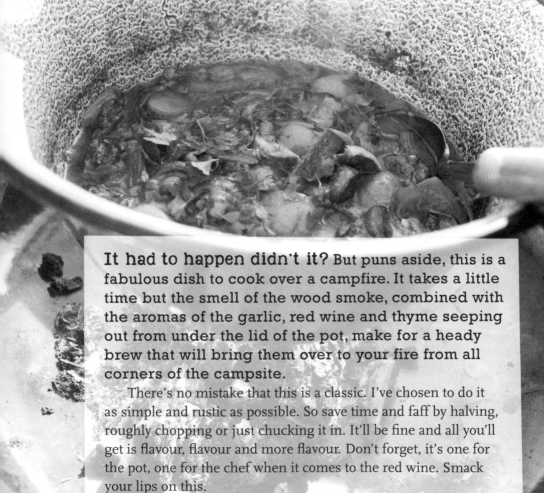

COQ AU VAN, rustic camper vin style

It had to happen didn't it? But puns aside, this is a fabulous dish to cook over a campfire. It takes a little time but the smell of the wood smoke, combined with the aromas of the garlic, red wine and thyme seeping out from under the lid of the pot, make for a heady brew that will bring them over to your fire from all corners of the campsite.

There's no mistake that this is a classic. I've chosen to do it as simple and rustic as possible. So save time and faff by halving, roughly chopping or just chucking it in. It'll be fine and all you'll get is flavour, flavour and more flavour. Don't forget, it's one for the pot, one for the chef when it comes to the red wine. Smack your lips on this.

For 4

6 skinned and
   boned chicken thighs
250g smoked **lardons** or
   smoked bacon
Olive oil
2 carrots
2 large white **onions**
½ **bunch** of **celery**
3 cloves **garlic**
1 bay leaf
A few sprigs of fresh **thyme**
1 chicken **stock cube**
1 heaped tbsp strong white **flour**
¾ **bottle** of heavy **red wine**
1 pint water
10 medium button **mushrooms**

6 small new **potatoes**
Seasoning
White crusty bread and
   butter to serve

Method

In your cookpot (over the fire or on the hob) brown the chicken with the lardons in a splash of olive oil for 5 minutes or so. Remove from the pot and put aside, leaving the juices. Add the carrots, onions, celery, garlic, bay leaf and thyme to the pot and soften for a few minutes, stirring from time to time. Add the stock cube and stir. Add the chicken and lardons to the veg and stir. Sprinkle the flour over the top and mix in well.

Now add the wine and up the heat a bit. Bring to the boil then add the water (just enough to cover everything) and bring to the boil again. Allow to simmer with the lid on for around 30 minutes. Add the mushrooms and potatoes and allow to simmer again for another 30–40 minutes, seasoning to taste.

Serve with the crusty bread and butter straight from the pot.

Asturian FABADA

Give your stew pot a treat with this wonderfully rustic and wholesome stew from northern Spain. I learned to cook it after having it a few times on trips in the van. So it has great memories for me, even if it does take an hour or so to make (with very little chopping time). But what's an hour when you have a cold beer to polish off and a sunset to savour…?

It's not very vegetarian (what do you expect from a Spanish dish) but it is tasty… and not a single bull was tortured in its making. Olé!

For 4
1 tbsp olive **oil**
1 onion, chopped
6 cloves garlic, coarsely chopped
1 red pepper, diced
500g belly pork (no skin), diced
A stick of spicy chorizo sausage, sliced
8 thick slices of black pudding
½ tsp hot smoked paprika
2 x 400g tins butter beans
1l chicken stock
Seasoning
Chunky bread and butter

Method

Add the oil to your cooking pot over a medium heat and sauté the onion, garlic and pepper until just tender. Add the diced pork, chorizo and black pudding. Cook for about 5 minutes. Add the paprika and beans and stir. Add the stock and simmer for an hour. Season to taste.

Serve in bowls to hungry campers with a chunk of bread and lashings of butter.

ASTURIAN FABADA

MUSHY PEA SOUP
with frankfurters

Cor blimey, it's a right pea souper. And it is. It's great, too. This is a very simple version of the Austrian classic 'pea soup with frankfurters' that uses tins of mushy peas rather than fresh (for once) because frankly we don't have the time or energy (gas) to spend hours making soup. But we still like pea soup. Especially on cold days.

Okay, so it's tins of peas. But they will keep forever for a rainy day in the back of a cupboard. Everyone will love it, I promise. Slop it about, dunk your white sliced right in it, enjoy.

For 4
Knob of butter
2 shallots, finely chopped
1 carrot, chopped into cubes of about 1cm
1 stick celery, chopped
1 clove garlic, finely chopped or crushed
1 bay leaf
2 x 300g tins of mushy peas
300ml chicken stock
6 frankfurters, chopped into 1in pieces
A dash of double **cream**
Half a chilli, finely chopped

Method

In your cookpot (over the fire or on the hob) melt the butter and sauté the shallots, carrots and celery. When the onion is translucent, add the chopped garlic and the bay leaf. Sauté for another minute or so. Add the tins of peas and mix in with the veg. Add the stock and stir to mix well.

Bring to a gentle boil. Simmer for 15 minutes. Then add the chopped frankfurters and season to taste. Simmer for 5 minutes. Serve in bowls or mugs, adding a little cream and sprinkling chillies on to each.

SEAFOOD and sweetcorn CHOWDER

There are some foods that have the ability to transport you back to a time and a place. The merest smell of them can whisk you away to moments of food pleasure.

This recipe, which is my attempt at recreating something not unlike the very fine seafood chowder to be found at Eithna's By The Sea Seafood restaurant in Mullaghmore, Ireland, takes me straight back there. There are kids throwing themselves off the harbour wall at high tide, wet wetsuits are hanging on the line, and, of course, a hearty chowder is waiting for you at lunchtime. Good memories.

For 6 hungry campers

Olive oil
1 pack of smoked streaky **bacon**
1 white **onion,** sliced
2 tbsp plain **flour**
1 tsp cayenne **pepper**
½ litre of fish **stock, or water**
½ **pint of milk**
4 waxy **potatoes**

1 **sweetcorn** cob
1 fillet whiting, **haddock or coley**
    (cut into 1in chunks)
Large handful of peeled **prawns**
Handful of mussels
1 clove **garlic,** chopped
Cream
Parsley

Method

I like to cook mine in the Kotlich, but it could be any largeish
pan on the hob. Heat the oil and brown the bacon well until it is crisp
and golden. Add the onion and allow it to sweat for a few minutes.
Add the garlic. Stir in the flour and cayenne pepper and cook for
another couple of minutes. Add the fish stock or water gradually.
Add the milk and potatoes. Season well.

Simmer until the potatoes are almost cooked, then cut the kernels
off the sweetcorn and add to the broth. Then add the fish, prawns and
the mussels. Simmer for a few minutes, then add the cream and bring
to the boil. Remove from the heat and add the parsley.

Serve with the no bake brown scones (*see* page 248) and lashings
of butter.

No bake brown
SODA BREAD SCONES

The only **way to enjoy chowder** is with a brown bread scone, the way they do it in Ireland. This recipe should give you something close enough without an oven. Use lashings of butter to eat!

**Makes approx.
16 scones**

**8oz (225g)
wholemeal flour**
**8oz (225g) self-
raising white flour**
1 tsp salt
1 tsp baking soda
**1 tsp soft brown
sugar**
**300ml milk (add
more
if too dry)**
2oz oats for shaping
**Splash of olive or
sunflower oil**

Method

In a bowl mix the flour, salt, baking soda
and sugar together. Slowly stir in the milk
and add extra if the mix is a little dry. Knead
the dough and add oats if too sticky.

Sprinkle some flour onto a flat clean
surface, and roll out the dough to around
1in thickness. Cut round shapes; in this case
I used a small glass.

To cook the scones you need a flat griddle,
add a splash of oil, either olive oil or sunflower
oil. Heat the griddle, add the scones and cook
each side for about 7 minutes. When golden
brown and starting to rise, flip the scones over
and cook the other side until golden brown.
The scones will rise and cook through. When
done, leave to cool.

MEATY, BIG AND BOUNCY

Sometimes you have to have meat. Sometimes. And if you don't want a burger then it has to be something altogether different. Like a venison fillet. Or pork tenderloin. Both are great cuts and don't need much doing to them. Add a little spice and some *jus je ne sais quoi* and you're away...

VENISON FILLET with red wine, cranberry and baby veg

This is one for the meat eaters who don't like washing up. It's a one knife, one pan wonder and will also give you a bit of an opportunity to create cheffy little piles of baby veg cuteness that you can tweet at me or plop onto Instagram. Don't forget to include me @campervanliving.

Anyway, I first cooked this in the van in the Trossachs in Scotland on a very rainy night, and have been trying out various forms of it since. The red wine works a treat and the cranberry adds a little extra fruitiness that you just can't beat. It's fresh and fine but also dark and deep, the way venison should be. And it only takes about 10 minutes.

For 2

A **dash** of olive **oil**
1 **venison fillet**
   seasoned
A **glug (half glass of)**
   of light **red wine**
8 baby **carrots**
1 **courgette** cut into
   strips, or 8 baby
   courgettes
1 bulb **chicory**
A **few** sprigs of fresh
   thyme
1 heaped tbsp
   cranberry jelly
A dash of **olive oil**

Method

Splash a dash of olive oil in a heavy duty skillet or frying pan on a medium/high heat. Place the seasoned venison fillets in the pan and fry for a few minutes each side until browned. Do not be tempted to over cook the fillets as we don't want to create any charred debris in the pan.

Remove the fillets and place them on one side to rest. Deglaze the pan with the red wine (posh word for put the wine in the pan to clean up and use the cooking juices) and then, when bubbling, place the baby veg and thyme into the pan to steam. Don't let the pan dry out – add a dash of water if it's in danger of doing so.

Once the veg is still a little crunchy after about 5 minutes, remove it and plate up. Slice the fillets into thin strips and add to the plates. Next, add a tablespoon of cranberry jelly to the leftover juices and allow to bubble and dissolve into a rich *jus*. Pour over the fillets.

Stand back and admire what you have created.

DUCKY PORK FAJITAS
with plum sauce

Chinese five spice is a bit of a miracle. It's a bit like its Spanish counterpart, smoked paprika, in that there's not a lot you can put it onto that it will ruin. And that includes pork loin. In fact, this is one of the best ways of enjoying pork loin I can think of. The spices in five spice give it that unique Chinese flavour with a hint of aniseed, cinnamon and cloves. Oh goodness it's lovely.

So this is a bit like having crispy pancakes from the Chinese but not. Except, of course you still get the joy of making. Great for kids.

For 4
1 pork loin
Big shake of Chinese five spice
Sea salt and black pepper
Homemade plum sauce
    (see opposite)
8 plain white tortillas
Soured cream
Half a cucumber, chopped
Spring onions, shredded
Handful of watercress
Bunch of coriander, chopped

Method

Split the loin down the middle to open it out, then split again until it is like a flat fillet. Bash it a bit with your hand to tenderise and flatten it a bit more. Sprinkle five spice over it, along with a bit of salt and pepper. Place on a griddle, in a pan or on the BBQ. Cook for 5–10 minutes until it's starting to crisp up a little. Spice and season the other side and turn over to cook again for 5 minutes or so. When you are happy it's done, remove from the heat, leave to rest for 5 minutes, then slice.

To serve, pour a blob of plum sauce on the tortilla, followed by a dollop of soured cream, cucumber, spring onion, watercress and coriander. Spread a bit of pork on top, roll up and eat.

FOR THE HOMEMADE PLUM SAUCE

6 ripe red **plums**
1 tbsp **vegetable oil**
Half a glass of red **wine**
½ white **onion**, chopped
1 star anise

2 cloves **garlic**, roughly chopped
1 tsp finely grated fresh root **ginger**
1 tbsp red wine **vinegar**
2 tbsp light brown **sugar**
2 tbsp soy **sauce**

Method

Peel, chop and de-stone the plums. Place them in a pan with the oil, wine, onion, star anise, garlic and ginger. Simmer until all are soft (about 20–30 minutes). Remove from the heat and push through a sieve (you can use the same pan for this by spooning it out a bit at a time) until you have a nice smooth-ish consistency. Add the vinegar, soy sauce and sugar, and bring to the boil. Simmer for a further 30 minutes. Allow to cool before using.

VEGGIE TREATS

Have you had your five today? If you haven't, get stuck into these*. Nothing whatsoever was harmed in the making of these, except perhaps a few cherry tomatoes and some fennel. And that's okay because fennel was given to us by superior beings, who knew that our bodies and palates needed cleansing with something clean and delicious from time to time.

* These aren't the only vegetarian recipes in this book, BTW. Have a flick through and see where the little V is. That's for you guys. Sorry it couldn't be more.

MUSHROOM, lemon and fennel RISOTTO

Risotto is a dish that's great to fall back on at any point in the camping experience, although it can be a little fiddly creating stock. However, if you don't fancy making up a new one you can always just dissolve a stock cube in boiling water in a jug.

Risotto is all about the creaminess so the amount of liquid you add is all-important. Cooking time is important, too. I like my rice cooked but not mushy, and a little firm but not crunchy. So tasting is important. Same applies to seasoning. The major ingredients will keep well in any cupboard so it's a good one to pack away and forget about before you go.

For 4

50g **butter**
100g **oyster mushrooms**
1 medium **onion,** finely chopped
2 large cloves **garlic,** finely chopped
300g risotto **rice**
Large glass white **wine**
Vegetarian Parmesan cheese
Small bunch of fresh parsley, chopped
Squeeze of **lemon**
Seasoning

FOR THE STOCK

1 vegetable **stock cube**
1l boiling **water**
1 bay **leaf**
½ bulb **fennel,** chopped
Half a **lemon**

Method

Firstly make the stock by dissolving the stock cube in 1l of boiling water. Add a bay leaf, the chopped fennel and lemon. Bring to the boil and simmer for 5 minutes. Put aside for use later.

Melt half the butter in a large pan and add the chopped mushrooms, stirring as they cook gently through. Remove the mushrooms from the pan and put aside, retaining the juices. Add the remainder of the butter and fry off the onion and garlic until it is soft. Then put the risotto rice into the pan and stir so every grain gets coated. Add the white wine and allow to bubble over a medium heat for a few moments.

Then add the stock a ladle at a time (leave the lemon and fennel). Simmer the rice for about 15 minutes, stirring regularly. Add the mushrooms and the parsley and check for seasoning. Simmer for a few minutes more until the rice is firm but also deliciously creamy, adding more stock if it gets too thick or dry.

Take off the heat and grate a generous amount of vegetarian Parmesan, then a squeeze of the lemon. Serve with a fresh green salad.

FRESH PASTA with homemade pesto and cherry tomatoes

There is something wonderfully simple about fresh pasta with pesto. It's one of those go-to meals that pleases kids no end and fills up hungry stomachs with glee. And it's also ridiculously simple, which is why it's great for cooking in your van. So don't be lazy and reach for the jar of ready-made, do this instead! Making your own is much more delicious.

In the spring and summer you can make this with half basil and half wild garlic leaves (but don't forget to leave out the chopped garlic); just pick it, wash it and treat it like basil.

For 4

4 tbsp pine **nuts**
Bunch of fresh **basil, finely
  chopped**
2 large cloves **garlic, finely
  chopped**
About 3 tbsp olive **oil**
4 tbsp finely grated vegetarian
  Parmesan
300–400g fresh egg **pasta**
A dozen fresh cherry **tomatoes**
  (halved)
Sea salt
Ground black **pepper**

Method

Crush the pine nuts in a pestle and mortar (or if you haven't got one, chop everything up finely and improvise, using the end of a rolling pin and a bowl or similar). Add the basil leaves and garlic and crush together. Add half the olive oil, a little at a time. Season and stir in the vegetarian Parmesan. Add the remaining oil and mix together.

Cook the pasta until it is ready (add a dash of olive oil to the pan as it cooks. This will help to stop it sticking). Drain and mix in the pesto mix and the tomatoes. Garnish with a basil or wild garlic leaf and grated or shaved Parmesan. Season and serve.

Eat

259

Billy goat's GRATIN

This is my camper van version of the classic French dish. It's something we do at home all the time so I wanted to try it in the van. We may not have an oven but we do have a grill, and that's good enough. It works well, and the goat's cheese adds a slightly different taste that makes it the same but different from your common or garden version. Great with salad...

For 4, as a side

2 or 3 white **spuds**
½ **cup single cream**
½ **cup milk**
Freshly ground nutmeg
Sea salt and freshly ground black pepper
2 cloves **garlic**, finely chopped
Goat's cheese

Method

Firstly, peel and slice the spuds (between 0.5 and 1cm) then put them in salted water. Simmer them for 10 minutes or so until they are just cooked. Drain them and place them in your grill pan or a small frying pan and then pour the cream and milk into the pan. Grate about a quarter of a nutmeg into the pan, add a pinch of sea salt and black pepper, and the garlic. Mix well together and bring to a gentle boil. Pour on the cream mixture to just about cover the potatoes.

Next slice the goat's cheese as finely as you can and place it on the top. Place under the grill on a high heat until the cheese begins to brown and bubble.

SALADS AND SIDES

Crunchy, crisp and clean. Those are the prerequisites of a good salad. And if you get some extra flavours – some fish sauce, a little fruity grapefruit or a touch of mint, so be it. Things will only get better. Like all things, salad is best served simply, eaten with gusto and appreciated by all.

Ten-minute California
CHICKEN SALAD

This is an easy, warm salad with really fresh flavours. As with all the best recipes to cook in your motorhome it's unfussy and takes just a few minutes. Preparation is minimal, too. So, a quick lunch for when you've got better stuff to do than spend hours inside slaving over a hot stove.

For 4

4 chicken breasts, diced
Olive oil, for frying
15 cherry tomatoes
½ glass white wine
Juice and zest of 1 lemon
Handful of fresh tarragon leaves, torn
4 very generous handfuls of baby spinach and rocket
Pack of croutons (optional)

Method

Dice the chicken and heat a splash of olive oil in a frying pan. Fry the chicken pieces for about 5 minutes, turning regularly, until almost cooked. Season with a little salt and pepper. While this cooks, cut each tomato into four.

Pour the white wine into the pan and let that bubble away for a minute or so. Next add the lemon juice and the tarragon and stir. Let that bubble for a couple of minutes. Now add the tomatoes. Cook for another minute or so. It's best to allow the tomatoes to stay whole rather than start to break up.

Put a handful of each of the leaves on a plate and then serve up the chicken on top. Use the juices as a warm dressing for the salad. Before eating, zest a little of the lemon on top and chuck over a few croutons.

FENNEL and GRAPEFRUIT salad ⓥ

If you like sharp and zesty salads then you'll like this.
It's quick and easy and very fresh and fruity. It's simple,
too, and goes great with the fishy bits with homemade
tartare sauce on page 223.

For 4

1 bulb fennel
6 cherry tomatoes
4 spring onions
¼ cucumber
1 red grapefruit
Sprinkle of icing sugar
Handful of walnuts
Handful of pine nuts
**Handful of chopped
   parsley**

Method

Slice the fennel, halve the tomatoes,
shred the spring onions, dice the cucumber
and cut the grapefruit into chunks
(removing as much of the pith as you can).
Keep as much of the juice as you can, too.

Put all the ingredients in a bowl and
mix with the parsley. Then dust with a
little icing sugar and toss with a drizzle
of olive oil.

Amanda's amazeballs
ASIAN-STYLE SALAD

Amanda brought out this salad on a recipe testing night for this book round at her house. Shamefully, as it was tipping down, we sat around the kitchen table while her 1978 Westfalia languished in the garage, un-started. But, she assured me, this recipe was devised on a trip, in the sunshine, on vacation, somewhere on a campsite in the middle of nowhere.

And it still tastes okay in the rain. Good enough for us then.

For 4
For the dressing
1 tbsp lime juice
1.5 tbsp fish sauce
1 tbsp caster **sugar**
1 clove garlic, finely chopped
1.5 tbsp rice **vinegar (or white or red wine vinegar)**
1 red chilli, deseeded and finely chopped
1 tbsp water

FOR THE SALAD
¼ red **cabbage**, finely sliced
¼ white **cabbage**, finely sliced
2 small carrots, grated
Handful coriander, chopped
Handful mint leaves, chopped
Handful chopped salted **peanuts**

Eat

265

Method

For the salad dressing, place all the ingredients in a bowl and stir well (or put in a jam jar and shake!). Leave for a few minutes to allow the sugar to dissolve, then stir (or shake) again.

For the salad, simply toss all the ingredients together in a large bowl (except the peanuts, if you want to allow people to add their own) then stir in the dressing. Voila!

Jo's healthy, minty
POTATO SALAD

If you are used to eating potato salad with mayonnaise or salad cream (crass but dee-lish) then this will come as a pleasant surprise. It's just as lovely but tastes fresher and less of guilt. It's great with steak!

750g new potatoes
2 large free range eggs
3 spring onions
Bunch of flat leaf parsley
Bunch of fresh mint
Salt and pepper to season
100–150g low fat crème fraîche

Method

Wash and cut the potatoes in half (unless they are tiny) and put them in a saucepan of boiling water. Boil away for 5 minutes, then add the eggs (see the Brekkie section (page 187) for how not to crack them). Once the potatoes are cooked but not mushy, drain and put them in a bowl to cool.

Meanwhile, peel and chop the eggs into quarters and add them to the bowl. Chop the spring onions, flat leaf parsley and mint, and add to the bowl. Season and mix well.

Once cool, add the crème fraîche and mix everything together well.

PUDDING LOVELINESS

Some people love puds, some people love them more. It's the sweet finish, the end of day treat, the pick-me-up that you can't do without. The only word of caution? As long as you're active and buzzing around doing stuff there's nothing wrong with it. But if your idea of heaven is sitting down all day scoffing bread and butter pudding, perhaps you might need to think twice about it. Or have the Lemony gingery cheesecakey thingummy.

Eat and be active!

LEMONY gingery CHEESECAKEY thingummy

One of my best memories of childhood is my mum creaming cottage cheese through a sieve to make cheesecake. It was a sign that good things were about to happen and good tastes were about to pervade my being. However, she was never that good at it and didn't have a food mixer, so her cheesecakes always had a lovely grainy texture to them. It's the quality I still look for in a cheesecake today, even though today we might call it rustic rather than 'can't be bothered to whizz'.

I thought we should bring a version of this 1970s homeliness into our camper van world. So we added a little ginger, a little lemon and a little more love. But took away the gelatine, the eggs and the faff. And then we scoffed it right down. It barely touched the sides.

Makes 4 individual glasses

50g butter
25g rolled oats
4 ginger biscuits, crushed
300g tub cottage cheese
2 tbsp Greek yoghurt
1 heaped tbsp icing sugar
Juice of half a lemon and zest
Thumb sized knob of fresh ginger, grated
4 tsp lemon curd

Method

Melt the butter in a pan. Add the rolled oats and the crushed ginger biscuits. Heat until they start to brown. Then divide the mixture between four glasses. Leave to cool.

Sieve the tub of cottage cheese into a mixing bowl. Add the yoghurt, sugar, lemon juice and zest, and ginger. Mix. When the base mixture has cooled, spoon out 1 tsp of lemon curd onto each base, then add the cheesecake mixture. Top off with a few sprinklings of lemon zest and perhaps a few mint leaves for the look nice. Baboom! It's a sweet and zesty pud, that's easy to make and easy on the eye.

SEAWEED PANNA COTTA
with rhubarb and ginger

Okay. **This is where** you might think it gets a bit weird. But bear with me. Carrageen Irish Moss has long been used for puddings, particularly in Ireland, as it contains a natural thickening agent, agar agar. It behaves in a similar fashion to gelatin, only it isn't made from animal bits so it's suitable for vegans and veggies.

It is perfectly possible to make this in your van if the fridge is working, although it will take longer to set if you drive when it's in there!

The agar is extracted from the seaweed (a generous handful) by boiling it in a little water for a few minutes. Buy your Carrageen from **http://cornishseaweed.co.uk/**

Makes 4 in individual glasses
A handful of fresh or dried Carrageen Moss
300ml double cream
150ml milk
3 heaped tbsp caster sugar
Vanilla pod seeds
3 stalks of rhubarb, chopped
Thumb sized lump of ginger
Shortbread biscuits (optional)

Method

Boil a handful of Carrageen Moss for about 10 minutes in enough water to cover it. Strain it and keep around 200mls of the thick liquid. Add to it a mixture of the double cream, milk and 2 tbsp of the sugar, and bring to a simmer, along with the seeds of the vanilla pod. At this point you can add a little more sugar if it isn't sweet enough. Tip into ramekins or glasses and leave to set in the fridge.

In another small pan, boil up the chopped rhubarb with a little water and grate the ginger over it. Then add the rest of the sugar and simmer until the rhubarb begins to break apart. Leave to cool.

Tip out the set panna cotta onto plates and add a dollop of rhubarb to each serving. Eat with a shortbread biscuit (if you have any).

Naughty banana and
ORANGE STUFFED PANCAKES

This recipe reminds me of baking bananas in the fire at camp, but only when it's late. It's our take on the stoner classic. It's munchie food all right, and has a gooey, fruity stickiness but without being overly sweet. The orange zest might even help to make it feel like it's good for you – almost – but not really. Enjoy.

Makes approx. 8 pancakes

FOR THE PANCAKES
100g plain flour
1 free range egg, whisked
300ml milk
A pinch of salt
Zest of 1 orange

FOR THE FILLING
50g butter, plus extra for frying
4 level tbsp Demerara sugar
A pinch of grated cinnamon
Juice of 1 orange
2 bananas, sliced
Crème fraîche

Method

Sieve the flour into a large bowl. Add the eggs, milk, salt and the grated orange zest. Mix 'em all up with a whisk until smooth. Now get your frying pan hot and melt a knob of butter in it. Then spoon out a good three or four tablespoon's worth of the pancake mixture into the pan and move the pan around to spread out the mixture. You can cook all the pancakes ready for the filling or get the filling going at the same time if you have space on your hob and don't mind a bit of multi-tasking!

Now for the filling. Melt the butter in a small saucepan over a low heat, add the sugar and grated cinnamon and allow the sugar to dissolve. Then squeeze the juice of the orange into the pan and mix until you get a light golden syrup. Then add the sliced banana and simmer gently for a few minutes until the banana starts to get all gooey and lovely.

Spoon a little of the mixture on each pancake, along with dollop of crème fraîche. Roll up and devour. You might need a fork.

MARSHMALLOWS and s'mores

If there's one thing that kids love about camping it's marshmallows. My lot especially enjoy sitting around the fire watching them caramelise and catch fire, only to blow them out again and pull off the crunchy, burned coating. This leaves behind a gooey mess that can then be heated and burned and pulled off, so leaving a smaller sticky innard, and so on and so forth.

S'mores are a North American treat that traditionally use Graham Crackers as the bread in the sandwich, with a filling of melted marshmallow and a slab of chocolate as the filling. The s'more bit comes, apparently, from people being unable to resist 'some more' on eating the first one. However, in a little fascinating historical aside, I note that the Graham Cracker was invented by a puritanical Evangelical minister, Sylvester Graham. From what I read about him on the internet, his crackers were designed to be so bland that they could combat 'the greatest threat facing America' in the 1830s. What was that? Sexual urges!

Well. He obviously never went camping.

VEGETARIAN MARSHMALLOWS

As we know, marshmallows use gelatin to make them form, which isn't always the most animal friendly ingredient. I tried to make marshmallows with Carrageen for this book but, alas, I failed, which is why you'll have to make do with the original ones or those little ones from the health food shop. Sorry.

ENGLISH S'MORES

I don't know if anyone has ever called them this but we're all in favour of positivity on this side of the pond so we're going to do it our way. And that means going for a biscuit that's eternally optimistic, the chocolate digestive, rather than one that was designed to be so horrible it could stop good things happening. The original digestive biscuit was invented just nine years after the Graham Cracker by two Scottish doctors in order to aid digestion, but the chocolate digestive (the humble but good natured chocolate digestive) wasn't brought to life until the 1920s, by a well-known biscuit maker.

Anyway, the English s'more is made by melting a marshmallow over the fire and then plonking a milk chocolate digestive either side – chocolate side in, of course.

Ooh ooh TIRAMISU

Some people can't live **without** their coffee. What's that all about? They post pictures on Twitter of mad looking polar bears in tiny zoo cages and then add meaningless captions like, 'It's a one cup of coffee kind of a morning', and then expect retweets for it. And the saddest thing of all is that they get them. So there must be real people out there who really are 'coffee addicts', 'barista gurus', 'latte sages' and actual 'frappe wannabes'. Good for them.

However, if you want coffee, shut up and try this. It's a classic and it's never gone out of fashion… add a dash of brandy for extra hipster points and make it in a glass for post-modern retro chic. Sort of.

Makes 4-6 servings

250g mascarpone
100g whipped cream
75g caster sugar
1 tsp vanilla extract
2 cups of coffee
1 tbsp brandy
Ladyfingers (sponge fingers)
225g fresh raspberries
Chocolate/cocoa powder

Method

Mix the mascarpone, cream, sugar and vanilla together in a bowl. Make the cups of coffee, add the brandy and allow to cool. Soak the ladyfingers in the coffee and put a layer in individual glasses, upright around the inside of the glass.

Layer raspberries, then mascarpone and then cream in the glass, and garnish with a fresh raspberry and a sprinkle of chocolate or cocoa powder.

SLEEP

Good night.
Sleep tight.
We hope the bugs don't bite.
And if we ever meet again,
Our hearts will be as one.
Good night.

INTRODUCTION

Sleeping is what this section is all about. And that means getting a good night's sleep. We all know it's important and yet somehow on a camping trip we expect to come home more tired than we were when we left. It's supposed to be relaxing!

So what is it that's keeping you awake at night. Is it your pitch? Your camper? Your kids? The temperature? Or is it just the fact that you are a natural worrier and would be awake all night anyway?

Let this section help you. In it we'll talk about what makes a good campsite (and what makes a bad one), what's going to help you stay warm and dry, and what kind of things can help to give you the full 12 hours you fully deserve on your holidays.

It's all about you. And yes, I am all heart.

HOW TO GET A GOOD NIGHT'S SLEEP

The camper van experience is very poor if you can't get a good night's sleep. So while I can't get in there with you and rock you to sleep myself (even though I would surely love to) I can give you a few pointers as to how you might enter dreamland and stay there for the full 8 hours you need (or deserve).

This section is all about making decisions as to your own comfort. It's up to you how hard or soft your foam is, how many togs you lie under and how big you like your bed. It's all subjective anyway. All I can do is show you what your choices might be and let you decide. And if you can't sleep for the lumps in the bed, maybe it's proof that you really are a princess after all. Who put that pea under my mattress?

Nighty night.

How NOT to get a good night's SLEEP

Before we move on to getting a good night's sleep, let's ponder a moment how best to go about not getting a good night's sleep. We've all had them. I've had some terrible sleeps. There have been some camping trips where I've had no sleep at all, either through discomfort, children, animals, anxiety, weather, neighbours or motorway flyovers.

Park up late at night unaware of your exact location

I once parked up in Hossegor, a surf spot in western France. We arrived too late to see where we were and could only hear what we thought was the roar of huge surf. I stayed awake all night worrying about the size of the waves I'd face in the morning. As it turns out, it was a motorway. The surf was tiny.

Forget your best kit

I forgot my sleeping bag on one surfing trip and had to sleep in my surfboard bag, which wasn't very thick. Worst of all though was that the end was pointy like a surfboard. I had cramp all night, didn't sleep a wink and have never forgotten a sleeping bag since.

WHAT does a CAMPER mean TO YOU?

'Put simply, my van is my escape. *Escape from the world, escape from the set, escape from the executive producer who wants me to say it 'with more feeling'. But, most importantly it makes me feel like that eight-year-old boy from Blackpool who used his duvet and mum's dining chairs to make his den. The same den where I fought the Germans with my plastic water pistol, yet 27 years later, I'm embracing their technical innovation and genius. Like most Vdubbers, I'm hooked. There's always something it needs (not necessarily, of course), there's always a new car smell courtesy of those little trees and there's always a new adventure! No questions asked. No answers needed. Just a rough idea of direction, I turn the key and she takes me there! Technically, my everyday car does that too. But I don't smile the same way.'*

Barney Harwood *BLUE PETER PRESENTER*

Park up next to the ravers

A rookie mistake, but easily done if the ravers are away all day and only return once you've turned in. We did this once in Wales and barely got any sleep for the sound of their music. But happily we got our revenge once they had gone to bed, as we had to get up very early the next day. It was about an hour after they turned in. We left the site tooting our horn, shouting 'wakey wakey' at the top of our voices and with our music as loud as it would go. Childish, I know, but very satisfying.

Go to sleep in a rabbit burrow

Bob the dog loves to chase rabbits. So, one summer when we camped among some busy burrows, he was awake and whining, looking out of the window at first light. Stupid dog. What was worse, he could see them but they were oblivious to him. It drove him mental and, in turn, us too.

Weather events

We've all had these. I have slept in tents that have been about to blow away, been flooded in the night, and feared for my safety in thunderstorms. All valid reasons for getting a really bad night's sleep. How to avoid it? Check the weather before you leave. Plan an escape route. Carry a credit card.

282 *Sleep*

Children and their cold feet

Our old camper had a pop top so when the weather was bad we usually dropped the roof to stop it getting damaged. That meant we all had to sleep downstairs in the rock and roll bed. Great.

Stoat Olympics

This is the noise of animals outside keeping you awake. On one site in France we swear we were being lapped by a fast and agile animal. It ran around and around and around our tent. The site was known thereafter as 'Camp Stoat Olympics'. We never found out what it was that was causing the noise.

Black bag error

We've all done it and it's annoying as hell to wake up in the wee hours to the sound of rustling coming from the place you left your black bag. It's always a risk to investigate, as you never know what or how big the beast (or persons) looking for your chicken bones will be.

Big beasties

The biggest animal we have ever been bothered by is a cow.
They love to lick the road salt from vehicles. If you've ever had that
happen to you then you'll know they can make a real racket. Their
tongues are like rasps.

Everyday life

On a different trip to France we were so tired that we went to sleep
in a car park. We slept well, but awoke to the local market that had
set up around us. Was very useful for getting breakfast but not so
easy to get away!

SLEEPING BAGS, duvets, liners

While I, like many happy camper van owners, love a
trip to an outdoor store to prepare for a holiday, I have to confess to
finding them a little confusing sometimes, especially when it comes to
sleeping equipment. I've long been a fan of the on-board duvet (that's
tog territory – more later) but have found that they can be a bit bulky,
especially when we travel as a family. So, to make more of the space
I decided to buy a sleeping bag.

Choosing the perfect bag presented a world of mystery. I got it
desperately wrong the first time, which inevitably led to some very
uncomfortable nights, even in the height of summer. After a few nights
of shivering I figured it was time I found out more about how ratings
work and what they mean.

What I got from my research was this sage bit of advice: buy warmer
than you think you'll need. You can make a hot sleeping bag cooler by
opening the zip a bit, but you can't make a cold sleeping bag any warmer
on a cold night. And that, my snoozy friends, is the basic truth of it.

WHAT YOU NEED TO KNOW ABOUT SLEEPING BAGS

Sleeping bags are temperature rated. These are set by a European Standard (EN13537), which means that all sleeping bags must conform to the same standards and that the standards must be set in a predetermined laboratory standard test. The ratings are as follows, and they refer to someone with clothes on.

- **Upper limit/maximum rating.** This is the highest temperature at which you can sleep comfortably without sweating (based on a standard man aged 25 with a height of 1.73m and a weight of 73kg).
- **The comfort rating.** This is the temperature at which a standard woman (25 years old, with a height of 1.60m and a weight of 60kg) can have a comfortable night's sleep.
- **Lower limit/minimum rating.** This is the lowest temperature at which a standard man can have a comfortable night's sleep.
- **Extreme rating.** This is the point at which the standard woman will be protected from hypothermia.

Okay that's cool, or warm, or hot. But what about with jim-jams? Or what if you're not standard? Well, these ratings are given for the person with clothes on. They don't specify what kind of clothes, however, so your guess is as good as mine. I'll assume it's a pair of long johns and a tee shirt. How romantic. When it comes to standardness, it's also safe to assume that if you are skinnier than a standard man or woman, you'll feel the cold more, while the reason they cite both men and women is because men and women react to temperature in different ways. Women generally (and this is not me that's saying it) feel the cold more.

Pyjamas?

What do you think? If it's cold you'd be a fool to abandon some kind of nighttime attire. But then, who wears jim-jams on a camper van trip? Surely it's vest and undies all the way (including the girls)? It is for me. I haven't worn pyjamas since I was seven and I'm not going to start again now. So I'm going to need an extra warm sleeping bag. And there we are, back to the first bit of advice: buy warmer than you think you'll need. Because sleeping bags, as we now know, are rated for a clothed body.

WHAT BAG SHAPE TO GO FOR

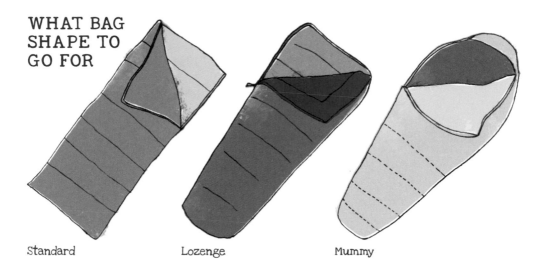

Standard   Lozenge   Mummy

The shape and style of your sleeping bag will determine how warm it is. The rule is that the more air inside the bag, the cooler it will be.

● **Standard/rectangular** shapes are standard in that they will fulfil your needs but may not be as warm as a mummy-shaped bag. BUT, on the plus side, you can zip two of them together to make a double bag. Handy, but not always.

● **Lozenge** shapes don't have the awkward corners of a standard bag shape so will still allow you to move about with a little extra warmth.

● **Mummy** shapes are the daddy, and will get warm quicker and stay warm longer. This is because there is less chance of colder air circulating, especially if you zip up tight and keep your head inside the hood. The shape can be restrictive for those who like to move about in the night.

For extra warmth and comfort, sleeping bag liners will add another layer and make it easier for you to keep the bag clean. You also get the added benefit of sleeping in a cotton sheet.

WHAT SEASON BAG TO GO FOR

To make it a little easier for the punters like us, camping stores divide their bags into seasons. These are set out below and will allow you to make a choice. Remember, though, that the temperature ratings still apply here, so when choosing your bag you still need to think about when you'll be using it and what the limits you expect it to cope with are. Remember also that the extreme limit is less about comfort and more about survival.

Sleep 287

- **One-season bags** are for use in a hot climate or indoor use.
- **Two-season bags** will see you through, as long as the temperature remains above 9°C. Basically you're looking at a British summer.
- **Three-season bags** are for temperatures as low as 0°C and can be used from early spring to late autumn.
- **Four-season bags** are designed for winter backpacking or climbing. Useful for people who really feel the cold, but rarely useful in a well-insulated van.

DARN THE SAVING SPACE, GO FOR A DUVET

Very wise choice! A duvet is a far more civilised way of sleeping (especially with a friend), although you will need to carry a bottom sheet. The only downside is the bulk of them. Even so, you still need to be mindful of the tog rating. It's actually a lot less complicated than sleeping bags and it goes like this:

What's the tog rating?

The tog is a measure of thermal resistance. That means that it's all about how a duvet will contain heat. So, for the layman: the thermal resistance in togs is equal to ten times the temperature difference (in °C) between the two surfaces of a material, when the flow of heat is equal to one watt per square metre (eh?).

And that, in turn, translates as:

Summer duvet	4.5 tog
Spring or autumn	9-10.5 tog
Winter	12-13.5 tog

If you want my advice, I'll say go for more togs than you think you'll need. You can always stick a leg out if you get too hot.

LOOKING AFTER YOUR SLEEPING BAG

Stuff it in, that's it. No need to worry. You might think that stashing your bag away into its stuff sack is the best way to store it – but it isn't, apparently. The more compressed you make your bag, the more it's going to lose its insulating properties over time. So while it's okay to stuff it for short trips, store it in a larger bag between trips. If you fold and roll your bag the same way each time you'll stop the inner fabric becoming creased and working less efficiently.

WHAT does a CAMPER mean TO YOU?

'Our first fully equipped camper van was a 25-year-old Mercedes, with blue and white retro lines and a squishy suspension that made it rock, roll and heave along those country lanes towards the beach. You see things differently at a slower pace, higher up and through larger windows, and that changes your perspective on life itself.

We bought the camper van with the intention of using it as a home from home after the birth of our second child who was only weeks away from delivery, but life had other plans. Shortly after our daughter arrived I had a major stroke, which I was lucky to survive. This was when our camper became a place of recovery, a safe haven and an escape from difficult times. Our family took on the life of a tortoise: slowing things down, carrying our home wherever we went and allowing the squishy suspension to comfort and rock us to sleep. That camper may have been an old metal box on wheels, but it felt like so much more than that. It felt like a loyal companion and one of the family. In fact, it had so many human characteristics... even failure! And just as we found we often had to fix it... it also ended up fixing us.'

Sarah Riley *FOUNDER OF INSPIREDCAMPING.COM*

WHY YOU NEED A QUILLOW

My friend Cath, who has a very nice camper van, swears by a night (or day) time device that is known as a quillow. It's like a quilt and a pillow all in one (in the same way that jeggings are jeans and leggings), and apparently is very, very useful on camper van trips. Why? Because it's a quilt and pillow – a magic pillow that turns into a quilt for sleeping and back into a pillow for driving. Get it? Quillow. Oh never mind. Soft cotton and fair trade, what more could you ask?

You need one of those. Unsurprisingly, available in batik.
www.naturalquilts.com

MOSQUITO **nets**

On balmy nights it's a real pleasure to sleep with the tailgate open and allow a gentle breeze to cool you while you snooze away. It's almost a prerequisite of any camper van dream. It's hot. You can't sleep. You open the tailgate and listen to the sounds of the night. Everything is wonderful.

Until the insects find you. Then you'll spend the rest of the night either swatting mozzies in the dark or scratching at your bites.

The solution, of course, is to fit fly screens or mozzie nets to your van. They can almost always be retro fitted to all types of modern campers. They can be extremely useful when travelling to areas where midges are prevalent. Having travelled in Scotland where the midges were a big problem I can safely say they would have made our trip a whole lot nicer. Choose from full screens for sliding doors to tailgate screens.

Or, if you don't want to go to that kind of expense, you can always use a standard mozzie net in the van. They are generally cheap and will protect the bed only.

Condensation

Having condensation inside your van won't stop you from having a good night's sleep – unless it drips on you – because it is just a by-product of sleeping in a tin and glass box. But stopping it will make for a more pleasant experience all round and will mean you don't have to wipe the windows down each morning.

Condensation is a common problem that affects all camper vans and motorhomes. It can cause a real problem if the water hangs around for a while and begins to corrode the bodywork. If you allow it to happen a lot it could well kill your van.

WHY CONDENSATION OCCURS

Whenever there are differences in temperature and moisture, condensation will occur. So, when you are cosy inside the van and breathing out hot moist air, the likelihood is that you will create condensation if the outside temperature is different. You'll find it happens a lot more on cold nights.

Condensation can also be caused by high moisture content in the interior air of the van – by wet towels, using a shower, damp wetsuits, whatever. As long as there is a difference it will happen.

STOPPING CONDENSATION

You can always stop breathing at night. But it's not a very practical solution. Alternatively, allowing air to circulate by opening a window or two will allow the moist air to escape and even up the difference between outside and in. Insulating the van and windows will also help as the insulation will provide a protective heat-proof barrier between the two temperatures. Insulation will also help to keep the van warm and to stop warm air escaping through the thin metal sides of the van.

STOPPING WINDSCREEN CONDENSATION

The windscreen is the place where you are most likely to get condensation. This is because it's a large area that isn't usually insulated. It's a pain in the backside to wake up every morning and have to wipe away gallons of condensation from a big windscreen, so anything you can do will be worthwhile.

Thermo screens that you can stick to the window interiors are a great idea that will stop a certain amount of condensation. Buy them or make them yourself with bubble wrap or foam insulation.

However, a more effective way to use thermo screens is to use them on the outside of the van, so stopping the warmth of the van (and a nice warm windscreen) from having direct contact with cold air. These are available, too.

BLOCKING out the DAYLIGHT

Blocking out the light is kind of essential when it comes to getting a decent night's sleep. Or at least sleeping in once the sun has come up. So getting the right curtains is important. It's also the first and most important soft furnishing you'll have to make decisions about.

Curtains can be about either blackouts or decoration or both. Most modern coach-built motorhomes will have some kind of blinds and fly screens so curtains are no more than a decoration to soften the edges a little. But for most campers, curtains are the way to go.

You can choose to match the interior and be damned by what light stopping properties they might have, line them and hope that helps, or go the full hog and make sure they are blackout lined. This will be more expensive, inevitably, but what price is a good night's sleep?

INSIDE OR OUTSIDE?

If this question has never occurred to you (because you already know the answer or have never considered such a thing) then I apologise for polluting your mind with such triviality, but it is something I have often wondered about: when you choose a material for your camper van curtains, does the design go on the outside or inside? Does it matter? The answer must be inside. But there are people for whom showing is everything... and for them I recommend double sided. Easy.

Curtain tips

- **Magnets sewn into the linings** can help to stop curtains from flapping about and letting in light.
- **Velcro strips** can be used to hold curtains together to stop light from coming in.
- **Thermo mats** can provide better light (and heat) insulation than curtains but have to be stowed away in the van somewhere. Curtains just tie back.
- **Blinds** are going to be more efficient than curtains, but not as pretty.

Levelling CHOCKS

Aside from a decent blackout set-up and a warm sleeping bag, levelling chocks are the most important items you'll need for getting a good night's sleep, especially if you have slippery sleeping bags and vinyl or leather seat covers! Sleeping on a slope is rarely pleasant and will always end unhappily, with all of you in a heap on one side of the van.

A pair of chocks will do, but on some sites two pairs will be essential. They will lock together for even the worst of inclines (within reason). If your handbrake is a little slack you can also get chocks that lock you into place using small wedges.

If you are level obsessed you can buy dashboard spirit levels to make sure it's inch perfect. Otherwise, get a friend to help you.

EFG 893V

Sleep 293

THE CAMPER VAN BED DEPARTMENT

This is what it's all about: what you sleep on. Often you won't have much of a choice if you are buying second hand but it is relatively easy to buy foam cushions cut to size and have them recovered to suit the interior or how you like to sleep.

The IDIOT'S GUIDE to bedding foam

Right then. So you're looking for some foam to fill your cushion covers for the van. Easy! Or is it? Well you'd have thought it was easy, but actually it's a little more complicated than just buying a bunch of foam, having it cut to size and hoping for a great kip.

The first thing to remember is that comfort is relative. Bony arsed folks are going to need softer, thicker seating than someone with natural padding.

The second thing you need to remember is to think about what your cushions are to be used for predominantly. Are they to be used as seating or are they to be used as bedding?

UNDERSTANDING FOAM GRADES

For a start you're going to have some numbers thrown at you that mean nothing to the average human and then you're going to have to make some decisions. However, I've done the graft (and by that I mean

I've spoken to an expert) and will do my best to make it as simple as possible. Stick with it, because this is important.

Foam is graded by TYPE, DENSITY, HARDNESS and VOLUME.

On your quest for a decent night's sleep you may come across foam grades such as 3 INCH V 38/200 or the heady combination of a classic 4 INCH R 40/180. You lucky people. Let's explain...

Type

Foam type is the basic name for any particular type of foam.

● **V is for foam** that is 'heavy domestic and contract quality'. A quality foam that is best suited for sitting and seat cushions and will last well. Generally 30% per cent cheaper than Reflex (below) and better suited to sitting than sleeping.

● **R is for Reflex**, a brand name. This is a very high quality latex foam that will retain its properties over time. The best quality for sleeping.

● **CMHR** is for 'Combustion Modified High Resilience Foam' that includes a lot of melamine for flame retardancy. It can tend to powder over time and can retain moisture, so is not recommended for camper vans.

● **RECON** is reconditioned foam. It is made up from all the off-cuts. It is generally poor wearing, very heavy and not much use to anyone, although it is cheap. Avoid.

Foam density

Foam density is the weight of the foam in kilograms per cubic metre. The higher the number, the higher the density. A high density foam will last longer and be of better quality. Expect to see density of around 38–40 for a decent foam.

Hardness

Hardness is measured in Newtons. It's all about the science here, so I shall skip that and say that to the layman, the hardness is all about the comfort. Typical foams for campers comes in at anywhere between 135 and 200 Newtons, depending on the comfort required.

The rule for choosing foam based on hardness:

🌰 If you're sitting more than sleeping, use a high density V grade foam. If it's less firm, go for extra thickness. V40/200 at 3in is a good bet for camper van cushions.

🌰 If you're sleeping more than sitting, use a thicker but less firm Reflex foam. Try something like a R38/150 at 5in for a cosy night.

Volume

Volume is basically the thickness of the foam, with increased volume offering you more support. However, after a certain point volume is pointless, as a dense foam can have the same support at 3in thick as at 4in thick, depending on how you use it.

Too much detail? Until the time comes to look for a mattress maybe.

CHOOSING FOAM OR MATTRESSES FOR YOUR HOME CONVERSION

Some good advice coming up! When the time comes to work out how big your bed is going to be in your home conversion, stick, if you can, to standard sizes, especially if you are looking at mattresses. While foam can be cut to size easily, it is extremely expensive to stray from standard bed sizes for some materials. So when planning your bed, stick to the following (in cm):

Sizing up your bed foam			
90 x 190	single bed	135 x 200/190	standard double
75 x 200	single bed	150 x 200	king size
122 x 200/190	small double	180 x 200	super king

MEMORY FOAM EXTRAS

Lots of campers like to top up their standard cushions with memory foam toppers, with the idea that a little extra comfort can make an uncomfortable bed more comfortable. And it can. However, in the camper van context, it does have limitations.

Memory foam has got a bit of a buzz about it. Everyone wants it because it moulds to your shape and cradles you in your sleep. It works very well in everyday life but its main property – that its hardness is determined by temperature – can work against it the moment you put it in your van.

Between room temperature and body temperature, memory foam will halve its hardness – it doesn't like the cold. So if you are creeping back from the pub to a cold van, it could well feel like sleeping on cardboard until your body temperature has warmed it up a bit. And if that memory foam is part of a multi-layered cushion (and therefore underneath a cushion cover as well as a sheet or sleeping bag), it'll take longer to heat up through

Top tip for an uncomfy mattress

If your camper van bed is uneven, lumpy or just uncomfortable, you can make it less so by adding a sleeping mat to it. Sleeping mats are often super light, self-inflating (to a point) and surprisingly comfy. Adding one to an existing bed will help to take out the lumps and bumps. As an added bonus they will roll up small and can be easily stowed. I use one and love it, even when I am actually in a tent. It's snoozetastic.

your covers (if at all) and therefore longer to be effective (if at all).

Also, memory foam requires three-way fabric to be truly effective and mould to your body shape – this won't work through a vinyl covering. So what's the point?

Stick with the Reflex maybe.

ROCK and ROLL beds

We all know what a rock and roll bed is, right? Well if you don't, it is a seat that turns into a bed. That's kind of it. But of course it actually isn't. There are lots of different types to go for, with lots of options, ranging from fully crash tested, 100 per cent compliant, touch-of-a-button British-made steel constructions, to wood and hinges kits that look decidedly un-crash ready. If you are converting or even buying a van, this is another important consideration. After all it'll be your seat, your bed and your life if anything happens.

Rock and roll beds for standard sized camper vans come in two sizes: full width and three-quarter width.

WHY A FULL WIDTH BED IS GREAT

Full width beds are fantastic for families that have children who like to creep in with mum and dad in the night. They are great for the whole family to lay about and even better if you like a lot of space to sleep in.

Notes on rock and roll beds

If you re-cover cushions for rock and roll beds, it is ABSOLUTELY VITAL to make sure that the cushions are fixed to the seat base if they are to be used with seat belts. Loose cushion covers can easily render seat belts useless as they can slide about in emergency stopping situations.

The drawback with a full width bed is that space is limited for other stuff, like cupboards, cookers and sinks. It means all your stuff is going to be up front, out of the way of the bed as it swings forward. The bonus is that there's more room in the back. Having travelled extensively in a T2 with a full width bed I can safely say it's great. You just gotta be tidy.

300 *Sleep*

WHY A THREE-QUARTER WIDTH BED IS GREAT

The three-quarter width bed is something of a standard with smaller camper vans. This is because it allows for a full set of units to be installed along one side of the van, so allowing plenty of worktop space and under-cupboard space for clothes, kit, cooking gear and fridges. Three-quarter width beds make it a lot easier to be tidy by using wardrobes and cupboards for clothes and suchlike, but the bed space is, of course, more limited. It also means that when not being used as a camper – as a day-to-day vehicle – they aren't quite so versatile.

And by that I mean less space for carrying wardrobes.

Which is no bad thing.

As usual the choice is yours. Wardrobes or no?

ROCK AND ROLL COMPLIANCE

Rock and roll. It was never supposed to be governed by rules, compliance and legislation. But sadly it is, especially if it's a rock and roll bed. Actually, I don't think it's such a bad thing, as we need to be responsible campers in every way, which means thinking about our passengers' safety.

Rock and roll beds are not only an important part of the camping set-up of many campers but also a vital part of the seating arrangements. That means they have two jobs to do: sleeping and seating.

The EU now dictates that new motor caravans (camper vans) need to be type approved, which includes testing and assessment against EU standards for seat belts, anchorage points for the seat belts, and the strength of seats and their mountings.

302 Sleep

However, when it comes to converting existing vans with rock and roll beds and converting them into motor caravans, the seats are not subject to the same demands, although they are subject to road vehicles' regulations demanding similar standards for seat belts and anchorage points, but not of seat mounting strength. What this says is: 'a motor vehicle, and all its parts and accessories; the number of passengers carried, and the manner in which any passengers are carried in or on a vehicle; and the weight, distribution, packing and adjustment of the load of a vehicle, to be at all times such that no danger is caused, or is likely to be caused, to any person in or on a vehicle or on a road' ('Carriage of Passengers in a Horsebox', UK Department for Transport).

Pull and crash tests

Some rock and roll beds are subject to testing. This is often a 'pull test', where the seat is pulled by a mechanism that exerts similar forces on the seat as it would get if a vehicle were to stop very suddenly (crash). Depending on the number of passengers that a seat is designed to carry, rock and roll beds get pull tested for 3 (one person), 7 (two people) or 11 tonnes (three people). This is a test of the strength of the seat and seat belts, not necessarily of the loading points of the seat (where it fixes to the chassis).

Some manufacturers also send their bed frames off for 'in-vehicle' crash testing, which will actually test the strength of the mountings as well as the seat itself. Often these manufacturers will add extra strengthening to the chassis in order for it to be able to cope with high loads.

Other manufacturers will also test their seats with 'sled tests', where the seats are tested on sleds that move backwards and forwards, so creating a more 'realistic' scenario.

Putting safety first

There are lots of rock and roll beds on the market. Some are pull tested, some in-vehicle tested, few sled tested. Many are compliant. Only you can make big decisions about the integrity and safety of the products you put in your van. However, if it were me making those decisions, I would go for the most rigorously tested, approved design I could afford. It's precious cargo aboard.

MAKES OF ROCK AND ROLL BEDS

Reimo rock and roll beds (Reimo are an approved VW converter based in Germany, with a base in the UK) are engineered differently and run on runners which are bonded to the vehicle's floor, so spreading the load over the entire floor rather than on a small number of mounting points. They can also be moved on runners up and down the van to make it easier to sit around a table to eat.
www.reimo.com or www.conceptmulti-car.co.uk

BEBB rock and roll beds are tested in vehicle and come supplied with extra strengthening. www.bebb.co.uk

RIB altair beds from Scopema are considered to be among the best rock and roll beds and also come with extra chassis strengthening.
www.scopema.com

Note: In the UK there can be differing restrictions on seats in vehicles in M or N classes, depending on the DVLA category.

WHAT does a CAMPER mean TO YOU?

'When I saw a lovely looking 1987 Volkswagen High Top T25 camper van for sale in a neighbouring street I knew I wanted to buy her! I happened to mention it to my mum and dad and they were interested too... as was my sister and her husband... and my aunt and uncle as well! So since October 2010, we've been the proud four-way owners of 'Twinkle' (named by my daughter because the bus has stars on its sides) and have had some fantastic trips and holidays with her, including regular family get-togethers, which generally involve bacon sandwiches and lots of tea and cake! A Google calendar ensures we don't double book Twinkle and when it comes to repair bills, four ways is much less painful! In the years we've owned her, we sadly lost my dad to cancer, but we've increased from one grandchild to three with a fourth due in November, and know Twinkle will play a role in our future family fun!'
Danny Pollard OWNER, T25 HI TOP

FIXED BED **campers**

This is the height of luxury: a bed that stays made all day long so you can simply crawl into it at night. No putting on sheets or zipping up sleeping bags or moving boxes. No putting everything in the front seats. No putting the seat up to drive away in the morning even. Plus, you get acres of space underneath for storage. And, on top of it all, you get to sleep on a real mattress, with springs and memory foam and all that malarkey.

The bad news? This kind of luxury is only for the bigger vans and motorhomes where it's not that important to make the best use of every inch of space. Often boxer sized vans will only sleep two with a fixed bed.

In some motorhomes, however, where the fixed bed is above the cab, this can significantly add to the available living space – and makes a good spot for storing stuff during the day (although if you do that, you'll still have to clear it all up to get into bed). And it's not so easy getting up the ladder after a couple of vino plonkos. Better to make it the kid's domain and let them use it.

Some Hymer motorhomes from the 1980s have beds that lower down over the cab at night. This is also useful, as you can leave the sheet and duvet on to stow – so saving time later and making more of the living space.

JIGSAW beds

Something I have noticed about campers and motorhomes – and I have been in a lot of them – is that it doesn't matter how expensive or well designed they are, somewhere, at some point, you will always find a little cushion that seems to fit nowhere in particular. This is part of the jigsaw bed, and I'll be damned if I know where it is supposed to go.

Jigsaw beds are usually the domain of either the pre-rock and roll camper – think of the early Dormobiles – or of latter-day motorhomes and larger campers, where seating can be arranged into day and night modes or changed around for 'lounge' or driving positions. Back-of-the-seat cushions double up as bed cushions then get used for the base of the day seat...

It's all a part of what it means to be a camper van. Unless you have a fixed bed you will, at some point face the making of the bed. In the darkness or the half light, in your drunken state and begging

to go to sleep after a long day, you'll forget where everything is supposed to go, get it all wrong and wake up in a pile of cushions. That's life. Sometimes you'll get it right and sometimes you won't.

JIGSAW BED TIPS

● **If your cushions have knee supports,** turn them around and put them under your head. Much better than having them under your bum, in the middle of the night.

● **Draw a map of your bed** and the way it is supposed to be. Tape it to the inside of one of your cupboards.

● **Take a bit of time** to work out all the options before you set off. Have a practice run. Try it out when you're drunk. Have a fall-back bed position that you can easily make and uses fewer cushions than usual.

Camper van TECHNOLOGY

Following on from the idea of the jigsaw bed, it always makes me enjoy a little chuckle to myself that even the most expensive motorhomes (and we're talking £50k upwards) still employ poppers, hinges, latches and the same kind of 'camper van technology' you'll find in almost every camper van the world over. The good news then, if you come into some cash and buy a really expensive motorhome you'll still get all the familiar ways of stowing, stashing and keeping tidy as you always have. The bad news is that, no matter how much money you have, you still can't escape the Velcro and poppers.

PLACES TO SPEND THE NIGHT

Everyone has a favourite place to spend the night...
it could be a campsite, an aire, a wild spot, a secret
spot, a Britstop or Passion site, or it could be on the drive.

That's part of the joy if it.

And everyone has their reasons for liking one spot or campsite
over another. Some people like busy sites, others like quiet sites. Other
people like no sites at all, preferring to go their own way in the world,
whether permitted or not.

Personally, I have often tried to define what makes one campsite
better than another. I have even harboured dreams of owning a campsite
myself. That was during a long trip in 2012 during which we visited a
different campsite every few days. In my frustration at not being able

310 *Sleep*

to find one that I really liked I began to note down what I thought would be perfect about my dream campsite. In fact, it became 'fantasy campsite', a game we played on long treks through the wilds of northern Spain. In my fantasy campsite I'd do away with all the stuff that annoys me about other people's campsites and, of course, keep in the kind of stuff I like.

And probably the only person who would want to stay there would be me.

So why is it that two similar sites could have the same facilities and outlook yet be totally different? Why should it be that I could pull up to one and instantly drive away and then pull up at the other and want to stay forever? Let's work it out.

Campsites

Location is everything. This is fact. Location is everything.

Recently I was shown to a tiny little site a few miles from my home. It's not really a site as such, and I am pretty sure it doesn't have a licence (which is why I am not going to disclose its location). The only facility it has to speak of is a portaloo that's plumbed into the mains and a tap for fresh water. The loo is, to be honest, pretty shabby, but we don't care. It's there for when we need it and that's okay.

Sounds pretty rubbish, doesn't it?

It isn't made any better for the road that leads to it, which is long and difficult. It's rutted and pitted and almost impossible in the wet. But that's immaterial really, as this campsite that isn't a campsite is a field on the edge of a cliff, with a steep goat track leading down to a secluded little beach where nobody goes. The only people you'll see

up there are walkers and ramblers taking a jaunt along the coast path, and perhaps other campers.

At the right state of the tide, on the sand bar below the field, there are waves. Very good waves for a surfer like me. On days when it's good you can see all the way up the coast to other surf breaks. From the cliff you can count the other surfers in the water less than a mile away, and see them jostling for waves, while below you, at the bottom of the path, wave after wave rolls in unridden.

The grass in the field is long and uncut and the ground uneven and undulating. There are no pitches or electric hook-ups, no washing-up facilities, no showers, no bar, no shop, no amusements. Just sea, sky, sand and fields of green.

This site might be your idea of a barren camping hell. But for me, it's just about as perfect as it's possible to get.

As I said. Location, location, location. (See my list of great campsites on page 331).

DENSITY OF SITE

The Camping and Caravanning Club has a 6m rule that they expect all their campsite owners and campers to adhere to. The 6m rule says that all tents should be at least 6m apart, a distance recommended as sufficient to stop the spread of fire from one unit or tent to another.

However, not all campsites or campers stick to this rule. On busy periods you might find yourself hemmed in a bit by windbreaks, tents and all sorts unless you go to a site that insists on this. If this is the sort of thing that bothers you (it does me), go to a Camping and Caravanning Club site or check with the campsite owner before you go. And if someone pitches too close, ask them politely to move and explain why.

BEING AMONG YOUR OWN KIND

One way to make yourself feel comfortable on a campsite is to hang out with people who think like you. Of course you can't ever tell if you're going to get on with your neighbours before you arrive at a site, but you can increase the chances by going to sites where your kind might gather. Whatever your kind is.

TYPES OF CAMPSITES

Adults only

So you don't like kids? That's okay. Other people don't like them either. And it may be best if you all stick together so you can find a little peace and quiet on your just-for-grown-ups campsite. It's a shame that some sites prefer not to hear the joyous laughter of kids being healthy, outdoor children but that's the way it is. We were all children once.

PROS ▶ If you are allergic to kids then this is your kind of camping. No brats.

CONS ▶ If you have kids, you can't go.

Naturist clubs and sites

There is something beautiful about going wild when you are going wild. I am not a naturist but I see nothing wrong with the thought of stripping off and baring all. I have done it myself, but only on secluded beaches (see page 136 of my last book, *The Camper Van Coast* (Saltyard Books, 2012) if you want proof).

Anyway, if your camping experiences include wanting to let the sun see the whole of you, then there are lots of options, with more in Europe than in the UK (perhaps for obvious reasons).

See **www.naturistguide.eu** for a list of naturist campsites and reviews in the UK. Alan Rogers, provider of guidebooks and camping directories, has a list of naturist campsites all over Europe: **www.alanrogers.com**

PROS ▶ If you want to be among naked people there's no better way to camp.

CONS ▶ Can get chilly sometimes. Or people make smutty *Carry On* jokes.

Holiday/touring parks

At the other end of the scale from the adult-only site is the family holiday park. These kinds of sites usually include a mix of touring pitches for caravans, mobile home pitches and camping pitches along with hardstanding pitches for motorhomes and camper vans.

A lot of holiday parks also include family activities and attractions, with some of the larger parks having pools, bars, restaurants, golf course, amusements, whatever. In any case, expect to be among families, kids and the whole of humanity in its many forms and all of its wondrous beauty.

PROS ▶ Lots for everyone to do. Fun for the kids.

CONS ▶ Not everyone likes big sites with lots of chalets and mobile homes.

Pop-up summer sites

Some campsites pop up in the summertime only, taking advantage of the 30-day rule (in the UK), which allows campsites to have a temporary licence. These can often be just for camper vans and motorhomes as they have no real facilities, or they can share facilities with a shop, bar or café.

PROS ▶ It's normally about the location, so they can be situated in great places.

CONS ▶ In my experience, there's few facilities other than loos and water, if that.

Large tent and camper van-only sites

We have been to a lot of great sites that have a fair mix of hardstanding and tent pitches, and perhaps some glamping pods or bell tents. We love these as they often have shops or pools or a café or bar, but without the glitz of some of the larger holiday parks. Includes well-run Camping and Caravanning Club sites.

PROS ▶ Well organised sites, with wardens, good quality showers and often extra facilities.

CONS ▶ Might be too organised and well run for some.

Small/independent sites

Lots of campers like to turn their backs on 'civilised' camping and go for a more natural camping experience. When you want to see countryside or beach out of your camper van window rather than a sea of mobile homes and static caravans, the small site is the way to go. This is camping as it should be (if you ask me), the way I remember it from when I was a boy, except the shower block and facilities have been upgraded.

PROS ▶ Camping how it should be. In a field, away from the trappings.

CONS ▶ You might not get wi-fi.

Certificated sites

These are small, privately run sites that may accept no more than
five caravans, camper vans or motorhomes at any one time. You must
be a member to stay, and it is often advisable to book. These sites are
often out of the way, in interesting places where big sites wouldn't
be allowed. For more see **www.campingandcaravanclub.co.uk**

PROS ▶ Great locations on private land, often secluded and quiet.

CONS ▶ Fewer facilities than bigger sites.

'*Our camper van* is a 40-year-old orange
and white Westfalia named Harlow. He came
by his name four years ago in Harlow, Essex.
Moments after buying the bus it broke down
with an indicator electrical fault. A quick fix
on the side of the road saw us gingerly driving
the van back to our hometown of Gosport.

On reflection, the reason we bought Harlow was to try and
give my wife and boys something special, a unique perspective
of the world with some good memories that would last a
lifetime. For me it's also been a challenge and a great hobby,
finding ways to maintain the bus, all on a slim budget.

The reason we enjoy Harlow is his charm and appeal, often
getting a wave while driving, and a friendly chat with fellow
camper van owners at our local beach. It's a step back in time,
taking us away from the humdrum of everyday living, giving us
some precious moments of freedom. Slide the side door wide
open, take in the view, have a nice cuppa, a breath of fresh air,
a chat, cook a good meal, and maybe spend a night or two.
It's just magic.

Our experience in ownership is that over time the intrinsic
value of our bus has now outweighed the monetary value.
He really has become part of our family.'

Tom Trubridge *OWNER OF HARLOW*

Sleep 317

WILD camping

For some the perfect campsite is a wild site, where you park up somewhere that takes your fancy. It's what camper vans were made for. Right? No hassle, no stress. You park up, sleep the night and move on the next day. Paradise.

Unfortunately, it's not so simple.

I love wild camping. I've done it regularly ever since I learned to surf way back in the 1980s. It was a necessity back then. I was a skint student and didn't live near the coast. The only way to do it was to hitch a lift with friends who owned camper vans and kip down with them wherever the surf took us. We slept in boatyards, on quaysides, among dunes and in pub car parks, just so we could go for an early surf the next day. And it was brilliant fun. I still do it now; at home in Devon I have a few of my own wild camping spots that are near great surfing beaches. From time to time we camp to make the most of the sunset or just to get away from home. We are lucky.

But the fact remains that wild camping is illegal in England and Wales.

I have never enjoyed wild camping more than on the Isle of Arran with Maggie in the summer of 2015. We parked by the beach and did nothing much at all for a couple of days. It was blissful. You might even say it's what this whole camper van business is all about.

As ever, the choice to drive a camper van is something that I do for all the right reasons. I do it because I don't want to have to pitch my tent on overcrowded and expensive campsites and I want to have a little more luxury than a few wet nights under canvas. The camper van is all about freedom, about choosing your own path and seeing where the road takes you. Oh yes... until you realise that you are committing an offence just by parking up and kipping the night.

There are some tolerated spots in England and Wales where it is okay to wild camp, but these are few and far between and closely guarded, and you probably shouldn't be camping there anyway because the law says no. And whether or not the law is an ass is up to you to decide.

The Caravan Sites and Control of Development Act 1960* makes it a civil offence to pitch your tent or park your camper without permission on someone else's land or to operate a caravan site or campsite without a licence. There are exceptions (for clubs and societies and for licensed gatherings) but on the whole the Act means that you are causing an offence by camping on unlicensed sites without permission.

Landowners too, are restricted by the amount of time that they can allow anyone to camp on their land, even with permission. They may allow one caravan, motorhome or camper van to stay overnight, for no more than two nights in succession and for no more than 28 days in any 12-month period. However, wild camping is a civil offence, which means that it is a matter for the courts, not the police. You make your own choices there, but it is as well to remember that parking up on the hard shoulder or in a layby (that is a part of the public highway) means that the police do have the power to move you on. Although in my experience a policeman in a good mood would rather see you snatch a few hours kip than drive tired.

How many times have you found a beautiful parking spot only to find you can't stay for the night because of the 'no overnight parking' signs? It's infuriating.

* You can read the Act in full at this website: http://www.legislation.gov.uk/ukpga/Eliz2/8-9/62

WHY LANDOWNERS AND CIVILIANS HATE WILD CAMPING

Whatever the reasons behind the Caravan Sites and Control of Development Act 1960, there is no doubt it controls unrestricted growth of campsites, prevents travellers parking up freely where they like and does contribute to the unspoiled beauty of our countryside.

No matter how respectful you might be when you wild camp (some people call it free camping or offsite camping) there are some who feel it is their right to camp as and when they will, with no respect for local residents, good sense and concern for the natural world. These are the minority that move in, get out the windbreaks and barbecues, leave rubbish, empty their grey tanks (people who see you do this will fear the worst), empty their black water tanks in the bushes (this is illegal and highly antisocial) and damage the environment.

We know it happens because we see signs all over the place saying 'no overnight parking', or height restriction barriers at beauty spots. They're not there for no reason. Don't be that person.

LEAVE IT NICER

I have a philosophy that dictates I leave somewhere nicer when I leave than it was when I got there. I think it should apply to everyone and everywhere. It's very simple and means that you make sure you haven't left any mess when you leave. It also means that you should tidy up other people's mess, too, preferably soon after you arrive. If you do this, your pitch will be clean and no one will have anything to complain about (*see* page 387 for more).

THE RULES OF WILD CAMPING

I have read an awful lot of the 'unwritten rules of wild camping' here, there and everywhere. They are invariably the same and follow the same lines, namely of respect. This is something I feel very strongly about so I am going to do something positive and write them down. Anyone, at any time, is welcome to take these rules and distribute them freely. If it makes a difference and ensures that more of us are able to enjoy camping at its best then it's worth sticking my neck out.

WILD CAMPING IN NATIONAL PARKS

There are some areas in national parks where it is legal to wild camp. However, that's for the tented folk. If you want to, you risk being moved on by the rangers.

WILD CAMPING IN SCOTLAND

Then you have to look at Scotland. The Land Reform Act makes wild camping legal on public access land. It is a great and truly liberating thing that means Scotland is viewed as the holy grail of wild camping by wannabe wild campers all over the UK. I'm heading up there soon with my family and can't wait.

But it isn't without its problems. I have heard many stories of campers abusing the law and leaving the place a mess. In Lunan Bay on Scotland's east coast there have been bad problems with wild camping. Likewise in the Trossachs. On certain areas of Loch Lomond there are

Wild camping: The rules

1 Leave it nicer than it was when you arrived. Take your litter home. If you can, pick up others' litter and take it home too. It will create a good impression of you.

2 Do not empty tanks of any type anywhere you are not authorised. Take it with you until you are able to dispose of it properly.

3 If you can, get permission from the the landowner.

4 Do not light fires or BBQs unless you know that landowner approves of them.

5 Arrive late and leave early.

6 Don't set up camp, hang out washing or get out all your tables and chairs and windbreaks, etc. Others might see it as preparing to stay a long time.

7 Don't pitch up near houses or blocking anyone's views.

8 Be prepared to defend your right to wild camp by ensuring others don't break the rules either.

9 Don't play loud music or act in an unsociable way.

10 If you are asked to move on, do it with a smile.

areas where wild camping is now illegal. These measures came into force on 1 June 2011 and, as I understand it, are as a direct result of people making the choice not to respect the environment and to camp irresponsibly.

WILD CAMPING IN EUROPE

In my experience wild camping is easier in Spain and France than in the UK, with Spain marginally ahead in terms of ease. France's aire system takes care of a lot of the problems they have had with wild camping (mess and disrespect) in organised areas. But there are places where wild camping is tolerated, if not illegal. Don't be surprised if you get the knock in the night.

In Spain I have free camped all along the north coast without any problems. It is tolerated at many spots and has become a part of life at some surf destinations – even though it may not be strictly legal. There are laws that prohibit camping within 200m of the beach and in other places, like near military zones, national parks and plenty of other places. Some of the regions ban wild camping altogether while others allow it as long as there are no more than three units, fewer than ten people and you stay no more than three days. Whatever the rules and how you interpret them, respect is always the order of the day.

In Scandinavian countries, including Norway and Sweden, there are certain rights of the individual to roam and have access to land. In fact,

as a nation with rights of access and the right to commune with nature embedded in its culture and law, Norway has some of the most liberal access laws of any country. However, it also comes with rules, such as not camping within 150m of a house or on uncultivated lands, in young forest or where it may cause environmental damage.

For more information, ask the Google. There are plenty of sites offering suggestions for wild camping spots in almost every country.

Final tip: Leave it nicer.

'**Camper van,** *van conversion, motorhome, motor caravan – call them what you want they all offer the same thing: the chance to escape. They don't offer you that 'sense of freedom' so many journalists use as a lazy cliché when writing about holidays, they actually provide you with the reality. We discovered motorhomes when we had twins. No airport stress, no being forced to follow someone else's agenda and timetable, and no need to spend the Earth to have quality time as a family. Load up, drive, pitch up, enjoy.*'
Daniel Attwood *EDITOR OF* MOTORHOME MOTORCARAVAN MONTHLY MAGAZINE

PLACES **to stay** EN ROUTE

Got a long way to go? Then better plan for a stop along the way. There are some options open to you, however each one comes with a caveat. Of course it does. Nothing is ever simple.

THE FIRST RULE OF THE HALFWAY HOUSE

You may get asked to move on, wherever you stay without express permission, so the last thing to do is have a glass of wine with supper. If the police come knocking and don't like the smell of you, you could end up spending the rest of the night in gaol, or jail, or worse.

THE SECOND RULE OF THE HALFWAY HOUSE

If you stay in a public place then it will either be the police or the local authority that has the responsibility for that space. They have different powers, but ultimately they can move you on, wherever you are.

Be prepared to be moved on if you don't have permission.

TYPES OF PLACES TO STAY EN ROUTE

At the side of the road

Parking in a layby could lead to a ticket for obstruction. This could be because you are using up space needed for emergencies or that you are in a dangerous place. The hard shoulder, as we all know, is a stupidly dangerous place to stop and should only be used for emergencies.

Laybys should only be used if there is enough space and they are away from the traffic. But remember that they are usually governed by the police, who have more power than the local authority.

Caution!

Anyone can get access to you if you stay on the public highway. So be safety conscious. If you must, lock doors, be low key. Don't leave anything outside. Have your phone handy (and check for signal).

Car parks and motorway services

Every car park is different and will have different rules. Some motorway services will slap a ticket on you if you don't buy a ticket for time over two hours (supermarkets can do this too). Now I'm not saying that these are legal or not legal, but I have never paid one, writing very patiently

that I parked up because I was in danger of crashing, so stopped
to get some sleep. In the UK these 'fines' aren't issued by the police
or local councils and are usually just 'invoices'.

Truck stops

Looking for a good brekkie? This is the place to stop. Just be careful,
park away from traffic, don't block anyone in and steer clear of the
arm wrestling contest.

Oh, and lock your doors and windows and keep everything out
of sight.

Private land

Some pubs, cafés and restaurants will let you stay on their land
overnight, perhaps in exchange for having a meal or buying produce,
in a similar vein to France's Passion sites and Britstops.

In the UK an exception in the Caravan Sites and Control of
Development Act 1960 exists, stating that landowners may allow
camping on their land (if they don't have planning permission for
camping) as long as campers don't stay for more than two nights
and as long as the landowner
does not allow it for more
than 28 days in any year. This
exception also allows pubs to
let you stay overnight in their
car parks if they don't have a
caravan site licence.

Stealth camping

Some campers don't look like
campers. That enables them
to go under the radar of the
authorities and stay in places
other campers wouldn't even
consider. It's at your own risk.
But same applies: if you get
moved on, go. If you have
a drink, be prepared for the
consequences.

PASSION sites

There is something wonderful about combining great food with camping. Let's face it, I'd be in trouble if I didn't think that. But combining great camping locations with finding out about new foods, learning about agriculture, horticulture or viniculture can only be a real winner.

The France Passion Scheme does exactly that. It's quite simple. The guide costs £25 or so and gives you a year's worth of 'invitations' to stay on more than 1850 sites all across France. These vary, from auberges to vineyards, farms and cafés, and all give you direct access to local produce and the people who grow them. The guide includes details of number of spaces, whether or not the owners speak English (or German or Dutch), whether you have to call ahead and if there are any facilities.

There is no charge for staying, only the obligation that you will say hello and goodbye as you leave. To take advantage of the scheme you must be self-contained and have the current guide. If you want to eat, buy produce or sample the wine, you can. And, of course, you will. If you are epicurious in any way, like wine or just want to see a little of the real France, then you'll enjoy special times on Passion sites.

We have a very particular memory of staying in a fabulous Passion site in Cauterets in the Hautes-Pyrénées. We parked up at an auberge and enjoyed a few beers in the sunshine. Then we booked in for a fantastic meal of local artisan food and wine, and stayed the night for free. The owner told us how much he loves welcoming France Passion guests, as they are polite, friendly and appreciate the food. We love that.

THE PASSION RUNNETH OVER

The France Passion scheme has been such a success that it has spawned a number of similar schemes in Spain and Italy, and even one in Britain.

Fattore Amico has been running for a while in Italy and has 521 farms and vineyards listed. The guide is available at **www.vicariousbooks.co.uk**

Espana-Discovery is the Spanish equivalent and is available from **www.espana-discovery.es**. It has 140 stopovers in Spain.

Britstops is the British version. It has been running for a few years now and is being added to all the time. The latest edition contains over 900 stopovers and includes Northern Ireland and the Republic of Ireland for the first time. Stopovers include farms and pubs and even the odd vineyard.

328 Sleep

AIRES and overnights

'Aires' is the common (UK) name for 'aires de camping car' (motorhome area). These are overnight parking places that are specifically designated for motorhomes and camper vans. The system is prevalent in France, although is spreading throughout Europe, with guides available for France, Belgium, Germany, Italy, Spain, Portugal, Holland and Luxembourg.

The idea is that local councils (or private individuals) provide an overnight stop for self-contained motorhomes. Tents and caravans are not allowed, neither is putting out tables and chairs or awnings. Most 'aires' have fresh water and facilities for emptying waste water and toilet tanks – these are known as service points. Some have electricity. Some charge for the privilege and others don't. Some provide showers and toilets, others just the basics – a parking place and somewhere to

empty the Porta Potti. Local police will often make daily rounds and take number plates to ensure no one abuses the system. We have used them a lot on our trips because they offer us a cheap alternative to staying on campsites.

I understand why the French have aires. They offer a neat solution to some problems. With designated places, they can police who stays overnight and control illegal camping on the roadside or at beauty spots. They can also control a little of the flow of traffic through busy summer resorts by signposting the aires via quiet routes or by placing them on the edge of town. It works. The system also works to attract people to a town and gives them a reason to visit. If there is a cheap place to stay, people will come and spend money in the town.

I wish there were more in the UK and Ireland and applaud independently minded councils who set them up (Torridge District Council, well done!) because they attract NEW audiences, do not detract from local tourism businesses and bring new revenue.

THE BEST-SITED CAMPSITES

I have been to a lot of campsites over the last 20 or so years. Some have been amazing. Some not so amazing. Each has its own special features and personality (thank goodness), which means that everyone will find something… whatever it is they need.

I have included just a few of the more memorable sites here for your enjoyment. There are plenty out there that I haven't been to but if you want something special, find it here.

England

DEVON

❧ Outdoor + Active, Roadford Lake, Lifton

If you ever wanted me to let you in on a camping secret, this is it. In fact, once you unlock one South West Lakes Trust campsite, you unlock them all. These are wonderful places to stay, right at the lakeside, with direct access to facilities and the surrounding area. Roadford is special because it's a vast playground with all kinds of activities on tap, level pitches with hook-up, good shower facilities and an eerie quiet once the day visitors have left. Early summer mornings are astounding if you get up with the birds. With the mist rising on the lake and dew on the grass you could be anywhere. There are also campsites at Tamar Lake and Wimbleball Lake in Devon, and at Stithians Lake and Siblyback Lake in Cornwall. **www.swlakestrust.org.uk**

Roadford Lake

What this site does better than any I know: *Direct access to sailing boats, silly games on the water and, if you need it, expert tuition.*

❧ Woolacombe Bay Holiday Park, Woolacombe

I don't like big, corporate sites, and this is the biggest. They send emails and brochures through the post (moral to that story: don't give them your details) and are terribly efficient and all that. They have hundreds of pitches, a small city of statics and touring pitches by the dozen. They also have a bowling rink, bingo, amusements and a bar with many screaming kids and the smell of chips. So it's far from my idea of a perfect site. But it does have a SURF MACHINE!! And that is quite something. There aren't many of them about. It's also very close to Woolacombe, one of the UK's best beaches (so they say), where you can ride real waves. The hardstanding pitches are good and facilities as you'd expect from a five-star site, but, you know... **www.woolacombe.com**

What this site does better than any I know: *They have a surf machine for crying out loud. Try it for shits and giggles.*

DORSET
The Red Lion, Winfrith, Dorset

There are plenty of campsites within easy reach of the coast in this area, however, when we went the choice was limited. We were really glad we found The Red Lion. The pub has a campsite in the field behind with hook-up, clean showers and water point. We were unable to park on the grass (for fear of not being able to get off again) but were able to stay on the car park and hook up to the mains. It turned out to be a great location as it's just 10 minutes from Lulworth and just about half a mile from 'Dorset's Best Village Shop', which sells just about everything you could ever want from a village shop.

What this site does better than any I know: *Obliging owners and open late into the season when everything else is shut.*

Wood Farm, Charmouth

Located about a mile from the beach at Charmouth, the site has lovely countryside views and most of the very generous pitches get a decent vista. In short it's very, very civilised. The thing I liked most about it was that the showers can be turned on and left on so you don't have to hit a

button every few seconds. The shower rooms are centrally heated, too, with loos, basins and mirrors. The indoor pool is also blissfully warm, with great changing facilities and an on-site café. I must admit I like a field with a bucket, but I'm coming around to this way too.

Wood Farm

All the pitches are hardstanding and perfectly level so you'll get a good night's sleep, it's just getting there that can be tricky. Then again, if I were able to get my old 34-year-old camper up and down the access roads, so can you. However, it's worth noting that their site says motorhomes over 8m cannot be accepted – so perhaps best to ring first! www.woodfarm.co.uk

What this site does better than any I know: *One of the best indoor pools the kids have ever dunked me in. Good for fossil hunting at Charmouth, too.*

CORNWALL
♣ Atlantic View Campsite, Porthcothan

If you want to get one of the best pitches here at Atlantic View you might have to have been coming for 20 years or more. It won't have changed in any of that time but you'll love it all the same for its simplicity and refusal to change. It's a classic farm campsite, with sea views and an easy walk down to the beach at Porthcothan, a gorgeous sandy haven on the wild north Cornwall coast. That means it's perfect for a good, old fashioned Cornish camping trip. No pools, no amusements, no nonsense, just camping on the farm. Book in 1995 to avoid disappointment (only joking, just turn up).

What this site does better than any I know: *Proper farm camping in an old fashioned Cornish way.*

● Ayr Holiday Park, St Ives

I met my missus here, we think, when I was cleaning caravans and working in a surf shop to fund a surfing summer. But don't hold that against me. Ayr has got a fantastic town and country location on the South West Coast Path, with the most fabulous views overlooking one of the UK's best beaches and St Ives itself.

I went back recently to see if the place had changed much and I am happy to say it hasn't. The park still enjoys fabulous views over St Ives and Porthmeor beach. However, it now has a brand new (and spotlessly clean) shower block and terraced hardstanding for camper vans with picnic benches, most of which also have hook-up, a tap and a drain. It's still a bitch of a walk from town with a few pints inside you but that's part of the appeal: no taxis necessary.

My recommendation? If they have space, go. This is one of the

Ayr Holiday Park

best-situated campsites I know. It's going to cost you in high season for two people and a camper van but it's worth it if you want to see the Tate Gallery, Barbara Hepworth Sculpture Garden, surf Porthmeor or eat in any of the town's restaurants. You could even go see my old house at 16 Teetotal Street. How very aptly named it was. Not.
www.ayrholidaypark.co.uk

What this site does better than any I know: *Amazing location next to one of Cornwall's most beautiful towns.*

Henry's Campsite, Lizard

If health and safety is an issue for you then it's your own lookout here on the southernmost tip of Britain at this quirky, interesting campsite with a lovely hippie vibe. Not that it's dangerous, far from it. It's just that the owner couldn't care for all that rules nonsense, as long as you do the right thing, be sensible and think like they do – which isn't hard once you've been here for 5 minutes.

The site has lots of quiet plots separated by hedges, granite posts and totems. Everywhere you look there are pieces of art, paintings, and bits and pieces. This is about as un-mainstream as it's possible to get and I love it! In summer they put on cider evenings and BBQs in the thatched roundhouse, a kind of tribal meeting area. There are about 50 pitches and a handful of hardstandings with electricity. Be warned though: I never told you about this place and, if you like neatly mown grass and whitewashed everything, it might not be for you!
www.henryscampsite.co.uk

What this site does better than any I know: *Makes you smile everywhere you go. Hippie vibe that spills over into your life for as long as you stay.*

Wooda Farm Holiday Park, Bude

Neat and tidy this is, with great views across the cliff tops to Bude and the Atlantic beyond. You can stay in luxury lodges here if you want to, or just bring your own van and hook up to the mains while your wetsuit dries off and your kids are off playing badminton, exploring the lakes or heading off to fetch you something from the takeaway. Heavenly? Not bad... heated loos off season means it's a cracking spot for a September surf trip, a summer holiday or a weekend away. **www.wooda.co.uk**

What this site does better than any I know: *Family camping that's organised, but not corporate.*

CUMBRIA
◗ Eskdale Camping and Caravanning Club Site

Oh lovely lovely lovely! That's what we say. This site is at the heart of Eskdale, the gateway to Scafell and the higher fells. Just a few hundred yards from the station at Boot, it's an amazing location, with really great staff, and everything a fell walker could ever want. There is a boot drying room and a pub that sells beer. Come on! That's enough for us. Amazing walks, great pitches and a high chance of rain. But hey. Last time we went it snowed, hailed and rained all at once. That's camping in the Lakes. **www.eskdalecampsite.com**

What this site does better than any I know: *Puts you right there among the fells in a well tended oasis with all the comforts.*

◗ Ravenglass Camping and Caravanning Club Site

This is a fantastic site that's really well tended and with a really friendly feel. There are 56 hardstanding pitches and 19 grass pitches, well-kept showers and toilets, a mini shop and very friendly and helpful owners. We really enjoyed it because of its proximity to pubs, restaurant, trains, coast and also the easy access to Eskdale. Jump on the steam train at the station and get a ride into Boot at the heart of Eskdale.

339 *Sleep*

You could pitch up here, plug in and enjoy a few days' walking, cycling and exploring without having to decamp. Especially if you get the weather, like we did – even in the hail the loos were warm and inviting, which is saying something. Great fish restaurant nearby. **www.campingandcaravanningclub.co.uk/ravenglass**

What this site does better than any I know: *A quiet spot close to the coast and with easy access to the mountains. Great fish restaurant close at hand.*

HAMPSHIRE
◗ Hollands Wood Campsite, Brockenhurst

This is a chain campsite, but feels very much not like one. With pitches in the woods bordering open meadows of the New Forest, it's a twitchers and naturalist's delight. With a pitch in the trees you can look out to see New Forest ponies graze carelessly in the fading evening light.

As usual with these kinds of site the facilities are spotless and clean, but that's irrelevant. Location is everything. Ask for a pitch close to the edge of the forest. **www.campingintheforest.co.uk**

What this site does better than any I know: *New Forest ponies! Need any more?*

NORFOLK
High Sands Creek, Stiffkey

It's another site that doesn't have a website that I can find. That generally means good things will come if you stay there. They did when I did. Direct access to the marsh makes it a heaven for samphire, seal watching, muddy kids, salty creeks and long walks in flat countryside. It's a good, flat site in a great position and with lovely views over the flats (if you get a pitch at the top of the gently sloping field). Wander the marshes, paddle the creeks, go wild. This is the place for it. **01328 830235**

What this site does better than any I know: *Gets you closer to the marshes than anywhere. Flatness supreme.*

NORTHUMBERLAND
Herding Hill Farm

I like this campsite because the bloke who runs it is a proper nice chap and is helpful and interested. That's a very good start. We turned up there after an epic drive from Scotland and were very glad we did. Our pitch was perfect, with hook-up and hardstanding. Great loos, and a very good eco policy. Posh pods, too, if you like that kind of thing. Perfect for checking out Hadrian's Wall. **www.herdinghillfarm.co.uk**

What this site does better than any I know: *Puts you right on the Wall, in wild, empty country. But no scrimping on the niceties.*

SUFFOLK
Southwold Camping and Caravanning Site

This is a popular campsite so you'd best book in advance before you go. And don't take too much notice of the mobile home park you have to drive through to get to the camping field. It might seem like the kind of place holidays go to die, but yours is yet to come. Once you pitch you'll

be in the company of all kinds of camping folk: motorhomers, mums and their kids, bell tenters and perhaps a few caravanners. That's okay. The best thing about this site is that it's situated right next to Southwold Harbour, a short walk from Southwold Pier and a trip across the river in a punt from Walberswick. It's the very next best thing to owning a beach hut in town; posh and proper and very well situated.
www.southwoldcamping.com

What this site does better than any I know: *The only campsite for Southwold if you don't want to drive. Classic walks and a great pub nearby.*

YORKSHIRE
Croftlands, Fylingthorpe, Robin Hood's Bay

This is an adults-only, no frills, C&CC certificated site with lovely views over the sea at Robin Hood's Bay. It's quiet and with limited facilities other than hook-up, chemical toilet disposal and water, so if you are truly self-contained then it'd be a great place for a weekend stop. It's a walk down the hill to the beach at Robin Hood's Bay but it's well worth it, even if you don't find any fossils. There are plenty of places to stop for a cuppa or a pint along the way. Wainwright's Bar, the end of Wainwright's Coast to Coast Walk, is right on the slipway so you'll never be short of refreshment. From here you can pootle off and park up for the day at any number of spectacular beachside spots. Put the kettle on at Sandsend, Runswick Bay or even Whitby itself.

What this site does better than any I know: *Quiet and in a perfect location overlooking the coast.*

Goredale Scar Campsite

This site completes the Malham trilogy (see opposite) in spectacular, if a little chaotic style. There is no doubt that this is one of the finest located campsites anywhere. And that's a tough one. But it's right there, on the flat bottom of Goredale, just below Goredale Scar and yards from Janet's Foss, a spectacular waterfall. All in all, it's an amazing spot.

However. The facilities aren't modern (to my knowledge) and haven't been updated in a while, so let's be kind and describe them as quirky. Yes. Quirky. And anyway, you don't go to a campsite for the quality of the housework do you?

What this site does better than any I know: *Puts you there, at the heart of an ancient and beautiful glacial wonder.*

338 *Sleep*

Goredale Scar
Campsite

● Town End Farm Shop, Airton

A Britstop (*see* page 85), so it's free for self-contained motorhomers, on the understanding that you'll go and say hello to Chris Wildman and buy some of his lovely goodies (the Yorkshire chorizo is very fine!) by way of thanks – that's how the scheme works! In other news it's a great stop on the way up to Malham. And particularly useful if you want to leave the van, walk into Malham and avoid the traffic on those teeny-tiny Yorkshire lanes. **www.townendfarmshop.co.uk**

What this site does better than any I know: *Food. Milkshakes. Local produce.*

● Town Head Farm, Malham, North Yorkshire

This is one of those campsites you used to stay in when you were a Scout or with the school outward-bound group. That means there are lots of notices around telling you not to do things, like take your backpacks into the shower block or talk after 10 p.m. or cough on a Wednesday. But never mind. If there are no rules then where would we be? It is a bit niggly but the location is so good and the owners are so friendly and easy-going that you forgive them their note-writing habits.

Unlike some farm sites you stand a good chance of coming out of the shower actually feeling cleaner than when you went in, which is a bonus at least. Camper vans can park on hardstanding while tents go on the grass.

Town Head Farm

Malham is a wonderful place to camp because it's ripe for adventure and has a little of everything. It's halfway between Malham Cove and town, so it's easy to ditch the car and wander everywhere. It's not even that far to walk to Goredale (where there is another legendary site) or Janet's Foss. Located as it is at the edge of town, it is dark at night – and a little eerie; we heard all kinds of twittering and screeching and quacking when we went. **www.malhamdale.com/camping.htm**

What this site does better than any I know: *Yards from Malham Cove and all kinds of natural wonders.*

340 Sleep

IRELAND

⚫ Atlantic Caravan Park, Enniscrone, Co. Sligo

Ireland isn't blessed with as many campsites as the UK, partly because of the weather. So there is less choice and you are likely to have to share the site with a large number of statics. Having said that, Enniscrone is a nice seaside town with a few good pubs and the all-important seaweed baths. And this campsite is close by to all of them. In fact, it's right on the beach. **www.atlanticcaravanpark.com**

What this site does better than any I know: *Gets you access to a massive sandy beach and yards from a seaweed bath.*

⚫ Wavecrest Caravan and Camping Park, Caherdaniel, Co. Kerry

I have gone on about this one before. That's because it has one of the most beautiful positions of any campsite I know of anywhere. Not only is it on the end of the Ring of Kerry in the west of Ireland but it is also very close to one of the finest pubs in Ireland, and to one of the prettiest beaches I know of anywhere. Do I need to say that again?

Thanks to some creative landscaping Wavecrest has a number of pitches that are right next to the water, with one or two enjoying their own little island. This is an area that I have visited on many occasions and absolutely love it. Despite the hordes travelling round the Ring by bus it remains quiet away from the main road. Actually, once on the site you'd hardly know it was there. **www.wavecrestcamping.com**

What this site does better than any I know: *Close to, if not on, the water. Best location anywhere.*

Wavecrest Caravan and Camping Park

Scotland

⚑ Craigdhu, Betty Hill, Sutherland

A well-situated site for exploring the north coast of Scotland. Set on a hill between Farr Bay and Torrisdale, it's in a fine spot overlooking the sea. Nothing fancy schmancy, just a good spot to get your head down in the Highlands. What more do you want? (*See* page 343 for Sutherland alternative).

What this site does better than any I know: *Gets you into north coast surfing country. Plus, if you want to paddle across the river, access to a deserted strand.*

❧ Eilean Fraoich Campsite, Shawbost, Lewis

Another wild and lonely site in the middle of nowhere. Actually, it's not in the middle of nowhere if you want to see Lewis and Harris in all its magnificent glory. As is the way in the Highlands and Islands, sites are few and far between, so this is as good as any. Get some washing done, have a shower and enjoy the oasis of this peaceful camping meadow in among Scotland's finest wildness. **www.eileanfraoich.co.uk**

What this site does better than any I know: *Offers a wash and a brush up on Lewis, a wild camper's paradise.*

❧ Lunan Bay Campsite, Angus

I stayed here before Scott and Bonnie, the owners, updated the facilities, installed hook-up and tidied the place up a bit. Even so, before all that happened I thought this was one of the best places I had ever been. The beach is spectacular and the welcome warm. The farm sells home grown pork and meats and it's all generally very wholesome.

What this site does better than any I know: *Camping by the sea with access to lots of good stuff.*

❧ Oban Caravan and Camping Park, Oban

For island hoppers or divers this site is great. Overlooking the Sound of Kerrera and with walks all around, this is a great stop on the west coast. It's handy if you're waiting for the CalMac ferry out to the Hebrides or just want to stay somewhere nice nearby the lovely Highland town of Oban. Puffin Divers are right next door so if you want to explore the waters of the north, this is the place. **www.obancaravanpark.com**

What this site does better than any I know: *Want to learn to dive? There's no better place than northern Scotland. Seriously? Yep.*

Oban Caravan and Camping Park

◀ Seal Shore Campsite, Arran

Down a little lane and around some twisty bends on the southern tip of Arran's undulating coast road lies Seal Shore, in a location that is, well, to use a cliché, to die for. It has its own private beach, wildlife galore minutes away and a semi-tame owner who fishes and takes kids on nighttime snorkels. Brilliant! We loved it when we turned up; however – and this is a big however – book early to avoid the kind of disappointment I saw on my daughter's face when I had to break the news that they were full. As one of the only two sites on Arran it's very popular, so do as Daddy says and book it now. **www.campingarran.com**

What this site does better than any I know: *Gets you close to seals and wildlife on Arran's wild coast.*

Sango Sands Oasis

◀ Sango Sands Oasis, Sutherland

Do you want to slip out of your camper, hop over a stile and then make your way down a goat track to one of the most beautiful beaches in the UK? Okay then, come and stay here at Sango Sands. It's a cracker of a site that's on Scotland's wildest northern shore at Durness. While it is popular with motorhomers making the journey to the far north, it is still very wild and one of the few sites available in this area. Great for a stop-off to recharge if you are doing the wild thing. **www.sangosands.com**

What this site does better than any I know: *Takes the breath away for just being so far from anywhere, and still looks north.*

◆ Cae Du, nr Tywyn, Snowdonia

Cae Du is a treasure of a campsite. However, it's also a bit of a darling among the camping press since it was 'discovered' by the Cool Camping gang some time ago. The good thing about Cae Du, though, is that it's hard to imagine fame will change it in any way. It's a rural, isolated spot on the wild west coast of Wales with basic facilities, a friendly farmer, fire pits and fresh meat and eggs for sale. It's also got the very best views. Access isn't easy, as you have to drive down a steep track and under a railway bridge, but it's worth it.

There is not a lot nearby so it would be a good idea to bring everything when you first arrive. That way you can hunker down and not move for a couple of days, which is something this site is all about. We stayed here on a trip to west Wales in early September 2014 and it was bliss. We took wood, supplies, wine (no pub nearby) and got busy doing nothing. Perfect. **www.caedufarmholidays.co.uk**

What this site does better than any I know: *Open fires overlooking the Irish Sea. High chance of seeing dolphins.*

◆ Cae Gwyn, Nant Peris, Snowdonia

I first went to Cae Gwyn on a mission to climb Snowdon. We hiked up, hiked down again and felt very good about ourselves, so making the experience of a few pints in the Vaynol, the pub across the road, all the sweeter. We earned it.

Cae Gwyn is a simple, farmer's field-type campsite. It's rough and ready and friendly, with mountains and sheep all around. Across the

Cae Gwyn

road you'll find an overflow car park for the busy car park at Pen Y Pass, the access point for a couple of trails to Snowdonia's summit. Here you can catch the Sherpa bus service for a quid each way. It means you can leave the van where it is for the day.

Of course it's not all about Snowdon here; walk in any direction from the site and you'll find spectacular scenery. We found a gorge with a perfect wild swimming spot and a natural slide in the rock about 8ft high. Kit off? You bet. Go, and explore. **www.nantperis.org.uk**

What this site does better than any I know: *The best base for climbing Snowdon. Or mucking around in the hills.*

Caerfai Farm

Caerfai Farm, St Davids, Pembrokeshire

I have written about this site before, but it's worth a second mention, purely because it's in such a great spot, has such a lovely, friendly vibe and sells good cheese. Do you really need any more? Oh yes, it overlooks its own private beach and gives easy access to the coast path. And they sell cheese. The field is sloping but there are plenty of level pitches and some hook-ups. Get a nice day and you could be anywhere... even St Davids. **www.caerfaibay.co.uk**

What this site does better than any I know: *Down the steps, onto the beach. Not bad!*

● Morfa Mawr, Aberdaron

When you book this site, make sure you ask for a sea view pitch. That'll put you in the smaller of the two fields on either side of the road into Aberdaron and will reward you with fine sunsets and great views, even if you have to cross the road (it's not very busy). You might also be best approaching the site from the Abersoch side if you don't want to take your unit over the narrow hump-backed bridge in the village. Getting stuck here causes all kinds of headaches and happens regularly. Better take on the hill over Rhiw mountain!

Your reward for the planning and pleading and crawling up the mountain will be a spot overlooking Aberdaron beach, just a few hundred yards from the village and in the right place to take some spectacular walks. Okay, so the facilities are basic – just showers and loos and a sanitation point – but you'll have everything with you anyway so what does it matter? This is camping like the old days.

What this site does better than any I know: *Easy access to pretty Aberdaron village, great sea views.*

● Newgale Camping Site, Pembrokeshire

I like the site at Newgale because it's in a great location right next to the sea. It's basic and clean and cheap, and that's about it. They rebuilt the amenities block a few years ago so it's also a lot better than it was before. Then again, it was never really the amenities that we'd go for – it was the location. The only downside is that they don't allow dogs – more's the pity, as they would love the beach, which offers miles of flat sands at low tide. In wet weather the field can get sticky (and it can rain a lot in Wales as we know) so best take your chocks to get on the upper levels of the field. You'll get a better view but it certainly isn't level.
www.newgalecampingsite.co.uk

What this site does better than any I know: *Great views and an early surf check.*

Newgale Camping Site

FRANCE

◆ Camping de la Côte d'Argent, Hourtin, Gironde

How much? Flipping heck! On hearing the price I whisked the family away quickly with a 'I'm not paying that for a night in the forest' to find somewhere cheaper in the vicinity. There isn't anything. Certainly not with pools and slides and kids' clubs and fun fun fun like my girls wanted to have. Oh well. If there is a French word for going back with your tail between your legs then I did it and booked in, blowing half the budget on five days of fantastic luxury! Did I regret it? Heck no, this is brilliant.

Okay, let's face it, if you want a good campsite you have to pay for it in France. But the location, in Hourtin, a very pretty seaside hamlet on the west coast, is lovely. You can cycle to the beach, through the forest or just try and get away with wearing shorts in the pool. They have a bar, too. And the rosé is cold. Very cold. See you there!

www.camping-cote-dargent.co.uk

What this site does better than any I know: *It's big and it's brash but it does it well. Everything for everyone. Perfect family site.*

Camping du Letty

Camping du Letty, Bénodet, Brittany

Everyone loves a lazy river. Yes they do!!! They also love indoor pools. And beach-side access? And neat little plots separated by tall hedges? Yes yes yes. This is one of Brittany's finest campsites, and you pay for it. But who cares, we're on holiday, right? Just bring your own loo roll (I never get that about expensive sites – can't they afford it?).

We found out about Letty from Cool Camping and were glad we had. The kids had a marvellous time in the pool and we enjoyed a little relax at the pool-side bar. We were a little put out that we couldn't get a pitch overlooking the beach but they had all gone by the time we got there so we had to make do with a quiet corner near the lazy river. Really it wasn't so bad, although adult males are expected to wear Speedos in the pool – shorts are banned. It's a walk from Benodet town for moules and chips but, you know, that's okay too. Order a pizza on site and keep an eye on the kids. **www.campingduletty.com**

What this site does better than any I know: *Great pools for the kids and easy beach-side camping – if you book early.*

Camping Inter Plages, Lafitenia

If you want to see the storm coming at you across the Bay of Biscay then you'll need to stay at this site in the Basque region. Some of the pitches, on the seaward side, face all the weather so if you get unlucky, you'll get it all. But, before the storm comes, think of the location. The site is positioned on a point between two lovely beaches. To the south is Lafitenia, a gorgeous surfing beach with a world-class right-hand point break, while to the north you'll find a tiny little beach called Mayarco that can be accessed directly from the site. There are restaurants nearby and easy access to Biarritz, St Jean de Luz and the Basque region. A top place to base yourselves. Just watch for those storms. They could catch you out. **www.campinginterplages.com**

What this site does better than any I know: *Camp on the point, between two beaches.*

348 Sleep

⚜ Camping La Bergerie, Gavarnie, Hautes-Pyrénées

Change your plans. Stay another week. Sack everything. We did when we found La Bergerie. Driving though the Haute Pyrénées I had been moaning about wanting to find a campsite that had a few basic things. I wanted to be somewhere wild, without masses of plastic lodges, in a spectacular location, with good facilities, next to a river. Was it too much to ask?

In finding this site we had planned to visit Gavarnie then keep on looking. Gavarnie is famous for its cove, an enormous 'cirque' of rock that's over 3km wide. It's really spectacular walking and the views are nothing short of incredible. On the way back from the cirque we spotted La Bergerie, one of the few buildings at the head of the valley. We noticed that there were tents in the field behind the building so asked if it was possible for us to bring our camper van. The lady who runs the place, a very tall, elegant and imposing woman, smiled (phew) and said it was fine (hoorah!). That was the moment when we changed our plans. We fetched the van, drove it up the narrow pedestrian street to the end of the village, crossed a wooden bridge and pitched up in the field next to the river, staying for a few unplanned days in this most beautiful of places. It was everything I had hoped for from a trip to this part of France. www.camping-gavarnie-labergerie.com

What this site does better than any I know: *The very best mountain view, bar none.*

Sleep 349

Camping
La Bergerie

Camping Panorama, Pyla, Arcachon

When you come to this part of France you have to stay here, just to have a glass of wine on the terrace overlooking the Arcachon basin. The views are spectacular from the bar, which sits almost at the top of Europe's tallest sand dune, the Dune du Pyla. As you sip away you might also see a few silent parascenders, riding the thermals above your head. It's quite something, especially after a few wines.

But wine aside, this is a good site, with nice facilities, a good pool complex and a relaxed vibe. It's in the pine forest like a lot of sites in the region so it's got a nice dappled mix of light and shade, heat and cool during hot summer days. Again, if you give them your email address they will send you emails but it's not the worst culprit and that means it's a little less corporate than all the others. Mind you, with that view, who cares? **www.camping-panorama.com**

What this site does better than any I know: *Views from the tallest dune in Europe? Okay!*

Indigo Noirmoutier, Vendée

Okay, so it's part of a chain and they send you emails. But it doesn't feel like that when you are here. And even if it did, you wouldn't care because you'll be looking out to sea anyway. And that's not a bad view to have.

The Indigo site at Noirmoutier is hidden in the pine forest at the edge of a beautiful sandy beach where you can swim at high tide and collect cockles at low. It's beautiful and peaceful, and when you are here you wouldn't want to be anywhere else. Noirmoutier is one of the Vendée's

Indigo Noirmoutier

'nearly islands' that are linked to the coast by causeways and bridges. The island's slightly more southerly and posher Île gets super busy but this one less so. It's a great place to ditch the van and cycle around for a few days. Epic! **www.camping-indigo.com/ en/noirmoutier-indigo- campsite-france.html**

What this site does better than any I know: *Beach access and easy foraging – if you like cockles.*

350 *Sleep*

Camping Leagi

Spain

❧ Camping Leagi, Leikeitio, Biscay

Spain isn't blessed with as many sites as France, so when you find a good one you remember it. We found this by chance, having been turned away from one because they were too busy and driven away from another because it wasn't up to much. How glad we were! The location is isolated but everything is there if you wanted a few days of relaxing. The pool is great and the restaurant good, too.

What this site does better than any I know: *An oasis in the wilderness of the area between Mundaka and Zumaia.*

❧ Camping Playa España, Asturias

A little to the east of Gijon, on the northern coast of Spain, lies a little gem of a site set in an orchard at the bottom of a steep sided valley. It's a peaceful and friendly sort of a place in a wild section of country where there's not much else but farming. Grain stores, hanging with maize drying in the sun, dominate the rolling hills. The site is adjacent to a small sandy beach and a bar and restaurant, and it's about 30 seconds' walk to the sea. Good enough reason for me to go again.
www.campingplayaespana.es

What this site does better than any I know: *A nice site with really clean toilets in an isolated valley on Spain's north coast.*

The Field, San Vicente de la Barquera, Cantabria

This is a cracking spot on the north coast of Spain about 50 miles west of Santander that we found by chance in 2012. There are no facilities so don't get excited; the only loo is on the beach opposite and it only opens when they fancy, which we worked out was from about 11 a.m. to about 9 p.m. There is a shower there too, but it takes ages to fill a water container (and results in long queues of irate, sandy Spanish beachgoers) so take your own supplies.

The Field

In fact, take everything (Porta Potti included) and you'll be fine.

This site isn't for everyone (and definitely NO TENTS) but it suited us. It's about 30 yards walk from the surf, about a mile along the beach to town (which is famous for seafood) and feels isolated come sundown. It's a favourite spot for weekending locals so expect some fiestas. That said, they were all very cool and very friendly.

Go, but keep it to yourself; we don't want any of that overcrowding nonsense. No internet. No website. Just go looking.

What this site does better than any I know: *Cheap and easy camping right next to the sea in northern Spain.*

Ruta Finisterre, Playa Estorde, Finisterre, Galicia

Okay, so it's across the road from the beach. But I'm not too bothered about that. Being a little way away means that it's in the pine forests, so has some shade from the hot Galician sun. The beach, like a lot of Galician beaches, is spectacular, with lovely white sand, clear blue water and plenty of facilities, such as easy access to ice cream and beer. It's also the nearest campsite to Cap Finisterre so it's handy if you are planning a trip out west, to the very end-of-the-world west.
www.rutafinisterre.com

What this site does better than any I know: *Close to the beach but with the advantage of great shade. Close to the most westerly point in Europe.*

352 Sleep

Website GUIDE to CAMPING

UK CAMPING GUIDES AND CLUBS

THE CAMPING AND CARAVANNING CLUB
    http://www.campingandcaravanningclub.co.uk/
THE CARAVAN CLUB
    http://www.caravanclub.co.uk/

CAMPSITE GUIDES

UK and Ireland
CAMP FIRES BURNING: A site dedicated
    to UK sites that allow open fires.
    http://www.campfiresburning
    .org/sites.php
CAMPR: Hand-picked selection of great
    sites in the UK.
    http://www.campr.co.uk/
CAMPSITED: Irish based site with online
    booking facilities for Irish and UK
    campsites.
    http://www.campsited.com/
COOL CAMPING: The original and best listing site, and hugely
    successful guidebooks to 'cool' camping sites in the UK and Europe.
    https://www.coolcamping.co.uk/
PITCH UP: Reviews and online booking for thousands of campsites
    and holiday parks in the UK and Europe.
    https://www.pitchup.com/

Europe
ACSI EUROCAMPINGS: European-wide campsite listings:
    http://www.eurocampings.co.uk/
ALAN ROGERS: Comprehensive guide to campsites in Europe.
    https://alanrogers.com/
CAMPING CARD ACSI: Off peak camping discounts in Europe.
    http://www.campingcard.co.uk/
VICARIOUS BOOKS: Publisher of camping guides, Aires reviews
    and listings, and all kinds of guides for campers. Essential.
    http://www.vicariousbooks.co.uk/

(REPEAT)

You refuse to be nothing,
  I cannot stand in your way,
I hope that heaven holds no bounds,
  for what you want to say.
And even if you spend your life
  singing out to sea,
Rest assured that nothing's lost.
  You're everything, everything to me.

© Martin Dorey

INTRODUCTION

It's okay to admit that camper van living is not always plain sailing. Things can, do and will go wrong. The secret to making your trips a success is making sure that you do all you can to prevent things going wrong, and if they do then you'll be able to smile through knowing that it was *force majeure* that spelled disaster for your camper van trip.

I hope.

Sometimes there's nothing you can do to stop the wheels of fate. At some point your tyres will wear down, your grey water tank will fill to the brim and your energy will face a low ebb. These are the times when you need to rouse the hardy camper inside and soldier on. These are the times when you need to reach down into your soul and find your inner Baden-Powell, the stoic, self-sufficient and ever chipper (but probably quite annoying) being that dwells deep inside us all.

This section is all about keeping going. It is about making one day run seamlessly into the next, about taking care of the places you camp, about keeping mind, spirit and body going in difficult times.

Goodness knows we've all been there.

So in the following chapter you'll find advice on everything from getting up in the morning to putting a camper away for the winter. It includes a few ideas of my favourite campsites and tips on long stay trips.

356 (Repeat)

We're also going to talk a little more about responsible camping. It's a big thing for me as it means the difference between being welcomed back and not being welcome at all. While there are some places I wouldn't want to go back to, there are many others that I would like to see again before my time is out. And I'd like to think that both you and I will be welcomed back with open arms should the opportunity ever arise.

KNOW **your** LIMITS

In 2012 my family and I left Blighty for a 65-night adventure in France and Spain. We took the kids out of school, rented out the house, left the dog with a nice neighbour and hit the road. We explored mountains and rivers and beaches and ended up as far west in Europe as it's possible to go on four wheels. We ate winkles and razor clams, squid and hot peppers, foraged for cockles and mussels, and cooked them alive, alive oh. We camped on huge commercial sites and in wild spots, by the side of *bergeries* in the Pyrenées and in a farmer's field in Cantabria.

We braved rainstorms and flooded campsites, searing heat and hot, dry days when we could do nothing but find the nearest river to cool off in. We hiked up mountain passes and swam in glacial cascades and faced near divorce in a kayak up the Contis River in western France. We survived.

On our last day under canvas we pitched our awning at a campsite above the beach at Lafitenia near Biarritz. It was September and the weather was beginning to turn. Glancing up from my half-made awning I noticed a storm approaching over the sea. Before I had a chance to finish things off – and too late to take it down – the wind whipped up and the rain began to lash down. The ground was hard so getting the pegs in

WHAT does a CAMPER mean TO YOU?

'It felt like we had it all; *a nice house, well-paid jobs, the latest tech. But we were sick with stress. Hoping there was more to life, we set a goal to slash our spending. A few years later our mortgage was gone. In August 2011 we bought an ageing Hymer B544 we called Dave. With £28k saved, we set off to tour Europe for a year. Living frugally was now an ingrained habit, and we loved life on the road so much, we accomplished two years by sleeping for free in car parks, on beaches, even on volcanoes. Returning home we knew we didn't want the stuff from our previous lives; we only needed what was in Dave. We've sold most of our belongings and learned about investing. Back on the road again we've enough money coming in each month, without working, to cover our costs. We're now free, unstressed and happy.*'

Julie and Jason Buckley *OURTOUR.CO.UK*

was tough. As Jo and the kids stood inside the awning, holding on to it to stop it blowing away, I stripped off to my shorts and grabbed an axe, banging pegs in with the back of it in a desperate bid to get it built before the storm took us all with it. I got soaked to the bone as the kids held on inside. I banged and banged but the pegs buckled and crumpled and the rain lashed down. Finally the clouds parted and we finished the job. But it was enough. 65 nights of camping was enough for me.

That night, lying in bed I turned to Jo and said, 'I'm ready for my own bed now.'

Quietly she replied, 'I was ready two weeks ago.'

The next day we packed up and hit the road to Bilbao and our ferry home.

What's the point of telling you this? Well, it's that everyone has their limits. Some people are weekenders, preferring to take their escape in bite-sized chunks, while others are full-timers, who think nothing of spending months on end on the road.

Just as it doesn't matter what you drive, so it doesn't matter how long you stay away. It isn't a competition. But if you can make the 'repeat' as easy as possible – even if it's just staying one more day – you just might have it cracked.

359

(Repeat)

GETTING UP IN THE MORNING

360 (Repeat)

Did you get a good night's sleep? We hope so. But, in case you didn't, here are a few tips for getting out of bed. Or, more precisely, for getting ready to get out of bed.

The five-minute
WAKE AND SHAKE workout

Andrew Blake is a man who gets hundreds of people out of bed every year. He runs a boot camp for early risers at Croyde Bay in North Devon and also trains big wave surfer, Andrew Cotton. This is his workout for the first five minutes after waking. The first three minutes are in the van, with the final two out in the open...

While still in bed, start with this simple routine to release tension in the lower back.

MINUTE 1: Pelvic tilts
Keeping your hips and pelvis on the bed, breathe through your diaphragm, inflating your abdomen for 5 seconds. On the exhale release your lower back into the mattress, so engaging your core for 5 seconds.

MINUTE 2: Lumbar rolls
Keeping your feet on the bed and bringing your hands out to the side, bend your knees and gently roll your legs from the left to the right.

MINUTE 3: Knees to chest
As well as muscle and bone you have connective tissue in your back called fascia. Hugging your knees close to your armpits while keeping your pelvis on the mattress releases the thoracolumbar fascia, which connects the top of your back to your bottom.

Out of your van Now jump out of your van and do an impromptu dance of your choice for 30 seconds.

MINUTE 4: Hindu squats

This will mobilise your legs, hip flexors and shoulders. Squat until your heels tickle your ankles (or just get as close as you can without pushing it!) and come back up to standing and repeat.

MINUTE 5: Downward dog
+ knee to left then right elbow

Waking up your core, getting some oxygen to the muscles and making you feel energised for the day. Do it on a mat if you don't want to get dew all over your hands, feet and knees!

Downward dog, in case you never tried it, is a yoga position. The best way to get into it is to start in a 'tabletop' position, on your hands and knees. Your hands should be below your shoulders, your knees below your hips. Keep the palms of both hands flat and spread your fingers wide, taking care to put equal weight through each finger and into each fingertip pad. Keep your shoulders down, away from your ears, which creates space in the chest to breathe. Then straighten your legs, press through the fingertips, and push your bum up in the air. Keep your head in line with your arms to make an upside-down 'V' shape.

When you are in this position, point each knee at the opposite elbow, repeating until your minute is up.

Note: If you're new to downward dog or struggle with flexibility, you'll notice that you won't be able to get your heels to touch the ground in this position. That's absolutely fine: it's more important that you straighten your back rather than sacrifice a straight back for your heels touching the ground. Both the straight back and heels-to-the-ground come with time, flexibility and practice, but for now feel free to bend your knees slightly to allow you to straighten that lower back – and don't forget to keep breathing!

The LAZY MORNING workout

If you decide to do nothing each morning in the way of exercise, then that's your lookout. But if you want to guarantee that you'll be able to repeat all those little rituals that make life worth living, you need to do something that's so simple but which makes a huge difference.

I am talking about pelvic floor exercises. Yes I am. I wouldn't normally, but I promised my dear old mum that I would help her to spread the word around the world. You see, in her studies (she is a professor of urology, among other things), my white-haired mother (bless her) has proven in clinical trials that doing pelvic floor exercises can not only cure urinal and faecal incontinence but also sexual dysfunction. This applies as much to men as it does to women, perhaps surprisingly, with trials proving that men can gain control where control has been lost through incontinence or even after prostate surgery. What this means for camping trips is that a little work every morning could well save you a night of getting up every five minutes.

PELVIC FLOOR: SOME FACTS

- **One in ten men** experience urinary incontinence.
- **Erectile dysfunction** affects more than 20 per cent of men under 40 years of age, more than 50 per cent of men over 40 years of age and more than 66 per cent of men over 70 years of age.
- **Research has shown** that 40 per cent of men who had experienced erectile difficulties for 6 months or more regained normal erections after performing pelvic floor exercises for 3 to 6 months. A further 35 per cent of men improved their rigidity (Dorey *et al*, 2004).

BEFORE YOU GET UP - PELVIC FLOOR EXERCISES

Lie on your back with your knees bent and apart. Tighten your pelvic floor as if you are trying to prevent wind escaping. Hold this pelvic floor muscle contraction as strongly as you can, for up to 10 seconds, without holding your breath or tensing your buttocks. Perform three strong contractions, holding for up to 10 seconds followed by a 10-second rest.

Now get up and get on with your day and forget I told you about any of this.

SAFETY

In order to keep repeating those wonderful adventures you're going to go on, it's quite important to keep yourself together in such a way that you can enjoy your life while you have it. So this is the small print, the nanny state, the overbearing but well-meaning words of wisdom to help you on your way.

For some of you it might even be the bleeding obvious, and I'm sure I'll get reviews about it, but at least I said it and pointed it out before you put that axe through your leg. This is your pre-fun safety briefing and my demonstration of due diligence. So please read carefully before setting out.

Thank you, and please be careful when you swing that axe.

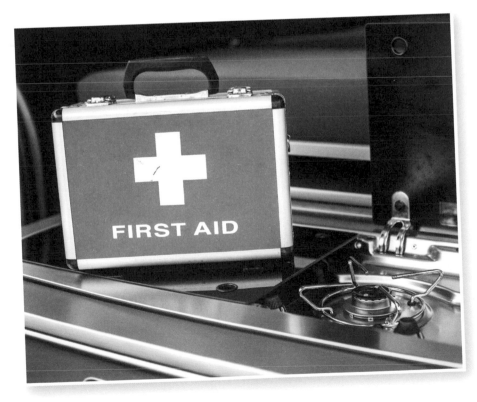

Seat BELT law

The following information refers to UK law, with guidance from the Department of Transport. Seat belt law differs across the world so what applies in the UK may not apply where you are, or where you travel. However, the advice given in this book concerns the safety of you and your passengers. In that respect it can be followed wherever you may be. Just because there may be no law about seat belt safety in the country in which you travel, it doesn't mean you shouldn't take safety advice. The consequences of ignoring advice are the same, whatever the law. **If you crash and you're not wearing seat belts then you are likely to suffer much more serious injuries than if you didn't. You may also injure others.**

Adults

When travelling in the front and rear, seat belts must be used if available. If they are not available, you are not obliged to use them.
But safety says, don't travel if seat belts aren't available. It's not cool or clever to be dead.

364 (Repeat)

Children

In the front, all those up to 135cm in height (or 12 years or over, whichever comes first) must use the correct child seat/booster for their weight, with no exceptions. If over 135cm or 12 years and above, the child is treated as an adult.

In the rear, where seat belts are fitted, the same rules as for front seats apply, but there are a few exceptions. If belts are not fitted in the rear, then those three years and above may travel unrestrained. Those under three must always use the correct baby/child seat.

Sideways facing seats

There is no legal requirement for seat belts to be fitted in sideways facing seats. However, in an impact, those in such seats have an increased risk of serious injury. If seat belts are installed then they must be used by adults.

Children may not travel on booster seat or child seats facing sideways as their use prohibits it. Children may not use adult belts in sideways facing seats as they must be in the appropriate seats for their weight and age.

Seats without belts

Adults may travel in seats without belts. However, my advice is don't. Besides, the police can take action against you if you carry passengers so that 'the manner in which they are carried is such that the use of the motor vehicle or trailer involves a danger of injury to any person' (UK Department of Transport).

365

(Repeat)

Insurance and no belts

What view does your insurance company have on passengers in your vehicle not using belts? If you have a crash and are sued by a non-belt wearing passenger for damages, will they support you? Think about it.

Likewise if you are away from home and need medical treatment following a crash, will your travel insurance pay your medical bills if they found out you were driving without a seat belt? Read the small print.

Rear travel

Although it is not specifically illegal to travel in the accommodation area of a camper van, you should bear in mind that this area would not have been specifically designed for use when travelling. You may be liable for prosecution (in the UK) if your manner of carrying passengers is deemed to be a risk to their safety or the safety of other road users.

Basically, just belt up. That is all.

Driving in Europe

Under EU law, drivers and passengers must wear a seat belt in any seat fitted with one.

Children under 1.35m tall, or travelling in cars/lorries fitted with safety devices, must use an approved device for their size. Taller children may use an adult seat belt. Rear-facing child restraints are no longer allowed on front passenger seats unless the airbag has been deactivated.

Seat belt law in the USA

The laws in the USA differ from state to state, with some states only demanding that those in the front buckle up. In one, New Hampshire, there are no rules at all. If in doubt, buckle up.

CAMPSITE safety

I don't think of myself as accident-prone. I really don't. Even so, things keep happening to me on camping trips. But, I wonder, why? I am not a five-year-old boy. I am a fully grown man.

However, I am also someone who likes to do things and be damned. Chop first, ask questions later. I don't go much on risk assessments when the only person I could sue would be myself. And I certainly wouldn't think about writing one for chopping wood in a field at 11 at night, in the dark, having consumed a few ciders; otherwise I would have had to sit in the dark and cold. The evening with my family would have been very much poorer without the fire.

Sometimes you have to take risks to enjoy life's best stuff. It's inevitable. That, to me, is camping. It's not always safe, this going out business. And that's why it's brilliant. Because it makes us challenge ourselves. It makes us get out from under the cotton wool duvet, away from the comforts of home and into the 'wild', even if it's nothing more than a campsite with all mod cons. The wild, however tame, as we all know, can still be a dangerous place. Campsite safety is of importance here because camping can be a dangerous thing, if you don't watch yourself.

GET **proper** COVER

No book on camping and travel would be complete without a mention of travel cover. Whether you are accident-prone or not, it is an essential piece of kit whenever you hit the road, especially when it's overseas.

VEHICLE COVER

What if you break down while towing in Turin? Or clap out in Clacton? Would you know how to get yourself home? Or would you leave it to chance and hope for the best? The sensible camper would make sure the vehicle is roadworthy when they set off (obviously) but would also have a plan B tucked away somewhere (usually in the back of the wallet) that would enable him or her to summon their roadside assistance provider at the touch of a few buttons. Some services will get you home, put you up, talk to local garages and even send drivers out to meet you if things go wrong.

And don't forget that if you break a windscreen or lose a wheel, you'll be losing your transport AND your house all in one fell swoop. So best get cover that will understand.

The Caravan Club's Red Pennant service does all that for their members – with the added benefit of the fact that they know what you're like. **www.caravanclub.co.uk**

367

(Repeat)

PERSONAL INSURANCE

Okay, so the unit is covered. Who is covering you? Personal travel insurance is another vital part of your camping kit, especially if you travel abroad. Medical bills can soar into the thousands for people who break things or get cuts and bruises while abroad, with bills for more serious conditions spiralling out of control – into the hundreds of thousands, in many places. Medical care isn't cheap.

Travel insurance will cover all the other replaceable bits – like luggage, paperwork and gadgets – but will also provide you with the peace of mind you only get from knowing that you will be well taken care of if something happens to your health. Even in Europe, where the European Health Insurance Card (EHIC) gives EU citizens access to basic care, travel insurance is vital.

World First offers travel insurance cover for people up to 100, covers hundreds of sports for free and will also cover thousands of medical conditions that other insurers won't touch. **www.worldfirst.co.uk**

The EHIC myth

EU citizens are entitled to carry a European Health Insurance Card (EHIC) while travelling in Europe. This entitles them to the same free healthcare that citizens of that country would automatically receive. While this is okay for people visiting the UK, where healthcare is largely free at the point of care (for now), it is a different matter for people travelling to other countries. Why? Because in some countries, healthcare is not free, with private clinics working alongside government clinics. In some places you may have to pay for an ambulance while in others you may be required to pay for prescriptions or to see a doctor.

What does this mean? Always take an EHIC as it may give you access to certain services. However, ALWAYS make sure you have personal cover, in order to cover anything that doesn't come free. Like an airlift home, a doctor's appointment or even just a ride in an ambulance.

TRAVEL INSURANCE TIPS

● If you take medication, always carry a copy of your prescription so you can explain the presence of drugs in your luggage without any fuss.

● If you take medication, take enough with you to last the trip, as drugs can be expensive abroad compared with home.

● Always declare your medical conditions, as insurers won't pay out if you neglect to mention something and it leads to a claim.

● Be aware that being under the influence of drink or drugs can invalidate claims (*see* page 395).

● Remember that your vehicle is also your home so make sure your cover includes hotel stays or alternative accommodation if your van becomes unusable. This is essential for older vans as parts can take days to arrive sometimes – even a broken windscreen can put you out of action for days.

● Don't forget your EHIC for Europe, but don't rely on it providing you with anything but the most basic care – get another policy, too.

SWING AN AXE SAFELY

Axes are dangerous things. But you can minimise the damage they cause to you by remembering something I learned as a Cub Scout; that is, to chop with your legs open wide. If you then miss your target and the axe continues its trajectory, your legs won't be in the way and the axe will swing between right between them.

Also, don't chop on soft or spongy surfaces. Make sure you have a block or another log to chop on. If the surface is soft, the wood you're chopping can bounce up and hit you. It happened to me.

When chopping kindling, hold the piece you're splitting and tap your axe into it a little so the axe stays in place. Then hit the wood harder against a hard surface to split the wood. Don't try to split it with the first blow if you're holding it or you could easily lose a finger.

(Repeat)

MIND YOUR HEAD IN THE VAN

If there was an injury typical of the camper van owner it is banging the head on the door-frame (getting into the van), and on a cupboard (when standing up too quickly or bending down to pick something up). Also at risk are those who forget where they are in the morning and get out of bed too quickly.

I'm not your mother but would like to let you know that head injuries can be serious. So, if you have hit your head hard and are knocked unconscious at all, seek medical help.

Concussion

Concussion can occur if the head is shaken at any point. After a period of unconsciousness (usually less than 3 minutes), perhaps with vomiting after, signs of response improve and you should recover.

Compression

Compression is very dangerous and occurs when the brain is placed under extreme pressure, caused by bleeding or swelling. Response worsens over time, even though recovery, at first, may seem to be normal. Seek help.

TRIPS, SLIPS AND FALLS

The one thing I guarantee you will do on your next camping trip is to fall over a guy rope. Annoying though it is, it's your fault. Keep your eyes open. Better still, use hi-vis guy ropes that you can actually see, even in the semi-darkness of twilight when your guard is down. For goodness' sake kids, stop running around the awning!

CARBON MONOXIDE

This is no joke. Carbon monoxide is the silent killer. And it is a killer that visits some campsite or other every year. The reason is that people burn barbecues in their tents or awnings or keep the gas on in the van (to keep warm) without any ventilation.

There are rules about this: DO NOT EVER, UNDER ANY CIRCUMSTANCES, light a barbecue in a tent. This includes awnings or tent porches. It also includes BBQs that have been used and are still smouldering. They still give off carbon monoxide. No excuses.

If you cook in your van, make sure there is always plenty of ventilation.

Warning!

Install a carbon monoxide alarm in your van TODAY. Service all your equipment (fridge, cooker) regularly.

FIRE WHILE COOKING

Fire is a genuine risk in camp as we tend to be a little freer about it than at other times. So here are a few pointers for fire safety:

- Have you got a fire extinguisher in your camper? Get one.
- Also consider a fire blanket, which can be very useful for smothering cooking fires.
- If cooking over open fires or BBQs, do it where there is no risk of grass or scrub catching light. Only light a fire or BBQ with permission from the campsite owner.
- Cook well away from any awnings or tents.
- If you want to use candles, consider tea lights inside jam jars. If they fall over there is much less risk of fire spreading. Don't light candles inside tents or vans. Better still, use fairy lights.
- Avoid cooking with lots of hot fats.
- Extinguish any fire before you go to sleep. Never leave a fire smouldering.
- If you must have a fire, do it where it can be contained, for example, in a fire pit surrounded by stones, in a man-made fire pit such as an old wheel or washing machine drum that is off the ground, or on sand.
- Have a fire bucket full of water handy whenever you light a fire or BBQ.
- Don't use disposable BBQs as they are wasteful and encourage littering.
- Don't leave your fire unattended at any time.
- All campsites should have fire points. Find out where they are.
- Don't pitch your tent or awning closer than 6m from the nearest neighbour.

BITES AND STINGS

I've forgotten the number of times camping trips with my family have been ruined by bites from insects. One of my earliest memories of camping is of my mum going to A&E in Devon with a lump on her arm the size of a tennis ball. She had been bitten by a horse fly. I'm not immune to the odd bite but I'm not going to make a song and dance about it like my dear old mum did (I think she would have preferred to stay in a hotel).

It's going to happen so make sure you are prepared: carry insect repellent, Anthisan cream and antihistamine in your first aid kit.

CAMPING ON OR NEAR WATER

Water of all types – pools, lakes, rivers and the sea – are potentially lethal to all of us. But they are more dangerous to small children than anyone, so it's vital to watch them at all times if you are near water. If you're very close to the water it might not be a bad idea to insist they wear a life jacket while playing around in it. At the very least, make sure they can swim!

Warning!

If you or anyone has a near-drowning incident and has taken in water or has been resuscitated, seek medical attention, even though they may seem okay. Secondary drowning – when a person has water on the lungs – can occur hours later.

On the river or lake

- Only swim if you know it is safe.
- Don't swim near fast flowing water or overhanging trees/branches.
- Don't jump into water unless you know how deep it is.

At the beach

- Only swim on lifeguarded beaches.
- Only swim between the red and yellow flags where the lifeguards can see you.
- Don't swim when the beach is red flagged as it means it's unsafe.
- If you get caught in a current, swim at 90 degrees to it, then swim in. Don't try to swim against it.

KEEPING YOUR SPOT

In **previous sections** I have talked about awnings and sunshades and pup tents as a means of storing gear you don't need in the van while you tour around enjoying all kinds of camper van capers. Well, in case you hadn't noticed, they also provide a secondary, but much more useful purpose, and it's a purpose that addresses the perennial problem of campervanners. And that is marking the territory and hanging onto it.

374 (Repeat)

When you put up an awning, that is when your territory is clearly defined. It's the same with the pup tent. But it's less clear if you carry everything with you and all you have to say 'This is our spot!' is a windbreak or a chair and table. It's a tricky one. If you don't feel that you can leave your gear lying about while you pootle off to the beach (for security reasons) then there is a bigger problem. How do you keep your spot?

There's nothing more annoying than returning from a day out to find that someone has stolen 'your' spot or has pitched too close (remember: the recommended minimum distance is 6m) to your van or tent. It happens and it's extremely inconsiderate, but what can you do about it? What's the 'answer'?

Bugger orf, I'm HERE now

The answer of course, for campervanners, is simple. Get a duplicate of your number plate, affix it to a metal spike or tent peg and bash it into the ground where you park. Then, when you go out for the day, other motorhomers and campers will know you're already there.

This is not a joke. Some people do this. It sounds like a fine idea but it does seem a bit like towels on the loungers or windbreaks on the beach, doesn't it? You can if you want but, well, whatever. If we catch you at it you might just find us in your spot when you get back. 'Cos it's our spot now.

The secret to keeping your space? Don't go out, or live with the consequences.

SACRED SPOTS worth hanging onto

There used to be a campsite in a field at the southern end of Hell's Mouth beach in North Wales. The location was perfect but the facilities – one stinking, broken loo in a tumbledown shack and a fresh water tap – left a lot to be desired. It was basic and cheap but somehow perfect. On a low cliff overlooking one of the area's best surf breaks, it provided a base for surfers riding the waves of this famous spot. We'd leave a few quid on the window sill of the farmhouse as we passed and pitched our tent as we wished.

The only problem with the field was that it had no shelter, so when the wind blew you really knew about it; even in August a fresh south-west wind could tear apart the camp and keep us awake with flapping canvas and lashing rain.

It must have been howling the night we decided to pitch in the dunes, because we left the car on the campsite and trekked some way across the stream. There would be no other reason for leaving the flat, clean grass of the field other than to escape the wind. We went off to the pub, came back and went to bed. I was woken at first light by wet canvas across my face, my duvet drenched and the dome tent billowing like a sheet in a storm. The flysheet had worked loose (probably something to do with the pegs being in sand) and was flapping madly, while the inner tent, which wasn't waterproof, was leaking water all over me. This was because the wind had changed and was now blowing straight down a gully between the dunes. With the funnel effect making things worse, we were being battered. The gusts were so strong that they were blowing

the tent almost flat on my side, creating a bulge above Nick. He slept on, snoring quietly in his drink induced stupor.

Unable to sleep any more, I got up, wrapped myself in the damp duvet and trudged off down the beach to the car. When I got there I found that there were other campers on the field. They had arrived while we were at the pub. It was a family of four: parents and two children. Dad and son wore khaki shorts with long socks and tank tops while mum and daughter wore pretty flowered dresses under their cotton storm smocks. They made a startling sight, more like a company of cheery Nazi Youth than campers making light of a storm in North Wales in 1987. They were up and about, making breakfast, hanging out their washing and getting ready for the day ahead. The fact that it was five in the morning was odd enough, but what was more disturbing was the way their tent, a heavy-duty A-frame in grey canvas, barely moved, let alone flapped. Dad's Brylcreemed hair remained staunchly parted.

If they were surprised to see me appearing from down the beach wrapped in a duvet they didn't show it, and carried on about their business as I clambered into the back seat of the car and attempted to go to sleep again. They were clearly better at this camping lark than we were and had had an awful lot more sleep than I had.

The last thing I remember before nodding off was the dad banging a large wooden peg into the ground in front of their Ford Transit van with a wooden mallet. Nailed to it was a copy of their number plate. I could only assume that this was to show the other campers (me) that this was where they parked and that other cars should not park on that space. Later that day, when they had gone off to buy groceries, we moved my car right in front of it. You know, just because.

Ours was the only car on the campsite.

WHAT does a CAMPER mean TO YOU?

'We bought our first VW camper, a 1967 Canterbury Pitt, to travel overland to India via Iran and Afghanistan and back in 1976. We covered 30,000 trouble-free miles on some of the worst 'roads' imaginable, yet only had one puncture! Though we had to sell her on returning to the UK, in 1978 we bought a 1966 Devon camper from a family; the family's children cried as we drove off in her.

There's something special about an old Split bus. Partly the classic looks and the smiley face, partly the simplicity of the design meaning you can fix most things yourself. Yet there comes a time in life when something more comfortable, luxurious and economical beckons and so in 2012, after 34 years of adventures, we sold our Split Screen and bought a brand new VW California. While it may lack the cuteness and nostalgic appeal of a Split, it suits our needs now, and it's always packed, ready to head off on a journey.

In the immortal words of Mr Toad: 'Here today, up and off somewhere else tomorrow. Travel, change, interest, excitement! The whole world before you, and a horizon that's always changing!''

David Eccles
EDITOR OF VW CAMPER AND COMMERCIAL *MAGAZINE*

377

(Repeat)

KEEPING COMFY AND WARM

Stay WARM, stay HAPPY: get the RIGHT GEAR

(Repeat)

As a surfer I have known cold. Bitter cold. I have surfed in the snow and hail, brushed frost off my wetsuit and woken with more ice on the inside of my camper van than on the outside. I have driven my camper in a sleeping bag (feet poking out) with thick motorcycling gloves on. So I know what it feels like to have chattering teeth, frozen toes and dripping nose. I know the misery that cold can bring, despite wearing all the clothes you brought.

Apart from the fact that it can be dangerous to allow yourself to get cold, it's just not any fun to be cold on a camping trip. However, with the right gear, a cosy space to return to and the promise of a hot cuppa, it can be an awful lot of fun camping out in the cold.

I'm not your mother but one of the wisdoms that comes with being over 30 is the knowledge that buying once and buying well is the secret to a happy – and clutter-free – life. And all the more so when it comes to wet and cold weather gear. It's the same for sleeping bags, as I have explained earlier.

BUY GOOD SOCKS

Decent socks are hard to come by these days; it's all nylon and cotton blend rubbish. But if you want to stay happy in the cold, your socks are the single most important piece of camping gear (almost, IMHO). Once cold hits your feet it's all over, so don't scrimp on the socks. Keep fibres natural and consider the extra expense of merino, alpaca or good old fashioned wool.

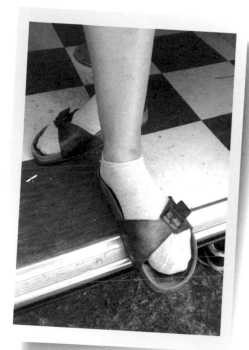

Merino is antibacterial (so you can wear it every day for a few days and not stink up the place), it actually heats up when wet (so even if your feet get wet they won't get cold) and it is soft. Merino also wicks water away from the body when you sweat, so you won't stay wet. Likewise alpaca and wool.

Oh, and wool is harder wearing, so it will last longer than rubbish cheap socks – so enabling you to justify a higher initial price tag. It's also sustainable, natural and non-polluting. And if you leave them in the woods by accident they'll biodegrade down to nothing... just like that. Can your nylon socks do that? Nope.

www.finisterreuk.com
www.jarbon.com

BUY DECENT BOOTS

Again, don't scrimp on the footwear, for reasons outlined above. Decent boots will pay you back many times over when compared with cheap shoes, trainers or sneakers. As someone who has stood around a lot on very cold days I can tell you this in confidence. Gore-Tex will breathe but won't stay waterproof forever, whereas leather, when treated properly

with old fashioned stuff like dubbin (grease used for softening and weatherproofing leather), will continue to stay waterproof and supple for years to come.

I wear Brashers because I think they are good. And I don't even mind mentioning them, even though I haven't ever had a pair for free. Maybe there's still time.

GET A GOOD WATERPROOF COAT

I like waterproofs but I don't like it when they sweat or when they weigh a ton. So, again the message is to invest in Gore-Tex or Vapour -Tex or Tex-h2o or hydrophobic, or whatever the latest breathable

waterproofing is called. You'll feel the benefit. Kagoules are awful unless they are breathable, and wax jackets eventually lose their waterproofing and have to be rewaxed, which is tedious.

INVEST IN LONG JOHNS

Oh yes. Sexy they may be. Long johns will make a cool night warm. Surprisingly effective, a good pair of leggings or long johns (preferably Merino) can make a massive difference to any camping trip. Can even be worn under a pair of shorts if you get caught out being optimistic.

For cool nights go for cotton. For cold nights, it has to be Merino or silk.

LAYER UP

Do I have to give you this lecture? Layering enables you to regulate better as you can take layers off when you get too hot and put them on again as you cool off. There is a lot to be said for a super-warm Arran or Fairisle sweater, but it's either boiling hot on or freezing cold without. Layering gives you control.

GO LIGHTWEIGHT BUT WARM

I have a jacket that weighs practically nothing but keeps me really warm in all but the coldest weather. It's not waterproof but I have an outer shell for that. This coat also packs down really small, is super light and makes a really cosy pillow. It's the ultimate two-in-one camping coat. Okay, so it's yellow. I don't mind that.

FINALLY, LOOK AFTER YOUR KIT...

...and it will look after you.

On-board HEATING

Whatever camper you own, there will come a time when your life would benefit from a little ambient warmth. It could be because you want to head north or just because you want to camp outside the summer season. Either way, this is the time to think about on-board heating.

We're not talking about your engine heater here. On-board heating, though costly, is one investment worth making. It extends the camping season – at the very least – and will make the whole thing a lot more civilised and fun. As I have said before, there's nothing worse than being cold on a camping trip. And there's really no need to be.

If you are retro-fitting a heater into an existing camper van, the most popular choice would be either an LPG Propex or petrol/diesel Webasto or Eberspächer unit. Petrol or diesel powered heaters draw fuel from the vehicle's fuel tank, so the heater's fuel supply is topped up with

WHAT does a CAMPER mean TO YOU?

'From the moment I was handed the keys for the 1974 Type 2 VW camper van, I felt like the queen of the road. Winning Visit England's 'Fan in a Van' competition and being given the opportunity to explore our green and pleasant land in such an iconic vehicle was a dream come true. I've admired campers for as long as I can remember! 'Rosie' was particularly striking, as she'd been given a vinyl wrap featuring images of famous English landmarks. We attracted attention everywhere we went and it was a pleasure to raise so many smiles on our epic 5000m journey. Spending 70 consecutive nights sleeping in the camper van was not without its challenges (especially as it was the wettest summer on record for 100 years!) but it was an experience I'll never forget and I would do it all again in a heartbeat.'

Rachel Kershaw *TOURED ENGLAND IN A VINTAGE CAMPER VAN CALLED ROSIE AS SHE FOLLOWED THE OLYMPIC TORCH IN 2012 FOR THE NATIONAL TOURIST BOARD*

383

(Rspool)

every visit to the filling station. Although more expensive, running costs are lower and fuel is more readily available. These heaters can also be thermostatically controlled and typically use around 0.1l of fuel per hour, making them suitable for all-night running.

DO NOT use the burners on a gas stove to keep warm. Prolonged use of a stove inside a closed camper van will gradually reduce the oxygen content of the air and then start to produce carbon monoxide, risking suffocation and carbon monoxide poisoning. Always carry a carbon monoxide alarm.

PROPEX HEATERS

These are the easiest way to heat a camper and use a similar system to many other heaters. They are gas powered and create heat by combusting the gas in a closed combustion unit. Clean outside air is heated via heat exchangers inside the unit and then blown into the cab of the van. Propex heaters can be controlled via a basic thermostat, which regulates the temperature and then cuts in when it drops. They are extremely effective when they work properly, but can be temperamental.

WHAT does a CAMPER mean TO YOU?

'VW camper vans have been part of our family and a passion of ours since we bought our first, a 1977 Westfalia, in 2001. We got engaged in him two years later in the West Highlands of Scotland, before he was our wedding transport the following year.

We currently own 'Chester', a Split-Screen 1963 13 window deluxe, and use him at every possible opportunity, be that a holiday in the UK or Europe, a weekend with friends, or popping to town for the shopping. We've also shown him in the local Steam & Vintage show where he's gone down very well.

We love that the adventure starts the moment the key turns, that we're never in a rush to get anywhere, the smiles and waves we get wherever we go, and even the hours spent in the garage keeping him tip-top and making him our own. In short, VW buses make us smile, and ours are very much part of the family!'

Will and Petra Rayner (and Chester!)

Propex heaters will run off both propane and butane but it's worth remembering the following:

- If you intend to camp in weather below around 5°C then you'll need propane.
- Butane, while burning more efficiently, will not convert to a gas below −1°C, so there will be no pressure in your gas bottle and therefore no heat, as there'll be nothing to combust.
- Butane generally comes in blue bottles and is characterised by Camping Gaz (it's actually a mixture of the two gases). *See* page 172 for more information.
- Propane comes in red bottles and will work at temperatures as low as −45°C, which is why it's always been more popular for cooking and domestic heating.
- Most motorhomes will use propane, whereas the leisure camping market tends to rely on butane.

EBERSPÄCHER

This is another piece of kit that can be retro-fitted to your camper van. They are popular in more modern vehicles and tend to cost more than the Propex heaters. They work in the same way as Propex heaters, with closed combustion and inlet and exhaust ports outside the van. The only difference is that they take fuel directly from the fuel tank (about 0.1l overnight) so you don't have to worry about extra gas bottles or the type of gas you use. One thing to remember is to use it when you're not running on fumes, or you'll not go anywhere the next day.

BLOWN AIR

Similar in working to Propex heaters, blown air heating systems are often the first choice of motorhome manufacturers. Same principles apply here except they work off gas and electricity, so are useful on sites with hook-up. Gas, though, remains more efficient than electricity. So set the thermostat, get into your long johns and relax...

TRUMA CONVECTION

These are gas powered heaters and are similar to blown air heaters. They are popular with many caravanners and can even come with a gas fire effect. Get you, with your home comforts! These will require a flue to be operated safely.

WEBASTO DUAL HEATER/COOLANT

These are heaters that heat up the engine to aid cold starting, but that can also provide heat into the cab through the standard heating ducts. They are popular with lorry drivers but can be used in motorhomes to clear windscreens and provide instant heat in cold climates.

WOOD BURNER

For large home conversions, a wood burner can be a good alternative. It's also got a lot more personality! But it does come with problems, such as needing to make sure everything around it is heatproof, and that you have a decent fireproof hearth and a two-part flue to keep the heat away from the roof. You'll also need adequate ventilation and a carbon monoxide alarm. But oh those flames!!! Cosy.

Water STORAGE in cold weather

However you store your water, in an on-board tank or in jerry cans, it makes sense to think about camping in freezing weather – and prevent any damage.

Most motorhomes and larger van based campers have water systems and tanks that are underslung and not part of the inside of the van. Therefore they can be at risk of freezing, with the added risk of cracking due to expanding ice, just as might happen in freezing weather at home.

Motorhome manufacturers can insulate underslung grey and clean water tanks to reduce the risk of freezing and also add heating elements to the tanks to keep the water above freezing. If you are planning on camping in extreme weather, this is something to seriously consider when you buy your motorhome. For camper vans without on-board tanks it's a simpler solution – keep your water inside the van.

386

KEEPING OUR ENVIRONMENT ON REPEAT

If there was one message I'd like you to take out of this book it is this: leave it better. What I mean by this is that we should leave anywhere we stay – a campsite, wild spot, wherever – nicer that it was when we arrived. This can work on many levels but on a basic one it means making sure your spot is immaculate when you depart.

Get over yourself – PICK UP litter

I don't really care if it isn't your litter, just pick it up. It really won't kill you and you'll feel great for doing your bit. If it's on your patch you should pick it up and dispose of it properly, irrespective of the source. God forbid I ever catch you leaving it (and I know you wouldn't)! If you leave somewhere and there is a mess (even if it isn't yours) we will all get the blame for it. And the consequences of that are that there will be fewer and fewer places where we are welcome. Height barriers will go up, rocks will appear on laybys and the dreaded 'No camper vans' signs will breed like rabbits.

I don't mind orange peel and banana skins as they biodegrade, but plastics are absolutely, definitely out of order. Plastics don't biodegrade and will eventually end up in rivers, watercourses, storm drains and sewers, where they will enter the sea, become toxic and kill. There is no nice way of putting it. Plastics, especially single-use plastics, are a terrible symptom of the selfish and wasteful way in which we live.

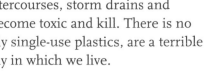

Do your body a favour: forget SINGLE-USE plastics

Everything comes in plastic these days. Salad, bananas, cucumbers, water, hummus, potato salad. It's frankly ridiculous the amount of packaging that our supermarkets and food stores force on us. Even when we don't need it. It's almost as if bananas, cucumbers and apples didn't have a protective outer casing on them anyway.

When you think about it, it doesn't make any sense to use a piece of plastic to carry your food home and then discard it. Unless, of course, you consider your personal convenience to be more important that the environment. So if you can, please forget the single-use plastics. The problem with them is that they don't biodegrade, turn toxic in water and break down into microplastics that will, in time, hurt us all. So, take your tin mug into Costa, refill a water bottle instead of buying bottled (Europe's tap water is the best in the world), refuse plastic knives and forks, and only take on plastics that can be recycled (if at all). Do this and you'll be doing the shopping equivalent of leaving it better, because you'll create less waste and less demand for plastics. If we all did it, things would change.

Of course I know that it's not easy being green sometimes, but there are choices we can make in the way we buy our food that can have a positive effect on the places we visit, so helping to make them better too.

Hug a FARMER - buy LOCAL

Buying local makes so much sense. Why? Because you are putting your money directly into the local economy instead of into a supermarket that cares for nothing but profit. If you give your money to local shops you generally get local produce that hasn't been halfway around the world (and therefore has fewer food miles) and have a chance to enrich the entire local economy. You might also meet some nice people, too; people are nice in general, and it's great to meet them. You might also discover something unusual or very special when you buy local. And it's a darn sight better than a soulless supermarket experience.

EMBRACE the season, eat with the HARVEST

There is a green leafy cabbage-like plant called 'hunger gap'. It's a really tasty green and I love eating it when it's in season, which is during the 'hunger gap', between winter greens and spring vegetables. It's a wonderfully evocative and quite humbling vegetable, simply because it has a job to do and it does it well. It's available when nothing else is. You can buy it locally when it's just been picked so it'll be as good as any green.

It's the same throughout the year with other foods. If you can eat with the seasons then you'll save lots of carbon (the old footprint issue) and will eat food that is local, fresh and about as good as it gets. Okay so you might have to do without strawberries from Argentina or samphire from Tel Aviv. But who wants to eat stuff that's been on a ship or plane for thousands of miles anyway? (And yes, I know it's hard to do sometimes). Again, as I have already preached to you about it (soz), buying local enables you to positively benefit the economy of where you are staying. It's a simple as that.

How to be an AMATEUR ECO HERO in ten easy steps

You might think you can't make a difference but you can. Voting with your feet, inspiring others and rolling up your sleeves is the most effective way of making change – for the better – happen. And if you just don't care, well, whatevs.

Anyone who camps cannot fail to be an environmentalist too, by default. Why destroy the thing that you camp to enjoy? It doesn't make sense.

1. Refuse single-use plastics.
2. Take your own bag shopping.
3. Don't damage the environment in which you camp.
4. Pick up and dispose of all litter, even that which isn't yours.
5. Eat locally as much as possible.
6. Eat seasonally as much as possible.
7. Recycle EVERYTHING. If it can't be recycled, refuse it.
8. Reuse water bottles or packaging.
9. Buy staples in bulk to save packaging and decant as you need it.
10. Choose clothes that are natural fabrics, well made and will last more than 5 minutes. Buy once, buy well.

Thanks for listening.

KEEP THE MOTOR RUNNING

This isn't a book about motor vehicle maintenance. Don't worry. However, we are concerned with keeping the motor running, whatever vehicle it is you drive. And that means doing a few checks and top-ups to keep it going.

Sometimes you're not going to be able to do anything about breakdowns and blips because things happen that you have no control over. But you can do a few things to minimise the chances. The more you keep up your maintenance routine, the more chance you've got of keeping that motor running, even on an old banger.

391

Choose your VAN for the MECHANIC you are

392 (Repeat)

The most sensible advice I can give you, after more than 20 years of owning classic campers, funny vehicles and quirky rides, is to choose your ride according to the mechanic you are, or the budget you think you'll need to keep it on the road. Over the years I have spent thousands on repairs and services. If you don't mind that or don't mind fettling and fiddling with your camper on a weekend then go for it. Otherwise, think hard about what you're going for.

So if you can't check your points, change the oil and set your tappets (I can't), owning a classic camper may not be for you, no matter how cool it may make you appear. Old campers have shorter service intervals and need more coaxing than modern campers. And that means big bills or lots of oil on your hands.

ESSENTIAL vehicle CHECKS: AAA (another annoying acronym)

Everyone loves an acronym don't they? Well, not really. The acronym, useful as it may be in some circumstances, is the realm of the middle manager as far as I am concerned. And that isn't always a nice place to be. One minute you're whooshing up the M40 in your Sierra, the next minute you're hosting an important meeting at a Costa Coffee on the M42, spouting off acronyms like billy-o. And you're the only one who really understands them, which inevitably leads to someone shouting 'Bingo!' halfway through your presentation when you mention paradigm shifts, innovation or lean manufacturing. That's not good.

But anyway, I am digressing. From time to time I come across an acronym that I actually think might be useful. I call these BUMS (brilliantly useful mnemonics) and one of them is POWER, or POWDER or even POWDERY. It's an acronym that's been used a lot to describe the checks to make to your vehicle each time you get in it.

So, in the name of safety, here it is. Consult your vehicle manual for more detail.

393

(Repeat)

ℙ IS FOR PETROL

Is there enough in it to get you where you are going? Is it the right type? Are you running diesel, petrol, bioethanol or LPG? Start off on the right foot and get this spot on, because if you don't, not much is going to happen afterwards.

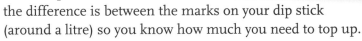

◎ IS FOR OIL

Check it. Check it again. And keep checking it, especially if you run an old machine that is more likely to spring leaks or burn it up fast. Find out what the difference is between the marks on your dip stick (around a litre) so you know how much you need to top up.

OIL also stands for your reservoirs, which may or may not include brake and clutch fluid, gearbox oil and power steering.

𝕎 IS FOR WATER

Simple enough, this. Check your reservoirs of water, if you are water cooled. These include your radiator/coolant, your windscreen washers and battery levels.

𝔻 IS FOR DAMAGE

Check the vehicle for damage to mirrors, lights and tyres. This isn't just cosmetic damage that may not affect the way your vehicle drives, but damage that will affect your safety.

𝔼 IS FOR ELECTRICS

Again this is important. Check your lights are working, that indicators are functioning properly and that your horn toots okay. Incidentally, I once owned a VW Beetle that had a horn that would go off unexpectedly on right-hand

bends. Most of the time it was fine but from time to time I had to
wave at imaginary people when the car tooted all by itself. Awkward.

R IS FOR RUBBER

This means checking your tyres are legal and have enough tread to be
safe. You should also check the wear pattern, as it may be an indication
of damage to your tracking or suspension if your tyres are wearing on
one side and not the other.

Y IS FOR YOURSELF

This is the final check and it's one you shouldn't really have to make.
You should know if you are fit to drive but it's worth remembering
anyway. Do you need glasses to read maps or drive in at night? Are
you healthy enough to drive? If you were out the night before, have
you left enough time to be within the legal limit for drink driving?
Are you taking any medication that may affect your ability to drive?

And now, if only I could think of something funny that included
the word POWDERY, I could finish off this section with an amusing
flourish. But no, it's not coming. Better, then, to end with an important
message. Check it. Check it again. Then check it again.

Drive safe. We need you for the next chapter.

Keeping it NEAT

Whatever kind of camper you drive, you'll want to keep it on the road for as long as possible. So in addition to the checks and regular servicing, there are a couple of extra bits of love and attention that you should be thinking of lavishing on your van, especially when winter comes around.

* **Avoid road salt.** It is extremely damaging to old vehicles that don't have the kind of rust protection most modern cars enjoy. So don't drive when it's been put down. If you have to, wash off the underside of the van with fresh water when you get home.
* **Get the underside** of the van protected with Waxoyl. Waxoyl is a layer that will protect the van from water ingress and therefore corrosion. Clean off the underneath of the van with a wire brush and then apply.
* **Get some mudguards fitted.** This will stop mud, stones and road salt from damaging paintwork, and therefore limit corrosion.
* **Keep the van clean** by cleaning off any dirt, bird droppings, tar or salt. Waxing will help to protect the paintwork even further.

396 (Re-loaded)

Bus BOOT camp

What if you could find someone who could show you how to avoid breaking down? What if there was a course that could show you the five most common problems affecting old campers and how you can get them fixed without calling for back up?

What if you could be more than just a tyre kicker?

Well, the good news is that it isn't that difficult. There are various organisations that run specialist courses on old vehicles, with a particular emphasis on Volkswagens. And if you don't own a Volkswagen then there's still no excuse for spending a fortune on garage bills. Most local colleges run evening courses on basic car and vehicle maintenance so that you can diagnose and repair basic problems, and perhaps even undertake basic servicing.

And if you want to learn how to tune your engine, how to set your points and even – God forbid – you wanted to learn how to drop the engine, they will show you how. No bother.

www.busbootcamp.com is run by Type 2 Detectives. Courses at the time of press cost £190 per day.

www.hotcourses.com is an online directory of evening courses of all types, including car maintenance.

WHAT does a CAMPER mean TO YOU?

'Well, we're complete novices. My old 1998 Nissan Almera began to fall apart last summer and I was looking around for a hatch with a good boot for our two lurchers. After a week visiting friends in north Wales (one with an old VW – Beryl – and another with a T5) we came off the ferry in Dublin and drove straight to County Louth to look at a 2005 T5. A few days later it was ours!

It started life as a panel van and was converted to a camper by a joiner who used it when cycling and travelling in Europe. He'd sprayed it Raven Blue, which, when clean and not covered in muck from the West Cork roads, looks stunning. I love driving it, peering over hedges into fields and gardens, and feeling like every day is a holiday! And it's got loads of room for the dogs in the back.

We've just had spots inserted into the bumper and are planning a few other things. We still haven't replaced the BMW badges on the wheels with VW ones or decided on curtain fabric. But we did get a shiny new blue whistling kettle to celebrate our first camper picnic. No overnights yet but we have had lunch out in various places in Cork, which is great as long as I remember to pack the mugs for drinks!'

Anne Harrington Rees, Cork

397

(Repeat)

DRIVING

DRIVING safety

I've been a naughty boy. I went too fast while driving home from work one day. I got flashed by one of those speed camera traps. A few weeks later I received an offer in the post to attend a driving course or have a whole bunch of points put on my otherwise clean driving licence. Let it be known that this would have never happened had I been driving the bus, simply because I don't drive that fast in the van. And, yes, it could if it wanted to. It was only a 30 zone.

Anyway, I went on the driving course and learned a lot of stuff. Afterwards I contacted the company running the course to ask if they would help out with this project, seeing as I was newly enlightened and all that.

Did they help me out? No. They put the phone down.

Oh well. Blame them.

398 (Repeat)

ONLY A FOOL FORGETS...

The 2-second rule is a great one to teach the kids if you are one of those rear-enders and tailgaters who spends too much time too close to the car in front. It's pretty easy. All you have to do is find a mark at the side of the road and start counting as the car in front goes past it. Count in seconds – 'one-and-two-and' – the time it takes for you to reach the same mark. If you get there before the 2 seconds are up, you are too close to the car in front. If the weather or visibility is bad, double it for extra caution. Simple.

The 2-second rule provides a distance of one car length per 5mph, no matter what speed you drive. The faster you go, the bigger the distance, so allowing you enough time and space to be able to stop if something happens to the car in front.

Using the 2-second rule can help to reduce accidents or reduce damage if a collision happens. It can also help to save fuel and will reduce brake wear. The chevrons on the road work in much the same way when you see them on the motorway.

DEFENSIVE DRIVING

Following the 2-second rule can also help to ease congestion in busy traffic, particularly those infuriating stop-start motorway journeys. By keeping a safe distance between you and the car in front you can have a significant knock-on effect on traffic and keep moving. How so?

When motorways are busy and slow, little things can bring traffic to a standstill: someone braking, someone changing lanes, a lorry going slowly. People react naturally to brake lights by braking themselves, so starting off a chain reaction behind them. In really slow traffic this will bring a line of cars to a standstill.

By keeping a safe distance between your van and the car in front you can slow down gradually and keep moving, albeit slowly. If you can crawl rather than braking and stopping then the traffic behind you should be able to keep moving too. If you time it right you will reach the queue after they have started up again so you can continue slowly without braking, and therefore without starting up that chain reaction of panic braking behind you.

Try it. You'll be surprised what kind of an effect your driving can have on the rest of the traffic behind you; even if it does nothing for the traffic itself it's better to keep moving than not move at all.

MAP READING: Getting there... and back

It's so very tempting to buy a sat nav. It really is. But, and it's a big but, sat navs will get you lost. They really will. And even if they don't get you lost, you'll have no idea where you are when you get there anyway. Sat navs are very clever and all that but they don't always give you context to where they send you. Okay... I will admit they can sometimes be useful if you were delivering a lot of parcels and didn't have an awful lot of time. However, in the days before sat nav plenty of parcels got delivered to the right place every day without electronic aids. We knew how to read a map.

A sat nav will tell you (in any number of hilarious voices) to turn left or right or whatever. It will show you where you are to the nearest foot or so but it won't always show you where you are in a local context, unless you work it a little bit harder. You'll need to zoom out and study the wider area. No one does that. All they do is blindly follow the directions down some dead end, footpath or industrial estate without knowing, really, where they are going. What then? Worst case scenario sees you

wedged between two cottages in a tiny village in Wiltshire, best case sees you driving around in circles or stopping to ask for directions because you really have no idea where in the hell your sat nav has brought you.

WHY I LOVE MAPS

Maps show you more than a sat nav ever could. They are the neatest, tidiest way of describing your surroundings in two dimensions. They show gradients, heights, footpaths and bridleways, monuments and more details than your sat nav ever could. You can tell everything you need to know just by glancing at a map. Or you can tell exactly where you are by looking around you and then looking for those features on your map. Information gleaned from maps stays with you, whereas the last yard of your latest sat nav journey is forgotten as fast as you drove over it. That means you build up a picture of where you are, what it looks like and how to get from A to B and back again without a machine. You begin to acquire knowledge instead of relying on a machine that will, eventually, stop working (because that's what machines do).

What will you do then, if you can't read a map?

Your driving LICENSE

Can you legally drive it? It all depends on your age and the size of the vehicle. This is particularly important for larger coach-built motorhomes, as some can exceed 3500kg. Most camper vans (apart from those built from commercial vehicles) will come under the 3500kg weight limit. But always check.

Category B vehicles

These are vehicles up to 3500kg with up to eight passenger seats. Anyone with a full driving licence of any age can drive these vehicles. They can also be driven with a trailer up to 750kg or with a heavier trailer if the weight isn't over 3500kg combined.

Medium sized Category C1 vehicles

These are medium sized vehicles between 3500 and 7500kg with a trailer up to 750kg. If you have a driving licence that was issued after 1 January 1997 you will need to pass a C1 test to drive this size of vehicle.

Category C1+E vehicles

You can drive a vehicle over 3500kg with a trailer over 750kg. If you passed your test before 1 January 1997 you are entitled to drive a vehicle and trailer combination up to 8.25 tonnes MAM (maximum authorised mass, the maximum weight of the vehicle plus load that can be carried safely on the road).

HOW FAST can you go?

Motorhomes and motor caravans are allowed to travel at the same speeds as cars on UK roads. Obviously it doesn't mean your vehicle is capable of going at that speed or that you should. But, if it were possible, this would be it.

Maximum speeds on UK roads *(allowing for driving conditions, special circumstances, etc.)*	
Built-up areas	30mph
Single carriageways	60mph
Dual carriageways	70mph
If a motorhome or motor caravan is towing then the upper limit on dual carriageways is 60mph.	

Motorhomes are considered to be commercial vehicles if they carry goods or are used for storage and therefore are limited to the same restrictions as good vehicles of similar weight.

Speed limits across Europe are similar and are mostly restricted to 50kph in built up areas, 80 or 90kph outside built-up areas and between 100 and 139kph on motorways.

STAYING ON FOR LONGER

We all dream of chucking it in and staying on, especially when Monday promises a return to the same old grind. And why not? The further you are from the job and the mortgage, the better as far as I am concerned – especially if you can get wi-fi and a decent enough pint without making too much of an effort.

Preparing for LONG-TERM stays

It's one thing to turn up for the weekend, but staying on a campsite for more than just a few days requires a little extra planning. For a start you might need to take extra kit to set up home. That may require towing a trailer.

You might also wish to consider how you intend to get around once you have arrived at your destination. It might seem obvious but if you stay somewhere for a long period of time it is reasonable to assume that you might want or need to drive your camper van while you

are there. So unless you are in wash one, wear one mode and have hardly anything with you, you're going to have to pack it all up each time you go out. Unless you are prepared.

FIND A CAMPSITE THAT'S PERFECT

Location is everything when it comes to campsites. This is particularly true of campsites that you intend to stay on for a while. I like to surf, so I like to stay on sites where I can either walk or cycle to the surf in the morning without having to disturb everyone and make them make the beds and ship out for the day. It's the same for going out in the evening. I don't want to drive in the evening (probably because I'd quite like a glass of wine with my dinner), so finding somewhere that's either got everything or that has restaurants, shops and bars nearby (or at least within cycling distance) is equally important.

SET UP A DRIVE-AWAY AWNING OR PUP TENT

Awnings are attached to either the sliding door or, in the case of vans without sliding doors, to rear doors. We have already talked about awnings. But they come in particularly useful when you are staying on a site for more than a couple of days. They provide an extra room so that you can use the van without having to pack up each day. They are perfect for unloading and stashing stuff you don't need and creating more space for eating or sleeping in small vans.

Pup tents, similarly are useful for storing equipment you don't need every day – clothes and cooking equipment, for example – so you can be more mobile.

405

(Repeat)

TAKE ALTERNATIVE TRANSPORT

If you're setting up for a long stay it can be a real pain in the neck to move a van once you are parked up with electricity plugged in and everything in night mode. So taking alternative transport to get supplies – a bike, skateboard or even a scooter – can be a boon. Besides, it's nice to enjoy a bit of life away from the cockpit of a van.

Some motorhome owners opt to tow cars – Smart cars, for example – in order to be more mobile when parked up at a campsite.

CARRYING BIKES

Pretty straightforward, this. We talked about it elsewhere. However, you could be breaking the law if your bikes are in the way of your lights and number plate, in which case you'll need a number plate board with working lights. That means having towing electrics.

Also, in some countries (Spain and Italy) you are required by law to have a red and white reflective square where your bikes overhang the back of the car. This is for safety. The same rules apply for motorcycles carried on racks at the back of your camper.

TOWING **more kit**

Okay, so there's no chance you're going to fit it all in. Better get a trailer.

Trailers come in all shapes and sizes, weights and legal limits, so it's important to get it right. If you are a VW owner your preferred trailer might well be a vintage Westfalia trailer or a cute teardrop trailer. Or even a Dub Box, a VW inspired caravan trailer. For some the look is all-important, but for others it's the space that matters. Either way, having more space separate from the van will give you much more flexibility and carrying capacity, and leave your mode of transport free for getting around. Never mind reversing in the supermarket car park.

WHAT CAN YOU TOW?

If you have a driving licence that was issued after 19 January 2013 and have passed a category B test (car and small vehicle), then you can tow a small trailer weighing no more than 750kg or a trailer over 750kg, as long as the combined weight of the trailer and vehicle is less than the MAM (*see* page 403). For towing heavier weights you need a further entitlement on your licence.

If you have a driving licence that was issued after 1 January 1997 and have passed a category B (car) licence, then you can drive a vehicle up to 3.5 tonnes towing a trailer up to 750kg MAM. You can also tow a trailer over 750kg as long as the combined weight of the trailer and vehicle is no more than 3500kg. For towing heavier weights you need a further entitlement on your licence.

If you passed your test before 1 January 1997 you are entitled to drive a vehicle and trailer combination up to 8.25 tonnes MAM.

Tow bars

Tow bars must be type approved for your vehicle, must be designed for the vehicle and meet EU regulations.

There is no need for type approval for cars first used before 1 August 1998. You must have an adequate view of the road behind you, therefore may require towing mirrors. If you tow without you may be prosecuted.

Trailer brake systems

Any trailer weighing over 750kg, including its load, must have a working brake system.

Number plates

You must display the number plate of the towing vehicle on the trailer. This should also include lights and indicators.

TOWING CARS ON A FRAMES AND DOLLIES

If you tow a car on an A frame (a rig that attaches to the car, keeping the four wheels on the ground) then it counts as a trailer, as does a dolly (a 'half trailer' that takes the front wheels of the tow car off the ground).

In the UK the Department for Transport has strict rules about towing vehicles. It regards A frames and dollies as trailers, which means they have to comply with trailer rules, as outlined above. These rules also.

state that if a trailer is fitted with a braking system, then the brake system must be operational. So your tow car's brakes must work in conjunction with your towing vehicles.

Dollies are mostly used for recovery but the law (in the UK) states that if a dolly is to be used for a functioning vehicle then it must have a braking system working on the wheels on the ground. There are also other rules that state the upper limits for speed using a dolly are 40mph on a motorway and 20mph on other roads.

For more detailed information on towing in Europe, we recommend seeking further information from motoring organisations in the country in which you are travelling. In the UK this would be the AA or the RAC. However, please be aware that towing cars on A frames may be interpreted by some police as being against the law, for which you may be liable for a fine.

POWER

Camping ELECTRICS: leisure batteries

Most campers will have some kind of camping electrics, running off a separate leisure battery. They are 'deep cycle' batteries and are different from your average car battery because they're designed to be regularly deeply discharged, using most of their capacity. They have to cope with a lifetime of being drained and then topped up instead of a burst (to start the engine) followed by constant topping up (from the alternator), as is the case for a car battery.

Leisure batteries are generally topped up via the split relay charger that delivers a topping up current when the engine is running, and by mains charging when plugged into a 240v hook-up, although not all campers have 240v chargers for their leisure electrics.

Different batteries have different ratings that are measured in AMP HOURS. This is the time the battery will run when drawing power measured in amps. If you have a 100AH battery and you run a lamp on it that draws 10 amps, the battery will last for 10 hours before it is fully discharged. However, it is never recommended to discharge a leisure battery more than 50 per cent, as they may not recover fully. Therefore, it's important to get one that will be able to cope with the demands you place on it.

HOW TO WORK OUT HOW MUCH POWER YOUR CAMPER DEMANDS

Every piece of electrical equipment in your camper will draw a certain amount of power, in amps. Times that by the number of hours you use it on average each day and add it all up together to get your power usage (say a TV draws 2 amps and you use it for 5 hours a day; it will draw 10ah). Add up all the appliances and the time you use them for and you will get some idea of the size of battery you might need (leisure batteries start at around 75ah to a whopping 170ah for more demanding motorhomes). However, since it is inadvisable to drain leisure batteries by more than 50%, double your average usage to get an approximation of your power needs.

It's also important to choose a leisure battery that will fit your battery compartment. And bear in mind that all batteries must now be properly secured for your UK MOT.

411
(Repeat)

Topping up with SOLAR

Solar panels will enable you to keep your leisure battery topped up when camping away from a campsite or if you are parked up and not running the engine for a few days.

Which solar panel to go for is a bit of a minefield (as I found out when I started looking into it). However, there are companies out there who can help you make the right decisions about which set up is right for you and your van. I sought the help of Colin from Select Solar, who very kindly gave me the benefit of his vast experience by passing on the following information.

In general you'll need to choose a solar panel that will produce the same amount of power that you use each day on an average trip. That way it will be powerful enough to top up your battery as you use up power the way you normally do. That depends on what kind of devices you have connected to your camping electrics. If you run an absorption fridge then it will require more power than a compressor fridge (for example), so you'll need more topping up power from your solar. Similarly, if all you ever do is charge your phone and use a few lights, something smaller – and much cheaper – will do.

TYPES OF PANEL

There are two main types of solar panel: amorphous and crystalline. In general, amorphous perform better than crystalline under low light conditions and don't suffer as much power loss in hot temperatures. However, in good conditions, the efficiency of amorphous panels is lower, and they are physically larger than crystalline panels of the same wattage.

CALCULATE YOUR SOLAR POWER NEEDS

You may already have worked out how much power you consume on a typical camping trip (*see* page 410), and therefore what size battery you may need. So all you need to do next is to choose a solar panel that can produce as much energy as you use.

The power generation rating of a solar panel is given in watts. In order to calculate the energy it can supply to the battery, multiply the number of watts by the hours exposed to sunshine, then multiply the result by 0.85 (this factor allows for natural system losses). So, in 4 hours a 10w panel will produce = 34wh of energy to the battery.

SIZE YOUR SYSTEM

The idea with a solar system is to balance the power going in with the power going out over a period of days or weeks. Here is a simple way to calculate the size of a system based on your power usage.

● **Find the wattage of your appliances:** If you can only find the figure in amps, multiply this by 12 to get the wattage.
● **Work out your daily watt-hour needs:** Work out how many hours you use an appliance per week, then divide by seven. Multiply each appliance's wattage by the hours you'll use it in a day. Add the totals together for your daily watt-hour usage.
● **Work out your panel size:** Divide the daily total watt-hours by the hours of useable light in an average day. In the UK you can expect 1 hour in winter, rising to 4 in summer.
● **What do you need?** Most motorhomes have panels 80w

Ready reckoner for solar panels from Select Solar				
VEHICLE?	Camper van, caravan and small motorhome, 110ah battery	Camper van, caravan and small motorhome, 110ah battery	Large motorhome, 200ah battery	Large motorhome, 200ah battery
WHEN?	Spring–Autumn	All year round	Spring–Autumn	All year round
60w	Lights, water pump, radio and TV for 2hrs/day	Lights, water pump, radio and CD	Lights, water pump, radio and CD	Lights, water pump, radio and CD
85w	Lights, water pump, radio, TV for 3hrs/day and 240v appliances	Lights, water pump, radio and TV for 2hrs/day	Lights, water pump, radio and TV for 2hrs/day	Lights, water pump, radio and CD
130w	Lights, water pump, radio, TV for 5hrs/day and 240V appliances	Lights, water pump, radio, TV for 3hrs/day and 240v appliances	Lights, water pump, radio, TV for 3hrs/day and 240v appliances	Lights, water pump, radio and TV for 2hrs/day

and above because of the typical gadgets that get used (fridges, phone chargers, radio, lighting, etc.). Bear in mind that laptops require at least 25w for a useful trickle charge.

● **Work out what space you have:** Panels come in various sizes, shapes and ratings, so it may be possible to fit two instead of one if the size was right.

DECIDING ON WHAT TO HAVE IN YOUR SYSTEM:

Bypass diodes
If part of a solar panel is in shadow, then output from the whole panel goes down, unless there are bypass diodes between the cells to isolate them.

Blocking diodes
These prevent power from going back into the panel from the battery at night. Larger panels tend not to have blocking diodes fitted, whereas the smaller portable panels generally do have them fitted. If you use a

charge controller you don't need a blocking diode, because the charge controller performs that function (among other things).

Charge controllers

The charge controller (or regulator) connects between the panel and the battery and protects the batteries from overcharging, while preventing power from the batteries from going back into the panel at night. It also helps to maintain battery condition by keeping the battery voltage high.

For more in-depth information about requirements, panels, fitting and a useful glossary of the terms used in solar power generation, please see **www.selectsolar.co.uk**

Cold weather
BATTERY PERFORMANCE

In cold weather the performance of a battery is reduced considerably (when you need it most), so it can help to have the leisure battery inside the van if you camp into winter. However, all lead acid and sealed-for-life gel batteries vent hydrogen as part of their normal working life so should always be in a separate compartment from the living space, and with a vent to allow hydrogen to escape.

Using a POWER INVERTER

Power inverters change direct current (DC) power from a battery into conventional mains alternating current (AC) power at 230v. This means that you can use one to operate all kinds of devices, such as your laptop, power tools or kitchen appliances.

The inverter draws its power from a 12v battery (preferably your deep-cycle camping battery). However, the battery will need to be recharged as the inverter draws the power out of it. You can do this by running the engine, with 10 minutes of running time per hour of inverter use being recommended. Most leisure batteries will provide an ample power supply for 30–60 minutes even when the engine is off, although actual time may vary depending on the age and condition of the battery, and the power demand being placed on it by the equipment the inverter is operating.

Again, see **www.selectsolar.co.uk** for more information.

THE OTHER LIFE

CAMPERS that DO other things...

Over the years the humble delivery van – whether Transit, Transporter, Comer, Citroën, Austin or any other make – has done many things. It's been courier, postman, fire truck, ambulance, mobile shop and a railway bus running on steel rails. Heck, it's even been white van man's daily ride, and a small and reliable workhorse that's built nations, kept economies on track, and brought goods and services to all corners of the world without fail. The van has, without a doubt, made us what we are.

Many new lives have begun between the metal sheets of our four wheeled friends. Those lives, begun in city traffic and country lanes rather than in the safety of a maternity ward, begin a little before time.

(Repeat)

But no matter, women have been giving birth for thousands of years. And who's to say breathing your first breath in the back of a van is a bad thing anyway?

Many of those born in transit (or transporter) will also have travelled to their nuptials nervously perched on the edge of a bench seat – a fitting start to any happy marriage, I would argue. A few, poignantly and tearfully, choose to make their final journeys recumbent between the axles of a much loved friend. We all make the same journey one day, so why not do it in camper van style?

But of course, let's not forget where life itself begins. There are equally as many – in fact I would argue, a whole lot more – who can attribute the first sparks of their existence to the rock and roll bed. It's one aspect of the camper van that cannot be ignored and should be fully embraced. What better start than love under the stars?

But, of course, this is not what concerns us here, now. What we're interested in is what campers get up to in their spare time, when they aren't driving dreams, sheltering from wind and rain or filling the air with the heavenly aromas of a top class curry. While it might seem like a double negative to talk about campers doing other things – because being a camper van is very much a secondary occupation for any van anyway – there are plenty of campers that are out there doing things other than their original purpose. In the same way that builder's vans all over the UK are now sleeping a new generation of camper van wanderers, so there are a lot of camper vans enjoying brilliant second lives beyond that of the mobile hotel. Being the cult vehicles they are, it is usually the VW Transporter that metamorphoses into something different. There are cocktail bars, mobile discos, vintage teashops, ice cream parlours and hearses, and each of them is guaranteed to bring a smile in times of need.

Camper van WEDDINGS

Any camper van is capable of taking a bride to her wedding day. That's a given. But there are a select few that are good enough for your little princess when she finally ties the knot. These are the best of the best, the fully restored, factory finished examples that would still turn a head or two in a field of classics. For brides looking for something unusual, quirky and very, very cool, the VW wedding delivers every time, on time. All you gotta do is say yes...
www.vintagevwweddings.co.uk

Camper van FUNERALS

Of course any camper van is capable of carrying somebody lying down. It's the way they were built. But it is extremely rare to find them converted to become hearses so that they can carry the eternally prostrate. The one owned by VW Funerals – they call it Hearseby – was a factory commissioned *leichenwagen* (hearse) and coach built by a firm called Fritz Freckinger in Augsburg, Germany, in 1972. It is one of very few still remaining in the world today and is unique in that it is the only one still in operation in the UK (if not the world). The company also owns a 1965 Split-Screen camper that has been professionally converted into a hearse called Ernie.

If it's your idea of a perfect send-off (and why wouldn't it be), make sure your relatives know in advance of your passing. **www.volkswagenfunerals.co.uk**

Hearseby is one of a kind. Converted in Germany by Fritz Frickinger to be a coroner's vehicle, he was bought by Clare Brookes at VW Funerals and converted into a hearse. Today Hearseby takes VW lovers in style on their final journeys. Clare, meanwhile, is one of the jolliest people I have met in a long time. I guess you'd have to be.

Camper van CAFÉS

Camper vans are good at serving food and beverages. They have been doing it for years anyway. One of the finest is the Camper Coffee Company, an outfit of travelling baristas who serve very fine coffee out of a lovely 1964 VW Split-Screen container van. They are one of many but a fine example among them. Campers can do anything. One lump or two? **www.campercoffee.co**

420 (Repeat)

↗ **Rosie is a very rare Splitscreen** VW container van from 1964. Restored and fitted with a state of the art coffee machine, she tours the south west in the company of Gary and Paul, who make people happy with some of the finest coffee known to man.

The World's Second Smallest ART GALLERY

In case you were wondering, the world's smallest art gallery is The Gallery on the Green in Settle, Yorkshire. It's an old red phone box, so easily qualifies and definitely beats any camper into second place.

With this in mind and knowing I could never take the title from this most teeny of establishments, I set up my old VW Type 2 as the World's Second Smallest Art Gallery at the World Belly Boarding Championships in St Agnes, Cornwall. The art contained within included images of previous competitions and a video show of belly boarding, the noble art of riding waves prone, like your grandparents did. We asked for voluntary donations of a minimum of 10p per visit and raised around £72 for the National Trust, although we are sure some gave more, as that would have meant that more than 700 people visited in just one day.

For once the camper became something entirely different from its usual job of reliable steed, home from home and bringer of good times for the four of us. It suited it well to make others happy, too. They came, two at a time, to sit inside and feel part of something timeless and pleasant. They smiled, too.

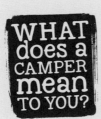

WHAT does a CAMPER mean TO YOU? 'Before we set off on a camper van road trip there is always a buzz of anticipation, not knowing what will occur when we travel to a new destination. 'Puffin' the camper van is our escape route to another way of life. Leaving the stresses and strains of everyday problems behind. Overnight trips to places we've always wondered about have now became possible. The biggest adjustment to camper van life was coping with our newfound freedom, being spontaneous and daring to go beyond our comfort zone. It takes some getting used to accepting that we are self-contained and we don't have to be back home before it gets dark. If only we had known it would be so much fun, we would have bought one years ago.'
Vaughan and Liz Southall *CAMPER VAN OWNERS*

That's the way it should be. Whether it's scooping ice cream, taking camper van wanderers on their final journeys or raising money for charity, the camper is all about the heart and soul. It brings people together, it shelters them, it makes their dreams come true and, as we all know, its spirit will always live on.

Long live the camper van.

THE ILLUSION OF FREEDOM AND THE TYRANNY OF TEATIME

A final word.

Do you remember when you were a little kid and you had to go to bed when it was still light outside? Or when you had to go home to have your tea at a certain time? If you didn't you were in trouble. I still feel that now, when the kids have to be up for school or meals have to be taken at sensible times. I feel it in the winter too, when teatime turns into telly time and telly time turns into bedtime. Suddenly a wet and windy week has gone by and nothing has been done except for a few episodes of *Mock the Week* and 40 hours of life draining graft. I feel I am wasting away. That's life sometimes.

Everything stops for tea. But it shouldn't. Teatime is a tyranny that holds us back and keeps us from enjoying the best part of the day. We wind down, hit the sofa and before we know it a large part of the day has passed by without the merest hint of an adventure. Often it's the weather that keeps us indoors, but more often it's ourselves. In northern Europe, where the seasons dictate our movements, it's tough to enjoy an evening *paseo*, a meal under the stars or a promenade before the light fades, for most of the year. We hunker down and wait for summer.

There is an internet story about camper vans that does the rounds from time to time in which it says that camper van drivers enjoy the illusion of freedom. Whenever I get it sent to me, again, for the hundredth time, I read it and think yes, it's true, but only to a certain extent. We don't have any more political or social freedom in a camper than in any other vehicle. We are still subject to rules and regulations, the laws of the land and our own – or our religion's – moral compasses. We live within limits.

But. And it's a very big but. The camper van – and camping and outdoorsyness in general – gets us off the sofa and out of the house when others are watching soaps and gritty northern dramas while their life slowly drains away. When you are camping, teatime isn't the end of the day. It's the start of the evening. You live with the light, away from the tyranny of teatime. So when we talk about freedom we talk about simple things that mean we get to live a little more, if living is not being confined by TV, tea and bedtime. The freedoms camping brings might be small but they are very real to an awful lot of people, me included.

WHAT does a CAMPER mean TO YOU?

'My van is my shed, it's where I put things that cannot go anywhere else. My van is a home away from home. Whether it's for a drive, a day out surfing or a camping trip with the family, it's an escape. My van is a friendly ear. I sometimes talk to it/at it and it always seems to listen attentively. My van is my distraction. Tinkering, fettling and fiddling with it helps my mind escape from the daily grind. My van is an extension of my family. When it's sick, I worry. I get nervous about MOTs like it's going for an exam (an almost pass is a C+); after a long drive I am proud of it for getting us there safely. My van makes me smile. It's no beauty queen but it makes me smile, and that smile broadens when it makes others smile.'

Jolyon Sharp *T25 SYNCRO OWNER AND BEACH RANGER*

445

Index

a

A frames 408, 409
A-Class motorhomes 36, 37, 45, 70, 74, 78
aires 84, 140, 324, 329–30
alternative transport, taking 407
art gallery in a camper van 422–5
Atlantic Caravan Park, Enniscrone 340
Atlantic View Campsite, Porthcothan 334
Auto-Sleepers 46, 50, 91, 97
awnings 134–7, 405
  drive-away 134, 136–7, 405
  fixed 134, 136
  skirts 137
axes 130, 369
Ayr Holiday Park, St Ives 334–5

b

baby wipes 144
Baden-Powell, Robert 29
batteries 107, 410–11, 414
BBQs
  equipment 164–5, 170, 173
  safety 370, 371
Bedford
  CA 40
  CF 18, 19
beds
  bedding foam 294–300
  bunks 74
  fixed bed campers 305
  hammocks 69, 75, 90–1
  jigsaw beds 306–7
  over cab beds 74, 305

rock and roll beds 72, 300–4, 416
bike racks 94–6, 110
  legal requirements 407
  rear mounted 94, 95
  roof mounted 94
  tow bar mounted 94, 96
bio fuel 48
bites and stings 372
Blake, Andrew 360
blinds 293
boots 380
breakdowns 367
breakfasts 186–96
briquettes 173
Britstops 85, 328, 339
buddy box 140
budget 65
Bulli 34, 50
bunks 74
buying a camper van 54–115
  budget 65
  camping styles 77–85
  carrying kit, capacity for 94–7
  day vans vs night vans 93
  new 54, 102–8
  reasons to buy 21, 23–5, 27–8, 62–4
  renting before buying 109–15
  roofs 86–91
  second-hand 55, 98–101
  sleeping capacity and layouts 66–75
  top tips 56, 59

c

Cadac Carri Chef 165
Cae Du, nr Tywyn, Snowdonia 344
Cae Gwyn, Nant Peris, Snowdonia 344–5
Caerfai Farm, St Davids 345
cafés, camper van 420–1
Cambee Picnic Pod 176
camper van 'technology' 308

camper vans
  better than tents 30–1
  criteria 32
  definitions 32
  distinction between motorhomes and 37
  history of 38–50
  international names for 34, 36–7
  naming 51–2
campfires 178–80
  lighting 179–80
  safety 371
Camping and Caravanning Club 29, 313
Camping de la Côte d'Argent, Gironde 347
Camping du Letty, Brittany 348
Camping Gaz camp stove 166
Camping Inter Plages, Lafitenia 348
Camping La Bergerie, Gavarnie 349
Camping Leagi, Leikeitio, Biscay 351
Camping Panorama, Pyla, Arcachon 350
Camping Playa España, Asturias 351
camping pods 93
  Camping Box Mk2 125, 127
  cooking pods 176–7
  Westfalia Camping Box 41, 124–5, 127
camping styles 77–85
  aires 84, 140, 324, 329–30
  Britstop/Passion camping 85, 328
  festival camping 79
  glamping 78
  small site camping 81, 316
  stealth camping 82, 88, 327
  touring park camping 80, 315
  wild camping 83, 145, 318–23

442

This kind of freedom is bursting out of the house or office when you have finished your work on a Friday night, it's the end to 'school night' restrictions at the beginning of the holidays and it's the opening of a door to adventures, however small they might be. It's the longest day, the smell of summer, the brilliant feeling of being physical, being out of breath, being giddy with excitement, of playing, of having fun.

Do you remember that?

I'll take your lifetime in front of the box and raise you with one glorious night under the stars, staring into a fire, telling stories and laughing while the kids squawk and scream in the stream, and we all go home feeling grubby and a little bit naughty like we skipped teatime and, honestly, we really don't give a hoot.

Make the most of it. You only get one shot.

GLOSSARY

$\mathcal{J}$argon, to many, is a dirty word. It exists because it describes things that cannot be described in any other way. Even so, I hate it. What's more, jargon is sometimes used as a weapon against the uninitiated to make them feel inferior or unknowledgeable. It happens often in sports, special interest clubs and business.

But not here. Everyone's welcome around our campfire. So, for a quick brush-up before the rest of the campers get here...

A Class type of motorhome that's built entirely by the manufacturer onto a chassis. Does not include a manufacture-supplied cab like a coach built. Typified by 1980s Hymer motorhomes.

aire designated parking for motorhomes and camper vans. From the French *aire de camping car*. A missed opportunity by many local councils in the UK (do you hear me?).

awning additional tent that attaches to the side of a camper van or motorhome to add another room or extra space to your van. Useful if you want to take the van away for the day and leave stuff behind. Don't drive away and forget to detach it.

Bay/Bay Window later edition of the VW Type 2 Transporter, with a curved bay window. Made from 1969 to 1979.

blue (or green) chemicals chemicals added to the waste reservoir of a chemical toilet.

black waste waste from a chemical toilet. Must be disposed of properly. Goes down the slophopper (*see* page 435).

buddy box/seat small box that sits behind the passenger seat and is used for sitting on. Typically a box without a backrest. Don't look inside; it's the most likely place you'll find the Porta Potti.

Bulli one of the original names for the VW Transporter that wasn't used but has now been adopted by fans. Also the concept car by Volkswagen.

Brick affectionate name for the Type 3 or Type 25 Transporter because of its brick-like shape. Insults are the sincerest form of flattery...

Britstop Not a type of music for campers, but the UK version of the French Passion network that allows free overnight parking at pubs, farm shops, farms and producers.

Camping Box removable piece of furniture made by Westfalia that fits into a camper for camping.

cassette toilet waste cassette of a toilet that is in-built into a motorhome and can be removed from the motorhome. Eeeew.

C-form type of waterproof 16-amp plug and socket used on campsites.

HDG 717D

chocks triangular pieces of wood or plastic that allow camper drivers to ensure their vans are level. Not to be confused with choc ices or chooks.

CO chemical symbol for carbon monoxide, the deadly gas that is created when fossil fuels are burned. Extremely dangerous, especially from disposable BBQs.

coach built motorhome that's built onto the chassis of an existing vehicle rather than built inside a van.

Combi name for VW Type 2 campers in the USA and Mexico.

Danbury UK brand of camper van converter and importer of VW Type 2s from Brazil.

designated seats seats with approved and crash tested seat belts to allow passengers to travel in the back of a motorhome. The only seats allowed for children when travelling in the back of a camper van or motorhome.

Devon UK make of camper van.

Dormobile UK based camper converter. One of the earliest converters.

dubber someone who loves V-Dubs (VWs).

Elsan make of camping, motorhome and caravan toilet that gives its name to 'Elsan points' on campsites.

Elsan point place where you empty your chemical toilet.

Fiamma popular brand of bike rack and accessories for camper vans and motorhomes.

fire pit off the ground container for lighting fires in places where they might otherwise be prohibited.

fly sheet outer layer of a tent, generally the waterproof outer skin but often the outside skin of a tent that isn't waterproof.

gin palace on wheels super swish motorhome with all the knobs, whistles and luxuries.

glamping glamorous camping. A form of camping that involves as much luxury as possible. As far from bushcratft camping as camping gets.

grey waste waste water from your shower, sink and basin run-off. Must be disposed of in the appropriate place.

hardstanding area of a campsite or pitch where motorhomes and campers can be parked without fear of becoming bogged in mud.

high top not a pair of sneakers but a high roof on a camper van.

J bars accessories for roof bars that can be used for carrying kayaks or adapted for surfboards.

Karmann German coachbuilder responsible for the Karmann Ghia as well as lots of other VW special editions.

Kombi common name for VW campers in Australia and Brazil.

433

leisure battery additional battery used to run camping electrics so that they don't run down the main battery.

Microbus early incarnation of the Type 2 Splitty in Germany, a passenger vehicle. Also a common term for VW in the USA.

micro camper camper van that's made from a small vehicle like a Bedford Rascal or similar. Small. Very, very small.

motor caravan term used by the UK Driver and Vehicle Licensing Agency (DVLA) for a vehicle with sleeping and cooking facilities, a side window, table and water tank.

outfit not something you put on for a club meet, but actually a generic term for your 'rig', 'unit' or van.

Passion site not what you think. Overnight parking for self-contained motorhomes and camper vans in Europe. *See* also **Britstop**.

pink chemicals term for the chemicals added to the water reservoir of a camping toilet.

pitch where you pitch your tent or park your van.

pop top extendable camper van roof to allow for more space.

pup tent little tent to chuck stuff in away from the camper van. Useful for storing children on camping trips when parents are frisky.

rag top convertible or cloth sunroof.

rat look/ratty camper that is purposefully made to look old and tatty.

rock and roll bed seat that converts into a bed.

RV recreational vehicle. Generally larger than your average motorhome and therefore not suitable for trips around Cornwall. More likely to be found stateside.

434

RV finger single raised finger from the steering wheel. A half-hearted acknowledgement of the existence of an RV that comes towards you and the driver waves.

shaka hand sign often used by VW drivers or by people being passed by VW drivers. Often followed by a bird or a V sign.

side elevating roof camper van roof that opens up from the side. Characterised by the Viking and Devon Moonraker roofs.

slider side opening sliding door on most camper vans.

slophopper brilliant German name for the place where you empty your Elsan, slop tank or Porta Potti. Literally, the place to slop out.

435

Splitty Split-Screen VW camper. Also known as the Type 2 Split-Screen. Revered by many, owned by few. Often appears printed on cushions and curtains, and used by clothing brands to appear cooler than they are.

Splitty salute that awkward moment when you wave at another camper and they don't wave back.

split charge relay switching system that will divert power from the alternator to the leisure battery in order to top up the charge when the main battery is fully charged during driving.

stealth camping camping in a van that appears to be no more than a standard panel van on the outside. Inside though, it's a palace.

Syncro 4 x 4 version of the T25 water cooled Transporter, production of which began in 1985.

thunderbox do we have to spell it out? Like a Porta Potti but more dangerous.

tin top camper van with the original factory roof rather than a pop top or high top.

top box ugly additions to car roof racks for extra storage. For use on people carriers and family saloons.

touring park large campsite often frequented by caravans and motorhomes. Usually with lots of facilities.

twin slider camper with a sliding door on either side.

unit colloquialism for motorhome or large camper.

Westfalia German company that converted the first VW campers. Much sought after.

wild camping camping away from designated camping areas or out of reach of standard facilities. Illegal in much of England and Wales.

Winnebago generic term for big motorhomes from Winnebago Industries, a US company that makes motorhomes. Favoured by pop stars and the film industry for their luxury and space on location.

zig unit basic control panel showing the state of charging of a leisure battery.

3-way fridge fridge that will run off battery power, mains electrics and also gas. Not what you might have thought.

437

ACKNOWLEDGEMENTS

With grateful thanks to the following people for their wit and wisdom and for helping me to make this book happen, in whatever small way it was.

The Team at Bloomsbury: Jenny, Clara, Lucy and Austin.
Tim and the team at PFD.
Bob Williams, for lighting up our lovely vans.
Paul, Amanda, Beth and Eva Bishop.
Martin, Cath, Tom and Jack Knight.
Ado, Rachel and Jack Shorland.
Ian, Kate, Sonny and Eva Boyd.
Jason, Simon, Matt, Daniel and all the team at Danbury Motor Caravans.
Nikki Nichol at The Caravan Club.
Daniel Attwood at *MMM* magazine.
Iain Duff at *Camping Magazine.*
John Greenwood at *Campervan Magazine.*
Jeff Gilmore at the Department for Transport.
Andy Brand and Emma Franklin at Marquis Motorhomes.
Clare Brookes at VW Funerals (and of course, Hearseby, one of the last remaining VW hearses...)
Rob Camber and his incredible Splitty, Norman.
Buzz and Marion Burrell and their lovely 1954 Split.
Jonny and Jane Ashworth and family and the Slidepod.
Paul and Sarah Greenings and the Bedford CF.
Terry Exell and his luxury Hijet.
Paul Potgeiter and his cheeky little Daihatsu Hijetta.
Alison Stubbs and her amazing Thermomix.
Martin Bellamy and his lovely T2 Brazibay Absinthe.
See them at **www.c13mpr.com**
Al Hesselbart, RV expert.
David and Cee Eccles.
Gary and Paul from the Camper Coffee Company. Brilliant fun times in the studio.

Allan Horne at the Dormobile Club.

Louisa and EVERYONE on the Eireball. Legends one and all.

All the camper van owners who opened their hearts to tell me what their campers mean to them. Thank you!

Nicky Green for all round support and administrative firepower.

Steve and Mandy at Britstops for... just being excellent.

Ali Ray, for the nice chats and shared experiences.

Jason and the Rothfink crew.

Tom and Julie Trubridge, and the boys, for being cool campers.

Josh Sutton, the Guyrope Gourmet.

Sarah Riley and her lovely family and way with words. An inspiration.

Terry O'Brien at O'Brien's Camping **www.obrienscamping.co.uk** for his knowledge of the camping fridge.

Mark Harris at the Foam Shop for his fantastic knowledge of foam and comfort.

Sam and Hilary at Concept Multi Car for their advice about Rock and Roll beds.

Martin Watts at the Classic Camper Club.

Scott and Bonnie at Lunan Bay campsite.

Andrew Blake and his 2 versions of the wake and shake.

Evren at Select Solar.

The team at Band Films, Bristol for their great studio and can do attitude.

439

440

CAMPER
COFFEE CO.

VW

BDV 47

447

Picture credits

All photographs are © Martin Dorey with the exception of the following:

p12, p96, p135 (top left), p364 © Georgia Glynn Smith
p25 © Damian Horner
p133 © Martin Knight
p162, p263 (all photos) © Joanne Dorey
p358–9 courtesy of Julie and Jason Buckley
p382, p415 (left) courtesy of Rachel Kershaw
p423 (all photos), p424–5 courtesy of Alexa Poppe
www.alexapoppeweddingphotography.com

All studio shots lit by Bob Williams
c/o **www.thescottidog.com**

BACKGROUNDS AND EFFECTS:

p1 © alanadesign, Shutterstock
p5, p64 © ulimi, Getty Images
p5, © niroworld, Shutterstock
p30 © Jamie Farrant, Getty Images
p185 © Mr Twister, Shutterstock
p187 © pockygallery, Shutterstock

The lyrics
on page 17 are
© Ben Howard and
are reproduced with
kind permission.